Business Studies

for CBSE Class XII

Question–Answer Bank

Business Studies

for CBSE Class XII

Question–Answer Bank

Karan Chadha BBS (pursuing)
Shaheed Sukhdev College of Business Studies
Delhi

Shefali Chadha BBS (Finance), MBA
Narsee Monjee Institute of Management Studies
Mumbai

CBS Publishers & Distributors Pvt Ltd
New Delhi • Bengaluru • Pune • Kochi • Chennai

Business Studies
for **CBSE Class XII**
Question–Answer Bank

ISBN: 978-81-239-2047-4

First Edition: 2012

Published by Satish Kumar Jain and produced by Vinod K. Jain for
CBS Publishers & Distributors Pvt Ltd
4819/XI Prahlad Street, 24 Ansari Road, Daryaganj
New Delhi 110 002, India.
Ph: 23289259, 23266861, 23266867
Fax: 011-23243014
Website: www.cbspd.com
e-mail: delhi@cbspd.com
cbspubs@airtelmail.in.

Branches

- Bengaluru: Seema House 2975, 17th Cross, K.R. Road, Banasankari 2nd Stage, Bengaluru 560 070, Karnataka
  Ph: +91-80-26771678/79 Fax: +91-80-26771680 e-mail: bangalore@cbspd.com
- Pune: Bhuruk Prestige, Sr. No. 52/12/2+1+3/2 Narhe, Haveli (Near Katraj-Dehu Road Bypass), Pune 411 051, Maharashtra
  Ph: 020-64704058, 64704059, 32342277 Fax: +91-020-24300160 e-mail: pune@cbspd.com
- Kochi: 36/14 Kalluvilakam, Lissie Hospital Road, Kochi 682 018, Kerala
  Ph: +91-484-4059061-65 Fax: +91-484-4059065 e-mail: cochin@cbspd.com
- Chennai: 20, West Park Road, Shenoy Nagar, Chennai 600 030, Tamil Nadu
  Ph: +91-44-26260666, 26208620 Fax: +91-44-45530020 email: chennai@cbspd.com

Printed at India Binding House, Noida (UP)

Preface

Today, as never before in history, there is a pressing need for an in-depth understanding of business and its nuances. The global economic environment is highly uncertain and several economies, industries and geographies are at their tipping point. The most important of many lessons that have emerged from the crisis is that corporations and businesses in a globalized world have an impact that transcends borders and various realms of life and that our understanding of this impact is extremely limited to say the least. Also, globally, there is an acknowledgement of the limitations of the existing business education framework in its ability to enable the students to appreciate the on-the-ground realities of business and bridge the gap between theory and practice.

Increasingly, we feel the need for learning tools which can improve the effectiveness of business learning by complementing traditional pedagogy. The essence of undertaking business studies learning is to create an understanding of the tenets of business and lay a strong foundation on which practice and experience can be built. This makes the synthesis of the subject to enable the deduction of key takeaways imperative. However, we also must appreciate that the existing framework of testing requires the students to present the knowledge that they imbibe during the course of their learning in an elaborate manner that will allow the examiner to assess their understanding fairly. Therefore, a fine balance must be struck between synthesis and detailing by a student.

This book is the culmination of a very well thought out effort to support the student's endeavour to develop an understanding of the subject by synthesizing learning from voluminous texts and presenting it in an easy to grasp format that will support the student in his/her arduous task. The book has been written to cover all content that is crucial from both the perspectives — learning and testing. We have put concerted efforts to structure the book in a question–answer format so as to include all content that can prove to be of essence to the student and have also made an effort to prepare the student from the examination standpoint by using suggestive alternatives on how a topic can be tested.

The book addresses all the challenges that students face in the subject as the authors have extended their experiences with the subject to make the book as student-friendly as possible. The book is a smart tool which simplifies content through intelligent organization of topics, fully prepares the student for testing and thus enhances the learning experience. We sincerely hope that this book will support each student of the subject in his/her endeavour to deliver in learning and understanding this dynamic discipline.

We have made every attempt possible to make this book a student's preferred read for conceptual clarity and examination preparation. We welcome inputs from our readers on how the book can be improved. Please feel free to contribute articles on topics relevant to the subject and we would be very happy to include them in the subsequent editions. Do write to us at with your suggestions; we would love to hear from you.

In the end, we would like to thank all those without whose inputs and support this book would not have been possible — our parents who have been a source of unconditional support and endless encouragement, our teachers who have been our guiding light, friends who have been our motivators, critics who have helped us improve, and most importantly all our readers with whom we embark on this journey of incessant learning.This book is dedicated to all of you.

Karan Chadha
Shefali Chadha

Contents

1

Nature and Significance of Management

Q1. Discuss the relation between *efficiency* and *effectiveness*.

Ans. The terms *effectiveness* and *efficiency*, even though different, are closely related.

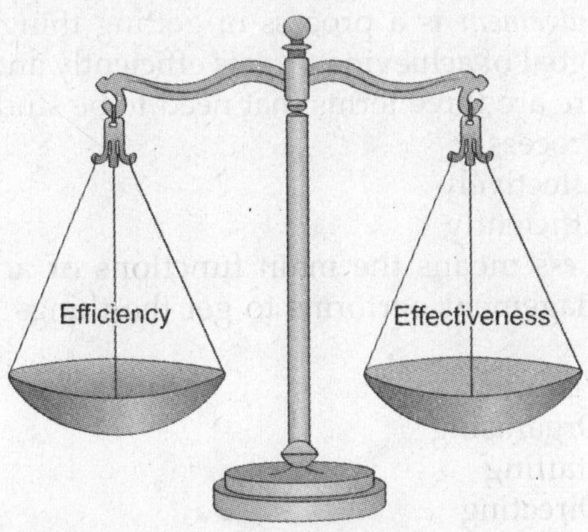

Fig. 1.1: There must be a balance between efficiency and effectiveness

Effectiveness in absence of efficiency: It is not desirable for management to complete a given task at a high cost. Suppose a company's target production is 5000 shirts. Due to power failure, most of the time, the manager has to operate double shifts thereby increasing the cost of production. Hence, the manager was effective but not efficient.

Efficiency in absence of effectiveness: It is not desirable for management to cut down cost but not achieve the end result. If a business tries to produce goods with lesser resources and is not able to achieve its target production, the goods will never reach the market and competitors will enter the market and the firm will lose its market share. Successful management requires a balance between effectiveness and efficiency.

High efficiency is to be combined with with high effectiveness but undue emphasis on efficiency without being effective is not desirable.

Q2. Targets have been reached but at a high cost. Which situation does it refer to?

Ans. Effective.

Q3. Explain the meaning of *management*.

Ans.

- *Management* is a process of getting things done with the goal of achieving targets efficiently and effectively.
- There are three terms that need to be studied:
  - Process
  - Effectively
  - Efficiently
- *Process* means the main functions or activities that management performs to get the things done. These are:
  - Planning
  - Organising
  - Staffing
  - Directing
  - Controlling
- Doing work *effectively* means finishing the given task. *Effectiveness* in management is concerned with:
  - Doing the right job and completing activities.
  - Achieving targets

  In other words, it is concerned with end result.
- *Efficiency* means doing the tasks in the correct manner and with the least cost. There is a kind of cost-benefit analysis involved and the relationship between inputs and outputs is as follows:

- If by using less resources (input), more benefits (output) are derived, then efficiency is increased. Efficiency also increases when for the same output, fewer resources are used and lesser costs incurred.
- When same inputs are used to achieve more output, then also efficiency increases.

Q4. What are the various features of *management*?

Ans. The various characteristics are:

1. ***Management is a goal-oriented process/purposeful activity***
   - *Goals* are targets, ends or the purpose of a firm.
   - Management is a means of achieving these targets/ goals.
   - Goals should comprise certain characteristics like:
     - Simple
     - Clear
     - Specific
     - Realistic

   For Example:

   Goal of a retail store may be to increase sales thereby increasing profits, but the goal of an NGO may be to impart education to children with specific needs.

   - It unites the efforts of different people in the firm towards achieving these targets.
2. ***Management is all pervasive/universal***
   - It is required at all levels of management:
     - Top
     - Middle
     - Lower
   - It is required in all departments in the firm:
     - Production
     - Finance
     - Marketing
     - Human resource
   - It is required in all types of organisations:
     - Economic
     - Social
     - Political

A petrol pump needs to be managed as much as a school.

3. *Management is multidimensional*
   - Management is a complex and complicated activity that has three main dimensions:
     i. *Management at work*
        - All organisations exist for some performance or work.
        - Management translates this work to be done in terms of
          - Goals or targets to be achieved
          - Assigns the means or methods to achieve these targets
        - This is done in terms of
          - Problems to be solved
          - Decisions to be made
          - Plans to be established
          - Budgets to be prepared
          - Responsibilities to be assigned
          - Authority to be delegated

     ii. *Management of people*
        - Human resources or people are a firm's greatest asset.
        - Getting work done through these people is a major task for the manager.
        - Managing people comprises two dimensions:
          - It implies dealing with employees as individuals with various needs and behaviour
          - It also means dealing with these individuals as a group of people.
        - The task of management is to work towards reconciling the individual needs in order to attain the overall group goal.
        - A good manager improves the strengths and minimizes the weaknesses of the employees.

     iii. *Management of operations*
        - Every firm deals with a product or a service.
        - This requires a production process which involves inflow of resources for production and outflow of products/services for consumption.

  - The mechanism of inflow and outflow is known as operation and this must be managed efficiently and effectively.
  - This is interlinked with both the management of work and management of people.

4. *Management is a continuous process*
   - The process of management is a series of composite, continuous (never ending, ongoing) but separate functions (planning, organising, staffing, directing, controlling).
   - These functions are simultaneously performed by all managers in the firm all the time.
   - Management as a process exists as long as the firm is in existence.
5. *Management is a group activity*
   - An organisation is a collection of diverse individuals (in terms of experience and background) with diverse needs.
   - Hence, coordination of individual effort in a common direction is a must for organizations.
   - Management must allow all its members to grow and develop as needs and opportunities change.
6. *Management is a dynamic function*
   - It is a dynamic function and has to adapt itself to the ever changing environment.
   - An organisation interacts with its outside environment which consists of various forces like:
     - Social
     - Economical
     - Political
   - In order to be successful, an organisation must change itself and its goals according to the changing needs of the environment.

   For Example:

   KFC, the fast food giant had made major changes in its menu to be able to survive in the Indian Market.
7. *Management is an intangible force*
   - It does not have any physical form or shape. It cannot be seen or touched.

- Its presence can be felt in the way the organisation operates
- Good management is reflected through the following features:
  - Orderliness
  - Happy and satisfied employees
  - Completion of targets/attainment of goals
- Bad management can be seen through
  - Unorderliness
  - Unhappy and unsatisfied employees
  - Falling short of targets

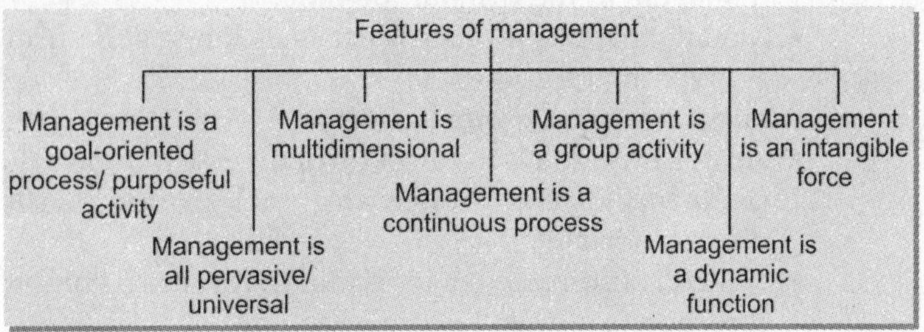

Q5. Identify the feature of *management* being referred to in the following cases:

Ans.

i. An organisation has to necessarily interact with the external environment

Dynamic

ii. Management is a series of continuous, ongoing functions.

Continuous

iii. A Spastic society and a retail outlet have been formed with varied and specific reasons.

Purposeful/goal oriented

iv. Despite the different goals of a school and a hospital, management is required in both organisations.

Pervasive

Q6. How are the objectives of *management* derived?

Ans. The objectives of management are derived from the basic purpose of business.

Q7. What are the main objectives of *management*?

Ans.

- Management seeks to achieve certain goals which are the desired results of an activity
- Management has to achieve all these objectives in an efficient and effective manner

Objectives of management can be classified as follows:

1. ***Organisational objectives***
   - Management is responsible for setting and achievement of goals for organisation. It has to achieve a variety of objectives in all the areas considering that the interests of stakeholders are taken care of:
     - Shareholders
     - Employees
     - Customers
     - Government
   - The main objectives of any firm should be to utilise human and material resources to the maximum possible benefit, i.e. to fulfill the economic goals of a business. The economic objectives are:
     - *Survival:* The basic objective of any business is to survive. Management must strive to ensure the survival of the business firm. In order to survive, an organisation must earn enough revenues to cover its costs.
     - *Profit:* Mere survival is not enough for a business firm. Profit plays an important role as it is a
       - Means of livelihood
       - Measure of success
       - Means for diversification and expansion

       Profit is essential for covering costs and risks of a business firm.
     - *Growth:* To remain in the market, management must exploit fully the growth potential and opportunities of the organisation.

       Growth indicators of a business may be the following:

- Increase in sale
- Increase in number of people employed
- Increase in number of products sold
- Increase in capital investments

2. *Social objectives*
   - It involves the creation of benefits for the society. This refers to creating economic values for various constituents (interest groups) of the society on a consistent basis.
   - This includes:
     - Using environmental friendly techniques of production
     - Giving employment opportunities to the disadvantaged and backward sections of society
     - Providing basic amenities like schools and medical aid to employees.
     - Avoidance of anti-social and unfair business practices
     - Conducting business legally and paying taxes accurately and promptly

   For Example:

   ITC's e-chaupal is a good example of a business organization fulfilling its corporate social responsibility.
3. *Personal objectives*
   - Organisations are made up of individuals who have different personalities, backgrounds, experiences, needs and objectives.
   - They all come to be a part of the organisation to satisfy their diverse needs.
   - Personal objectives refer to the objective of the business towards its employees which include:
     - Financial needs
       - Highly competitive salaries
       - Other perks
     - Social needs
       - Peer recognition
     - Higher level needs
       - Personal growth
       - Overall development

- Management has to reconcile the personal goals with the overall organisational goals for harmony in the firm.

Q8. Explain Management as a science.

Ans. Science is defined as a systematic body of knowledge that explains operations of general laws.

For management to qualify as a science, it must fulfill the following features:

1. ***Systematic body of knowledge***
   - Science is a systematic body of knowledge and theory which contains principles which are based on cause and effect relationship.

   For Example:

   Application of heat (cause) results in evaporation (effect).

   Management:
   - This is also true for management since it has its own theory and principles which have developed over time and they are also based on cause and effect relationship.

   For Example:

   Motivation of employees (cause) results in good efficiency (effect).
   - Management theory is based on other disciplines too, like economics, sociology and psychology, etc. (multidisciplinary)
   - Like science, management also has its own vocabulary of terms and concepts. Books of management are rated highly on bestsellers' list.
2. ***Principles based on observation and experimentation***
   - Scientific principles have been developed through observations and then tested through repeated experimentation under controlled conditions.

   For Example:

   Newton's law of gravity

   Management:
   - Principles of management are based on observations and experimentation and have evolved over time.

   For Example:

It was observed that a group of subordinates, receiving orders from more than one superior at a certain point of time leads to chaos and confusion. This observation was tested in various firms and thus a principle of unity of command was derived.

- However, management deals with human beings whose behaviour is unpredictable, varying and as a result, the result of certain experiments may not be fully accurate/predictable/replicated. Thus, management is called an inexact/soft/behavioural science.

3. *Universal validity*

- Scientific principles can be tested at any time and any number of times to give the same result over and over again.

Management:

- Universal validity does not hold true for management principles. Though the management principles provide standardised techniques and principles, they are not exact as they have to be modified according to the requirements of a given situation.
- Management principles are also used for training and development of managers.

Conclusion: Since management does not fully satisfy the criteria of science, it may be regarded as an inexact/soft/behavioral science.

Q9. Management is a science like physics and biology. Do you agree? Give reason.

Ans. No. Physics and biology are pure science whereas management is an inexact science which can be justified as follows:

Whole answer given above.

Q10. Explain management as an art.

Ans. Art may be defined as skilful and personalized application of existing knowledge/theory to achieve the desired results through the use of creativity, imagination and constant practice.

For management to qualify as an art, it has to fulfill the following features:

1. ***Existence of theoretical body of knowledge***
   - Art presupposes the existence of theoretical body of knowledge which contains the principles applicable to that particular art form.

   For Example:

   All music is based on the theory of seven basic notes

   Management:
   - This is true for management too, since it comprises theory in different areas of management like marketing, finance, human resources and the manager has to specialise in each of them.
   - A successful manager is one who has gained knowledge from various books of management and is able to apply this knowledge in his day to day working.
2. ***Personalised application***
   - The demonstration of art form varies from one artist to another artist since art is a personalised concept.

   Management:
   - A manager applies common management principles to a given situation in his own style and manner which is different from that of the other managers.
   - Hence, art and management are both, personalised forms.
3. ***Based on practice and creativity***
   - Art involves the use creativity and a continuous practice of the theoretical base of knowledge

   For Example:

   All music is based on seven notes but only a continuous practice and use of creativity makes a singer excel and achieve perfection.

   Management:
   - All managers equipped with the same knowledge, apply it in a creative manner by being:
     i. Imaginative
     ii. Innovative

     to solve various problems.
   - A continuous practice of handling different situations in a firm makes a manager perfect.

- It is rightly said, "The more you manage, the better you manage."

  Conclusion: Since the above criteria of art are satisfied, management qualifies as an art form. The distinction between a more and less successful manager is because of difference in their ability to put the principles of management into practice.

Q11. What distinguishes a successful manager from a less successful one is the ability to put the management principles into practice. Explain the nature of management highlighted above.

Ans. Management as an art.

Q12. Management is an amalgamation of both science and art. Explain.

or

Management as a science and art isn't mutually exclusive but complement each other.

Ans.

- It is true that a successful manager is one who is both a scientist as well as an artist. He requires technical knowledge of management as well as personal skills, continuous practice and creativity in order to attain the objectives successfully.
- Management as a science and art are two sides of the same coin. They are not mutually exclusive; rather they are dependent and complement each other.
- *Explain:* Features of Science (only for management) and features of art (only for management).

Q13. Explain management as a profession.

Ans. Profession is an occupation backed by specialised knowledge and training which can be acquired intellectually and organisationally. For management to qualify as a profession, it must fulfill the following criteria:

1. ***Well-defined body of knowledge***
   - All professions are based on a well-defined and specific body of knowledge that can be acquired through instructions.

Management:

- Management also has a theoretical body of knowledge comprising well-defined principles and theory. This knowledge can be acquired at different colleges, institutions and through a number of books and journals

For Example:

IIMs in India have been set up with a specific purpose of providing management education.

2. *Restricted entry*
   - The entry to a profession is restricted by a degree which has to be obtained after clearing the qualifying examinations

For Example:

Doctors have to clear MBBS Exam to obtain the professional degree before they begin to practice.

Management:

- There is no restriction on anyone designated as a manager.
- However, there is a greater demand for those managers who have degrees/diplomas from reputed institutes. Thus, this criterion is not strictly met.

3. *Professional association*
   - All professionals are affiliated to professional associations which grant Certificates of Practice and enforce the code of conduct as decided by the association

For Example:

In India, the lawyers have to be members of the Bar Council of India which regulates and controls the activities of the lawyers.

Management:

- Though, there are several associations of practicing managers in India like AIMA (All India Management Association), its membership is not mandatory for practicing managers. So this criterion is not strictly met.

4. *Ethical code of conduct*
   - All professions are bound by a code of conduct which guides the behaviour of its members.

- If this code is violated, it will invite penalty/ cancellations of certificate of practice

For Example:

Doctors have to take the oath of ethical practice at the time they enter the profession.

Management:

- In this case, though AIMA prescribes a code of conduct, but it has no statutory backing.

5. *Service motive*
   - The basic motive of a professional is to serve his clients' interests by rendering dedicated and committed service to them.

   Management:
   - Profit maximisation is the main objective of a business enterprise but it doesn't hold true absolutely nowadays and is fast changing.
   - Thus, an organisation having a good team of management automatically serves the society by providing good quality products at reasonable prices to them.

   Conclusion: From the above statements, we can see that management does not fully satisfy criteria of a profession. It is not a full fledged profession but an emerging profession, since it is slowly moving in that direction and demand for professionally qualified managers is increasing in today's scenario.

Q14. Is Management a profession? Discuss.

Ans. Management is an emerging profession but it is not a full-fledged profession. Refer to the previous answer.

Q15. Who is the CEO of HCL?

Ans. Shiv Nadar

Q16. What is meant by levels of *management*?

Ans. The authority-responsibility relationships between various individuals in an organization determine role and the specific tasks to be performed by each individual in the organization. These superior-subordinate (authority-responsibility) relationships give rise to the levels of management in an organization. There are mainly three levels of management:

1. Top Management
2. Middle Management
3. Lower/supervisory/operational/first line management

Q17. Explain the three levels of management.

Ans. The various levels of management are:

1. ***Top management***
   - This consists of the senior most executives of the organisation by whatever name they are called.

     Designations:

     i. Chairman
     ii. Chief Executive Officer (CEO)
     iii. Chief Operating Officer (COO)
     iv. President
     v. Managing director
     vi. General manager
     vii. Chief Financial Officer (CFO)
     viii. Vice-President (finance, marketing, etc.)

     Specific functions:

     i. Their basic function is to integrate the various elements and coordinate activities of different departments according to the overall goals of the firm.
     ii. Responsible for the welfare and survival of the business.
     iii. They analyse the business environment and its implications for the survival of the firm.
     iv. They formulate overall organisational goals and strategies for their attainment.
     v. They are responsible for all the activities of the business and for the impact it has on the society.
     vi. They appoint the middle level managers.
     vii. They issue instructions and guide the middle level managers.

2. ***Middle management***
   - It forms the link between the top and lower level managers.

Designations:

i. Departmental managers (like production, HR, finance, marketing)
ii. Divisional heads (northern div manager) or regional heads

Specific functions:

i. Interpret the policies made by top management.
ii. Ensure that their department has the necessary human resources.
iii. Assign necessary duties and responsibilities to lower level managers.
iv. Motivate the lower level managers to achieve desired objectives.
v. Cooperate with other departments for smoother functioning of the firm.
vi. Responsible for the proper functioning of first line managers.

3. ***Supervisory/operational/lower/first line management:***
   - This level provides a link between the management and the actual workers.

   Designations:

   i. Supervisors
   ii. Superintendents
   iii. Inspectors
   iv. Section officers
   v. Foremen

   Specific functions:

   i. Executing the plans and policies made by the top level and transmitted by middle level.
   ii. Organising a hygienic, safe and comfortable working environment for the workers in terms of lighting, ventilations, etc.
   iii. Appointment and training of the workers.
   iv. Issuing directions, instructions and guidance to the workers.
   v. Ensuring discipline among the workers.
   vi. Making efforts to reduce wastages and maintaining the quality of output.
   vii. Looking after maintenance of machinery, repairs and avoiding accidents.

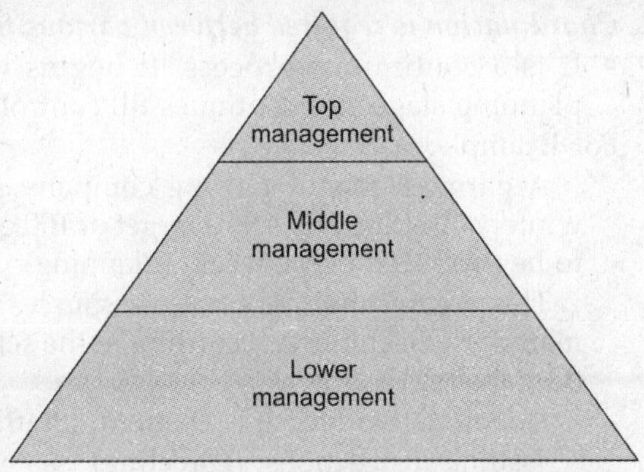

Fig. 1.2: Levels of mangement

Q18. Which level of management is entrusted with complementing and controlling plans and strategies developed by top managers?

Ans. Middle management.

Q19. Coordination is the essence of management. Explain.

Ans. Meaning:

- Coordination is a force that binds all the functions of management together. It refers to a process by which a manager synchronises the diverse activities of different departments.
- It is required for achieving harmony among individual efforts towards the accomplishment of overall organizational goals.

It is not a separate function of management; rather it is the essence of Management due to the following reasons:

1. ***Coordination is required between different individuals***
   - In an organisation, people from different backgrounds, intelligence levels and interests work together as a group to achieve common objectives.
   - It is the force which unifies unrelated or diverse interests.

2. ***Coordination is required between various functions***
   - It is a continuous process. It begins with the planning stage and continues till controlling.

   For Example:

   A garment manufacturing company plans its winter collection and sets a target of 100 garments to be produced every week. (Planning)

   This organisation assembles resources like raw materials, machinery, according to the set targets. (Organising)

   Adequate workforce is ensured. (Staffing)

   Issuing instructions. (Directing)

   Monitoring performance. (Controlling)
3. ***Coordination is required within the functions***
   - Within planning, it is required between main plans and departmental plans.
   - Within organising, it is required between authority and responsibility of various job positions.
   - Within staffing, it is required between skills of people and jobs assigned to them.
   - Within directing, it is required between orders, instructions, suggestions, etc.
   - Within controlling, it is required between actual and standard performance.
4. ***Coordination is required between various levels of management***

   i. *It is required at all levels of management*

   Required at the top level, middle level and lower level.

   For Example:

   Top level formulates plans which are interpreted by middle level and finally executed by the lower level.
5. ***Coordination is required between various departments.***

   Due to the inter-dependent nature of various acts performed.

   For Example:

On the basis of demand in the market, the marketing department communicates production targets to the production department which in turn communicates it to the purchases department.

Conclusion: Thus, like a thread in a garland, coordination is a part of all management functions.

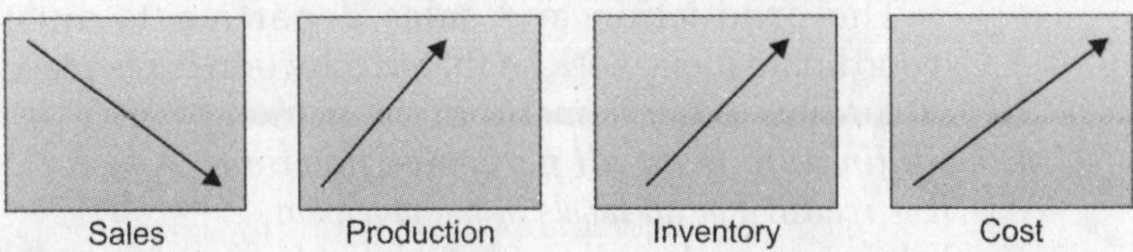

Fig. 1.3: Without inter-department coordination, the firm can not grow

Q20. Discuss the nature/characteristics of coordination.

Ans. The various characteristics are:

1. *Coordination integrates group efforts*
   - It unifies diverse interests of different individuals into purposeful work activity. It gives a common focus to group efforts to ensure that performance is in accordance with the plans.
   - Every organisation, whether big or small must integrate the efforts of individuals in the organisation.
   - In an organisation, a number of individuals from different backgrounds, intelligence levels work together under one roof.
   - Coordination helps to give a common focus to group efforts.
2. *Coordination is a continuous process*
   - It is not a one-time function, but a continuous and ongoing process. It begins at the planning stage and continues till controlling.

   For Example:

   Winter collection of clothes may be planned in June. (Planning)

   Required resources will be assembled. (Organising)
   Adequate workforce is to be ensured. (Staffing)
   Instructions to be given to workforce. (Directing)
   Production needs to be monitored. (Controlling)

3. ***Coordination ensures unity of action***
   - The purpose is to secure unity of action in the realisation of common objectives.
   - It acts as a binding force between various departments and ensures that all actions are aimed at achieving the organisational goals.

   For Example:

   The production and sales departments must coordinate their work so that production takes place according to the demand in the market.
4. ***Coordination is an all pervasive function***

   i. *It is required at all levels of management*

   It is required at all levels be it the top level, middle level or lower level.

   For Example:

   Top level formulates plans which are interpreted by middle level and finally executed at lower level.

   ii. *Exists between various departments*

   Due to the inter dependent nature of various acts performed.

   For Example:

   On the basis of demand in the market, the marketing department communicates production targets to the production department which in turn communicates it to the purchases department.

   iii. *Required in all types of organisation*

   Whether big or small, business or non-business, political or legal, etc.
5. ***Coordination is the responsibility of all managers***
   - It is the function of every single manager in the firm.
   - Top level managers coordinate between the external environment and the organisation.
   - Middle level management coordinates with both the top level and first line management and acts as a link between the two.
   - Operational management coordinates the activities of its workers to ensure that the work proceeds according to predefined plans. Lower lever managers coordinate between management and workers and act as a link between them.

6. *Coordination is a deliberate function*
   - A manager has to coordinate the efforts of different people in a deliberate and conscious manner.
   - Even where members of a department willingly cooperate and work, coordination gives a direction to that spirit of willingness.
   - Cooperation in the absence of coordination may lead to efforts getting wasted and coordination without cooperation may lead to dissatisfied employees.

   Conclusion: Coordination is not a separate function of management but is its essence. Like a thread in a garland, coordination is a part of all management functions.

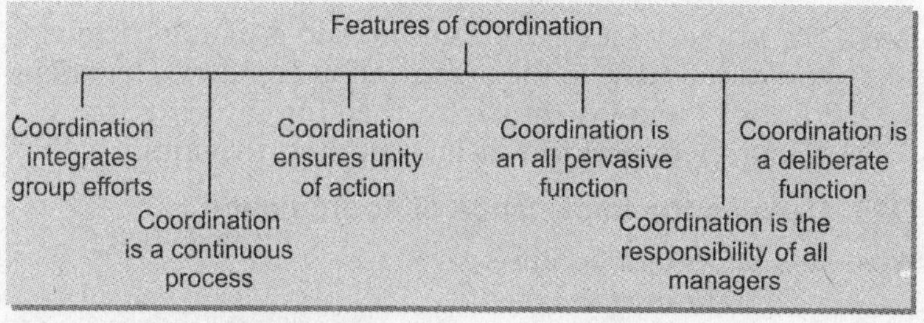

Q21. What is the relationship between *coordination* and *cooperation*?

Ans. Refer to point 6 of the above question.

Q22. "Like a thread in a garland, coordination is a part of all management functions."

Ans. For 3 marks (2nd, 3rd point of essence and conclusion) for 6 marks – Complete essence.

Q23. Define coordination or what is coordination?

Ans.

- It is the force that binds all the functions of management. It is the common thread that runs through all activities such as purchase, production, sales and finance to ensure continuity in the working of the organisation.

- It is however, the essence of management for achieving harmony among individual efforts towards accomplishment of group goals.
- Coordination is implicit and inherent in all functions of an organisation.
- According to the Haimann, coordination is the orderly synchronising of efforts of subordinates to provide people proper amount, timing and quality of execution so that the united efforts lead to the stated objectives, namely the common purpose of enterprise
- Not a separate function of management.
- Essence of management.
- Puts together efforts of individuals to attain common goal.

Q24. What is the primary reason for coordination?

Ans. The primary reason for coordination is that departments and individuals in the organization are inter dependent, i.e they depend on each other for information and resources to perform their respective activities.

Q25. Discuss the importance of coordination.

Ans. It is important because:

1. *Growth in size*
   - As organisations grow in size, the number of people employed by it also expands
   - At times, it becomes difficult to integrate the efforts and activities of so many people. All individuals differ in their habits of work, background, approaches to situations and relationships with other individuals.
   - It becomes mandatory to ensure that all individuals work towards the common goal of the organisation but employees do have their personal goals also.
   - For organisational efficiency, it is important to harmonise these individual goals and organisational goals through the process of coordination.
2. *Functional differentiation*
   - Functions of an organisation are divided into various departments, divisions and sections.
   - In an organisation, there may be separate departments of finance, production, marketing, sales, HR, etc.

- All these departments may have their own objectives, policies, protocols and their own style of working.

For Example:

The objective of the marketing department may be to increase sales by 12% by offering discount but the finance department may not approve this as it means loss of revenue. These conflicts arise as these units are performing in isolation with each other and barriers between departments are becoming more rigid. All departments and individuals are inter dependent and have to depend on each other for information to perform their activities for the achievement of common organizational goals.

3. *Specialisation*
   - Modern organisations often are characterised by a high degree of specialisation.
   - This is because of the complexities of modern technology and the diversity of jobs to be performed. Therefore, the organisation needs to employ a large number of specialists.
   - Specialists could also work in coordination with each other, taking suggestions from other specialists in their respective areas of specialisation.
   - Therefore, some coordination is required by an independent person to reconcile the difference in approach, interests and opinion of the specialists.

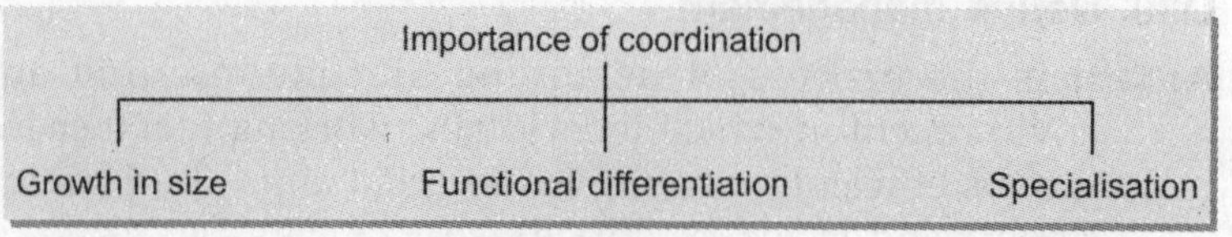

Q26. Who is a global manager?

Ans.

- A global manager is one who possesses 'hard' types of skills along with 'softer' types of skills. Managers who understand analysis, engineering, strategy and technology are needed and it is critical to global success.

- A manager must understand the various cultures in the world.
- The role of a global manager has changed from a single dimensional role in defined business context to being a multifaceted and multi-dimensional role that calls for diverse combination of technical skills, people skills, soft management skills and the ability to imbibe and learn from different cultural experiences.

Q27. Name the managers of some companies.

Ans. Nusli Wadia – Bombay dyeing
Bill Gates – Microsoft
Shiv Nadar – HCL
Indra Nooyi – Pepsico

Q28. What is common to every organization?

or

No matter what an organization is or what its goals might be, they all have something in common. Name it.

Ans. Management and managers.

Q29. Successful organizations don't achieve their goals by chance but by following a deliberate process. Name it.

Ans. Management

Q30. Define management.

Ans. It is the process of designing and maintaining an environment in which individuals, working together in groups efficiently accomplish selected aims. (by Harold Koontz and Heinz Weilhrich)

OTHER IMPORTANT QUESTIONS

Q1. Name the process of designing and maintaining an environment in which individuals, working together in groups efficiently accomplish selected aims.

Ans. Management (quoted definition by Harold Koontz, Heinz Weilhrich)

Q2. A Company's target production is 5000 units in a year. To achieve this target, the manager has to operate on double shifts due to power failure. He is able to produce 5000 units. Which element of management is being ignored?

Ans. Efficiency

Q3. In order to be successful an organisation must change its goals according to the needs of the environment. Which characteristic of management is highlighted above?

Ans. Dynamic.

Q4. A petrol pump needs to be managed as much as a hospital/school. Which characteristic of management is highlighted?

Ans. Pervasive.

Q5. State the 2 dimensions of management of people.

Ans. Dealing with individuals. Dealing with individuals as a group of people.

Q6. McDonald's, the fast food giant made major changes in its menu to be able to survive in the Indian Market. Which characteristic of management is highlighted?

Ans. Dynamic.

Q7. Despite all developments in technology, getting work done through people is still a major task for the managers. Which dimension of management is being highlighted?

Ans. Management is multidimensional. Management of people.

Q8. To meet the objectives of the firm, Asian Paints contributed large amount of funds to enable farmers to use the resources effectively. Identify the management objective it tried to achieve.

Ans. Social.

Q9. To meet the objectives of firm, management of Excel Ltd offers employment to physically challenged people. Identify the management objective.

Ans. Social.

Q10. Give the levels of management of manager for northern division of a corporate house, foremen, file managers and COO.

Ans.

Table 1.1

Designation	*Levels of management*
Manager of northern division of a corporate house	Middle level
Foremen	Lower level
File managers	Lower level
COO	Top level

Q11. Mr. Nitin has a good business of iron and steel. His father wants him to go to USA for MBA. What does this show about the nature of management?

Ans. Management as an emerging profession.

Q12. Ankit Enterprise Ltd. manufactures tea. The production department produced more tea than is required and the sales department is not able to sell the entire produce. Which quality of management is missing?

Ans. Coordination.

Q13. Give the levels of management which take the following decisions:

1. **Introducing a new product line.**
2. **Recruitment of casual labourers.**
3. **Give performance reports to top level.**
4. **Deciding the capital structure of company.**
5. **Devising a suitable advertising campaign.**

Ans.

Table 1.2

Decisions	*Levels of Management*
Introducing a new product line	Top level
Recruitment of casual labourers	Lower level
Give performance reports to top level	Middle level
Deciding the capital structure of company	Top level
Devising a suitable advertising campaign	Middle level

Q14. Differentiate between coordination and cooperation.

Ans.

Table 1.3

Basis	*Coordination*	*Cooperation*
1. Requirement	It is essential for the attainment of organizational goals.	It is voluntary by nature. It arises out of the desire of people to work together.
2. Scope and relationship	It is wide in scope. It includes cooperation. Coordination without cooperation will lead to dissatisfaction of employees.	It is narrow in scope. Cooperation in the absence of coordination leads to wasted efforts.
3. Nature	It is a deliberate and conscious effort of managers. It provides unity of actions to achieve common goals.	It is a voluntary effort of employees. It indicates merely the willingness of individuals to help each other.

2

Principles of Management

Q1. What is meant by *management principles*?

Ans. A managerial principle is a broad and general guideline for decision making and behavior

Q2. Distinguish between management principles and principles of pure science

Ans. The differences between management principles and principles of pure science are:

Table 2.1

Basis	*Management principles*	*Principle of pure science*
Nature	Management principles are flexible, not rigid.	They are more rigid
Deal with	They deal with human behavior	They deal with objects and phenomena
Scope for creativity	There is scope for creativity varying from situation to situation	There is no scope for creativity
Example	Unity of command, unity of direction	Law of gravitation

Q3. All management principles have to keep pace with changes in the business environment. Give an example to describe this situation.

Ans.

- In the absence of Information and Communication Technology (ICT), a manager can oversee only a small workforce within a narrow geographical space. The advent of ICT has expanded the capability of the managers to preside over large business empires spread across the globe

- Infosys headquarters in Bangalore boast of the Asia's largest flat screen in their conference room from where their managers can interact with their employees and customers all over the world

Q4. Distinguish between principles and techniques of management.

Ans. The differences between principles and techniques of management are:

Table 2.2

Basis	*Principles*	*Techniques*
Meaning	They are the broad and general guidelines for decision making and behavior	They are methods involving a series of steps to be taken so as to accomplish goals
Example	Principle of fair remuneration was given by Fayol	There are several techniques to ensure that this principle is followed like differential piece wage system

Q5. Distinguish between principles of management and values.

Ans. The differences between principles and values are:

Table 2.3

Basis	*Principles*	*Values*
Meaning	They are the broad and general guidelines for decision making and behavior	They are general rules of behavior of public in society
Derived	They are derived after research in various situations	They are derived from common practice
Nature	They are basic guidelines for behavior	They are desirable and have moral connotations
Example	Unity of command, unity of direction	Honesty, punctuality

Q6. How are management principles derived?

Ans. Management principles are derived through:

1. Research (observation and experimentation)
2. Continuous practice and personal experience of managers
   - i. Principle of unity of command was derived through research
   - ii. Principle of discipline was derived through personal experiences of managers

Q7. How do management principles contribute towards development of management both as an art and science?

Ans. Derivation of management principles may be said to be a matter of science and their creative application may be regarded as an art.

Q8. What is the difference between principles and functions of management?

Ans. The differences between the principles and functions are:

Table 2.4

Basis	*Principles*	*Functions*
Meaning	They are broad and general guidelines of decision making and behavior	They are the actions to be taken while practicing management
Example	Unity of command	Planning, organizing, staffing

Q9. Discuss the nature of management principles.

Ans. The nature of management principles can be described as follows:

1. ***Universal applicability***
   - They are intended to apply to all types of organization whether:
     - Business or non business
     - Public sector or private sector
     - Small or large
     - Manufacturing or service sector

- The extent of their applicability would vary with the nature of organization, business activity, scale of operation, etc.

For Example:

Division of work is applicable to a government office and also to a private limited company.

2. *General guidelines*
   - They are guidelines but do not provide straightforward solutions to all managerial problems
   - Real business situations are very complex and dynamic and are a result of many factors
   - However, the importance of principles can't be under estimated because even a small guideline helps to solve a given conflict.

For Example:

In dealing with a conflict between 2 departments a manager may emphasize on the primacy of the overall goals of the firm

3. *Formed by practice and experimentation*
   - They are formed by experience and collective wisdom of managers and by experimentation
   - Refer to Ans. 6.

For Example:

It is a matter of common experience that discipline is indispensable for accomplishing any goal

4. *Flexible*
   - The principles are not rigid prescriptions which have to be followed to the core. They are flexible and can be modified by the manager when the situation so demands. Thus, they give the manager enough discretion to do so.

For Example:

The degree of authority (centralization) or its dispersal (decentralization) will depend upon the situations and circumstances of each enterprise

5. *Mainly behavioral*
   - They are behavioral in nature and aim at influencing behavior of human beings

- It is not that these principles don't pertain to things and phenomenon. They enable a better understanding of the relationship between human and material resources.

For Example:

While planning the layout of a factory, orderliness would require that workflows are matched by the flow of materials and movement of men

6. *Cause and effect relationships*
   - They are intended to establish relationship between cause and effect
   - Accurate cause and effect relationships may sometimes be difficult to establish
   - These principles are less perfect as they mainly apply to human behavior
   - Yet, they assist managers in establishing these relationships to some extent and are therefore helpful

For Example:

If principle of discipline is not obeyed then it would cause indiscipline in the organization which results in chaos

7. *Contingent*
   - The application of these principles is contingent or dependent upon the prevailing situation at a particular point of time

For Example:

The employees deserve fair remuneration which depends upon contribution of employees, paying capacity of the employer and the prevalent wage rate for the occupation

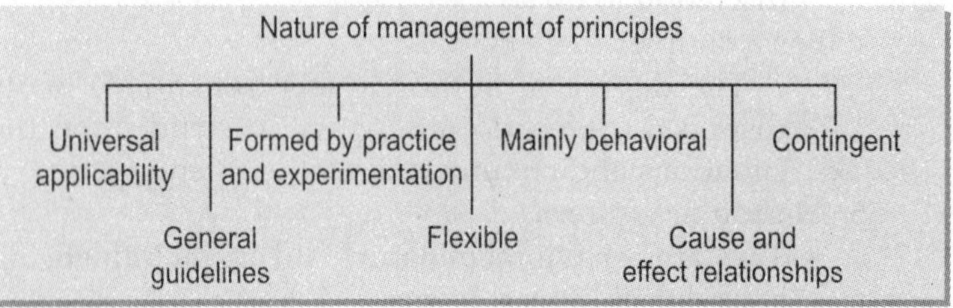

Q10. Identify the nature of principles of *management*.

1. **Principles don't provide readymade straightjacket solutions to all problems**
2. **Dependence on prevailing conditions**

Ans.

1. General guidelines
2. Contingent

Q11. Kiran Mazumdar shaw is a highly successful business woman and is CEO of Biocon. Who does she owe the success to?

Ans. Biocon owes its success to adherence to the principles underlying good management practices.

Q12. Explain Fayol's principles of *management*.

Ans.

- Fayol identified the activities of an industrial undertaking as:
  - Technical
  - Commercial
  - Financial
  - Accounting
  - Security
  - Managerial
- He published a book by the name of 'Administration Industrielle et Generale' which was published in english as 'General and Industrial Management'
- He was also called the father of general management

The various principles given by Fayol were:

1. *Division of labor*
   - According to this principle work should be divided into small specialized tasks/jobs

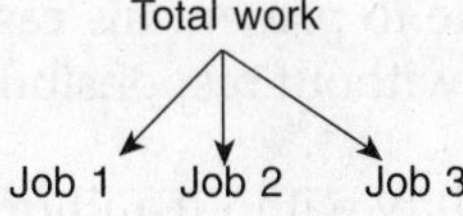

   - Each task is to be performed by a specialist or trained employee
   - According to Fayol the basic intention of this principle is to produce more and better work for the same effort

- It applies to all kinds of work whether technical or managerial
- It leads to specialization

For Example:

A person skilled in computer programming continues to do that work over a period of time. This helps him to ultimately become a specialist

- Benefits
  - Leads to specialization
  - Makes the task simpler
  - Results in effective and efficient output
  - Ensure better work and more production
- Because of division of work in an organization we have separate departments like finance, sales, etc.
- Adverse effects of violation (opposite of benefits)

2. ***Authority and responsibility***
   - According to Fayol authority is the right/power to give orders and obtain obedience
   - There are 2 types of authority:
     - Official authority (related to position)
     - Personal authority (related to personality)
   - Official authority is the authority to command and arises out of position
   - Personal authority is the authority of an individual manager enjoyed due to his personality
   - Responsibility of an individual refers to the obligation to perform the job assigned
   - According to this principle, there should be a balance between authority and responsibility i.e. a manager should have the right to punish a subordinate for not obeying a legitimate order but only after sufficient opportunity has been given to a subordinate to present his case
   - Authority without responsibility will lead to misuse of power
   - Responsibility without authority will make a person ineffective

For Example:

A sales manager is given the authority to grant a credit period to the clients for only 40 days. However, the client is asking for a credit period of 60 days and this deal would help the company to make profits of 50 crores. The management can't hold the manager responsible if the deal is not struck as there is an imbalance between authority and responsibility

- Benefits
  - No misuse of authority
  - Helps in increasing productivity by achieving targets
  - Makes a person more effective in decision making
  - Makes a person more responsible and helps him perform his duties on time

3. ***Discipline***
   - It refers to obedience to organizational rules and regulations and employment agreement
   - According to Fayol, discipline requires:
     - Good superiors at all levels
     - Clear and fair employment agreements
     - Judicious application of penalties
   - Discipline implies that both workers and management should honor their commitments without any prejudice towards one another

   For Example:

   Management and labor union have entered into an agreement where workers have agreed to put in extra hours and the management promises to increase the wages of workers when the company accomplishes its mission and revives out of losses. Management should honor its commitments

   - Advantages
     - Smooth and systematic functioning
     - Maintenance of a productive environment
     - Healthy relations between superiors and subordinates
     - Improvement in efficiency and achievement of goals

4. ***Unity of command***
   - This principle states that for a group of subordinates there should be only one superior who issues orders and to whom they are accountable and responsible
   - Unity means singleness and command refers to source of authority

- This principle is strictly followed in military organizations where dual subordination is avoided

For Example:

A salesperson is asked to give a 10% discount to customers by the marketing manager but the finance manager tells him not to offer a discount more than 6%. Thus, there is absence of unity of command

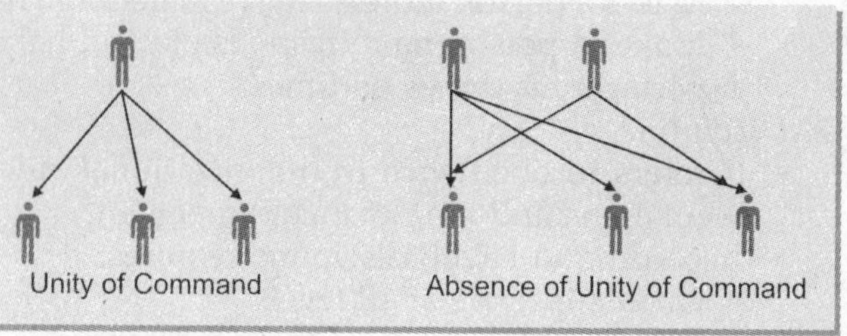

Fig. 2.1: Absence of unity of command results in chaos and confusion

- Adverse effects of violation
  - Confusion and chaos
  - Authority is undermined
  - Division of loyalty
  - Compromise in discipline and order
  - Threat to stability of the firm

5. ***Unity of direction***
   - Unity means singleness and direction refers to the path/plan to be followed towards achievement of organizational goals
   - This principle states that all activities having the same objective should be put under 'one head and one plan'
   - This principle implies unity of command, unity of plan and unity of objectives
   - Benefits
     - Increases efficiency
     - Clear direction of activities
     - Focusing of efforts
     - Optimum utilization of resources
     - Achievement of organizational goals

For Example:

A company manufacturing cars and motorcycles should have 2 separate divisions headed by different divisional managers and their respective plans

6. ***Remuneration of personnel***
   - According to this principle, the remuneration should be:
     - Fair
     - Just
     - Equitable

     To both employees and the organization
   - Remuneration refers to the compensation paid to the employees for the services provided by them to the organization
   - The factors that should be considered before paying fair remuneration are:
     - It should give a reasonable standard of living to the employees
     - It should be according to the qualifications and experience of the employees
     - It should be according to the paying capacity of the organization
     - It should be according to the rate prevailing in the industry
   - Advantages
     - Motivation and loyalty of employees increases
     - Good relation between employees and employer
     - Stability of the organization
     - Low rate of absenteeism and turnover

   For Example:

   A company distributes its profits to the shareholders in a fair manner
7. ***Equity***
   - Equity refers to:
     - Fair
     - Just
     - Kind

Behavior of superiors towards all their employees in order to ensure their loyalty and devotion

- This principle states that there should be no discrimination against employees on the basis of:
  - Caste
  - Religion
  - Gender
- However, Fayol doesn't rule out the use of strictness and force as and when required especially with lazy and non performing employees. He felt that in such cases use of force will help to strengthen the fact that everyone is equal in the eyes of management

For Example:

Many Indians are holding the post of CEOs even in MNCs

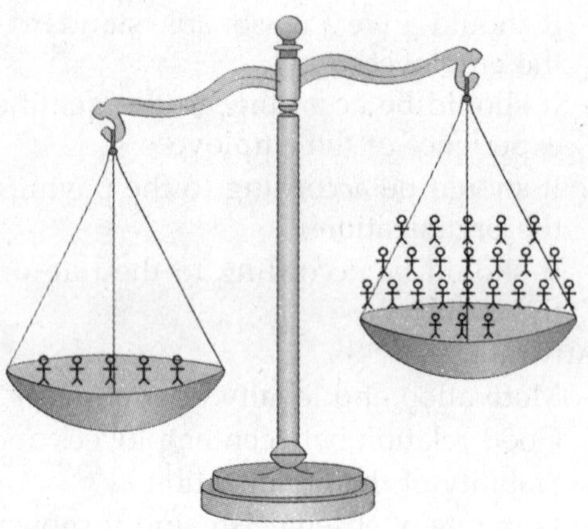

Fig. 2.2: All employees must be treated equally without any discrimination

8. ***Scalar chain***
   - Scalar chain is also called the chain of command/ chain of communication
   - Principle of scalar chain refers to the chain of superiors and subordinates from the top to the lowest level of management

- This chain allows for the flow of responsibility in an upward direction, authority in a downward direction and communication in both upward and downward directions
- According to this principle if one person in the scalar chain wishes to communicate with the other, all the intermediate positions should be respected and not bypassed

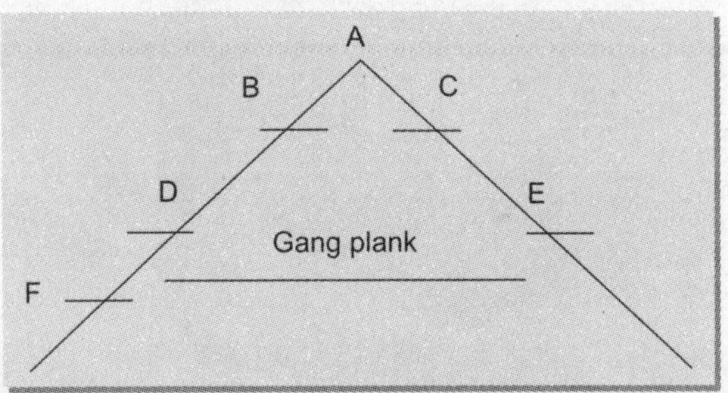

Fig. 2.3: Scalar chain

- Fayol had realized that the scalar chain will be very time consuming, he thus allowed a bridge of direct communication known as the gang plank which would happen only in the following conditions:
  - In case of emergency
  - People who wish to communicate should be at the same level
  - They should take permission from their immediate superiors before communicating
- Benefits
  - Ensures discipline
  - Smooth flow of communication
  - Maintains good superior subordinate relations
  - Avoids any confusion

9. ***Initiative***
   - Initiative refers to taking the first step with self motivation
   - With respect to management it refers to thinking about and executing the plan
   - The principle of initiative states that the superior should encourage initiative among their subordinates

and should reward any good suggestions which result in positive effects like reduction in cost and time saving

- However, it should not mean going against the established limits of the organization for the sake of being different

Fig. 2.4: Superiors must promote initiative among their subordinates

- Benefits
  - Encouragement, sense of belonging and participation
  - Feeling of motivation and satisfaction
  - Encouragement of creativity and imagination amongst the subordinates
  - Increased loyalty and stability of the organization

10. *Espirit de corps*
    - The literal meaning of espirit de corps is 'spirit of the body'
    - According to Fayol, the spirit which should govern an organization should be that of:
      - Unity
      - Harmony
      - Teamwork
    - This is because there is strength in unity and all managers should replace 'I' with 'We'

- Benefits
  - Feeling of mutual trust and understanding
  - Effective and efficient achievement of goals through synergy effect
  - Feeling of participation and belongingness
  - High degree of coordination

11. ***Subordination of individual interest to general interest***
    - Individual interest refers to the individual's personal interest.
    - General interest refers to the organization's interest.
    - This principle states that priority should be given to the organizational interest over the personal interest of the individual
    - If the interest of the individuals and the organization are in conflict then managers must guide the individuals to forget their differences and apply their efforts in achieving organizational goals since if the organization prospers the individuals will automatically prosper
    - Benefits
      - Cultivate teamwork
      - Improved inter-personal relations
      - Greater coordination
      - Improves loyalty, efficiency and productivity

    For Example:

    The organization is going through financial crisis and cuts down the salary of the employees. In this situation the organizational interest should be considered

12. ***Centralization and decentralization***
    - Centralization refers to the concentration of decision making authority in the hands of few in the top level of management
    - Decentralization refers to the dispersal of decision making authority to the middle and lower levels of management
    - There should be a balance between centralization and decentralization by including subordinates' involvement along with that of the superiors

- An organization should neither be completely centralized nor completely decentralized
- The degree of centralization or decentralization depends on:
  - Size of the organization
  - Ability of the superiors and subordinates
- Benefits
  - No over-burdening
  - Employees will be motivated
  - Same as subordination of individual interest

13. ***Order***
- Order means arrangement
- Arrangement may be with respect to people or things
- Arrangement of people is known as social order and arrangement of things as material order
- This principle states that there should be a place for everything and everything should be in its right place

For Example:

Files should be kept in the file cabinet and the manager should be in his room

Fig. 2.5: An orderly workstation is much better than an unorderly one

- Benefits
  - Orderliness
  - No wastage of time
  - Low level of fatigue since things are in order
  - Proper utilization of physical and human resources

14. ***Stability of personnel***
- This refers to continuity in the period of employment at a particular post or position in order to allow the

employees reasonable time for adjustment and performance

- According to Fayol, people should be selected after a vigorous procedure but once selected they should be kept at their post for a minimum fixed tenure
- Employees should not be shifted frequently as it would result in insecurity and instability
- This of course does not imply that employees should not be promoted or transferred as and when required.
- Benefits
  - Job security
  - Motivation and loyalty increases
  - Stability in the organization
  - Lower employee turnover
  - Reduction in the cost of training

Q13. What is meant by *rule of thumb*?

Ans. Personal judgment, hit and trial method which is not supported by any scientific reason is called the rule of thumb.

Q14. What is meant by scientific *management*?

Ans.

- It is an approach that was based on the method of science:
  - Defining a problem
  - Developing alternative solutions
  - Measuring progress
  - Anticipating consequences
  - Drawing conclusion
- It is the application of science in the field of management of different problems
- Taylor emerged as the father of scientific management
- According to Taylor, scientific management means knowing exactly what you want men to do and seeing that they do it in the best and cheapest way

For Example:

The Bethlehem Steel Company achieved a 3 fold increase in productivity by applying these principles

Q15. Explain the principles of scientific *management*.

Ans. The various principles of scientific management are:

1. ***Science not rule of thumb***
   - Rule of thumb is personal judgment, a hit and trial method which is not supported by any scientific reason whatsoever
   - Taylor believed that there was only one best method to maximize efficiency
   - This method can be developed through study and analysis
   - Scientific method should substitute rule of thumb throughout the organization
   - Scientific method involves different work studies developing a standard method which would be followed throughout all cadres in the organization

   For Example:

   Loading pigs of iron into box carts should be scientifically planned and managed. This saves human energy as well as wastage of time and materials. Use of internet has brought about improvements in internal efficiencies and customer satisfaction

2. ***Harmony not discord***
   - Managers serve as a link between owners and workers
   - A class conflict between managers and workers arose which is not good
   - Taylor emphasized that there should be complete harmony between workers and the management
   - Both should realize that each one is important. To achieve this, Taylor called for complete mental revolution on the part of both the management and the workers
   - It means that management and workers should transform their thinking. In such a situation even trade unions won't think of going on a strike
   - Management should share gains of the company, with the workers

   For Example:

   A paternalistic style of management is in practice in Japan. There is a complete openness between the management and workers. If at all workers go on strike they wear a black badge but work more than the normal working hours to gain the sympathy of the management

3. ***Cooperation not individualism***
   - There should be complete cooperation between the labor and the management instead of individualism
   - The principle is an extension of principle of harmony not discord
   - Competition should be replaced by cooperation. Both labor and management should realize that they need each other
   - Management should:
     - Allow suggestions by employees
     - Reward them for suggestions
     - Allow them to be a part of the management
   - Workers should desist from going on strike and making unreasonable demands on the management. There should be an open communication system

   For Example:

   Paternalistic style of management in Japan where there is complete openness between the management and workers

4. ***Development of each and every worker to his greatest efficiency***
   - Scientific management stood for worker's development. Worker training was essential to learn the best method
   - Taylor was of the view that the concern for efficiency could be built through:
     - Process of employee selection where each person should be scientifically selected
     - Work assigned should suit his physical, mental and intellectual capabilities
     - To increase efficiency, they should be given the required training
     - Efficient employees would produce more , hence earn more. This ensures their greatest efficiency and prosperity

Q16. What is meant by paternalistic style of *management*?

Ans. Refer Ans. 15

Q17. Which principle is an extension of harmony not discord?

Ans. Cooperation not individualism

Q18. Identify a scientific principle of management which emphasizes that competition should be replaced by cooperation.

Ans. Cooperation not individualism

Q19. Explain the various techniques of *scientific management*.

Ans. The various techniques of scientific management are:

1. *Functional foremanship*
   - This technique is an application of Fayol's principle of division of labor to the foremen's level
   - Taylor believed that a foreman's job is multi-dimensional and requires qualities like:
     - Intelligence
     - Honesty
     - Judgment
     - Skill
     - Good health

     All these qualities are difficult to find in a single foreman
   - Therefore, he proposed that 8 foremen would perform 8 different jobs which would help in:
     - Specialization
     - Increasing efficiency
     - Increasing speed
   - Taylor advocated separation of planning and execution function
   - In the technique of functional foremanship, the factory manager would have a production in charge and a planning in charge under him and each one these would be in charge of 4 foremen each.
   - Planning in charge
     - *Route clerk:* He is in charge of determining the path/route of the various stages in the production process
     - *Time and cost clerk:* He determines the time and cost involved in every operation

- *Instruction card clerk:* He issues various instructions to the workers
- *Disciplinarian:* He ensures the overall discipline

• Production in charge
  - *Gang boss:* He assembles all the resources needed for production
  - *Repair boss:* He is responsible for all repairs and maintenance of plant and machinery
  - *Speed boss:* He ensures that the work is progressing at the right speed
  - *Inspector:* He inspects the quality of the output

• This technique violates the principle of unity of command since the workers are receiving instructions from 8 different foremen

2. ***Standardization and simplification of work***
   • Standardization refers to the process of setting standards for every business activity
   • It can be done for:
     - Process
     - Raw materials
     - Machinery
     - Time
     - Methods
     - Product
     - Working conditions
   • The standards are the benchmarks which must be adhered to
   • The various objectives of standardization are:
     - To reduce a given line of products to fixed types, sizes, etc.
     - To establish interchangeability of manufactured parts and products
     - To establish standards of performance of men and machines

   For Example:

   Business processes like re-engineering, kaizen and benchmarking are aimed at standardizing work

   • Simplification aims at eliminating superfluous varieties, sizes and dimensions
   • The various objectives of simplification are:

- Eliminating unnecessary diversity of products
- Savings of cost of labor, machines and tools
- Fuller utilization of equipment
- Increasing turnover
- Reducing inventories

For Example:

Men's shirt sizes generally follow the range 38, 40, etc. and not superfluous sizes like 38.5, 39.25

3. ***Method study***

- According to Taylor, the objective of method study is to discover one best way of doing the job
- It seeks to determine one best method to do a job after weighing several parameters
- Right from procurement of raw material till the final product is delivered to the customer, every action is a part of the method study

For Example:

Taylor devised the concept of assembly line by using method study which was used successfully by Ford Motor Company and is being used till date

- The objectives of method study are:
  - To minimize cost of production
  - Maximize quality through proper combination of resources
  - Maximize customer satisfaction
  - Ensure accuracy and uniformity

4. ***Motion study***

- It refers to the study of movements like:
  - Lifting
  - Sitting
  - Putting objects
  - Changing positions

  Which are undertaken while doing a typical job
- Taylor identified 3 types of movements
  - Productive
  - Unproductive
  - Incidental
- He used stopwatches and various symbols and colors to identify different motions
- Unnecessary movements are sought to be eliminated so it takes less time to complete the job efficiently

- The purpose of the motion study is:
  - To eliminate unnecessary movements
  - To increase efficiency and productivity
  - To save time and energy of workers
  - Helps in design of machines and equipment which avoid unnecessary movement
  - Provide the basis for time study because unnecessary movements are eliminated before standard time for performing a job is determined

5. *Time study*
   - It is the study of the time taken by an average worker of reasonable skills in performing a well defined job
   - This study helps to determine the standard time with the help of time measuring devices like stopwatch
   - The result of the study is fixed only after taking several readings
   - Methods of time study depend on
     - Volume of task
     - Frequency of task
     - Cost involved
     - Time cycle of operation
   - The purpose of time study is to determine
     - Standard output/fair day's work
     - Number of workers to be employed
     - Suitable incentive schemes
     - Labor cost involved

   For Example:

   On the basis of several observations let the standard time to make one cardboard box be 20 minutes.
   Number of boxes in 1 hour = 3
   Number of working hours = 7
   Standard output per day = 21 boxes

6. *Fatigue study*
   - A person is bound to feel tired physically and mentally if he does not rest while working
   - The purpose of fatigue study is:
     - The rest intervals will help one to regain stamina and work again with the same capacity
     - Increase in productivity
     - Job satisfaction and loyalty

- Fatigue study seeks to determine the amount and frequency of rest intervals in completing a task

For Example:

In a plant, work takes place in 3 shifts of 8 hours each. Even in a single shift a worker has to be given rest interval to take his lunch, etc.

- There can be many causes for fatigue like:
  - Long working hours
  - Doing unsuitable work
  - Bad working conditions
  - Having uncordial relations with the boss

7. ***Differential piece wage system***

- This refers to a system of wage payment on the basis of number of units produced by them
- Workers producing less than the standard output are regarded as inefficient and are paid a lower piece rate
- Workers producing more than or equal to the standard output are regarded as efficient and are paid a higher piece rate
- The rate of payment depends on the worker's level of productivity

For Example:

Standard output for a day is equal to 20 boxes
Higher piece rate = Rs 55 per box
Lower piece rate = Rs 45 per box
Worker A:
Actual output = 21 boxes
Wage = 21 × 55 = Rs1155
Worker B:
Actual output = 18 boxes
Wage = 18 × 45 = Rs 810

- According to Taylor, this technique was to provide an incentive to the inefficient workers to reach the standard output. He also aimed at continuously motivating the efficient workers by paying them higher piece rate
- This technique aimed at 'Produce more earn more'

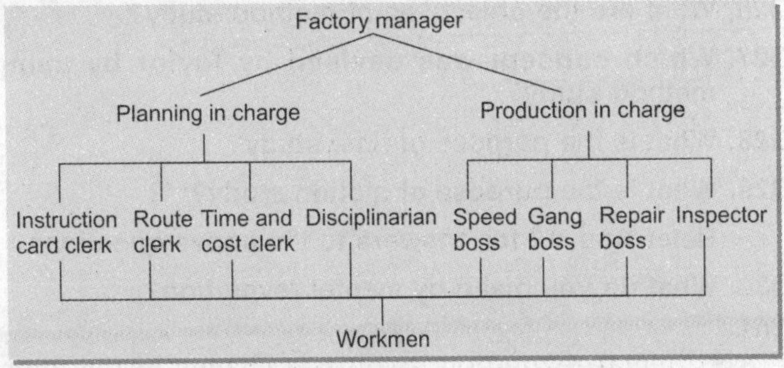

Q20. Identify the principle of management on which the technique of functional foremanship is based?

Q21. Which principle of management is violated in the technique of functional foremanship?

Q22. What prompted Taylor to suggest the technique of functional foremanship?

Q23. What are the objectives of simplification?

Q24. What are the objectives of standardization?

Q25. Differentiate between simplification and standardization.

Ans. The differences between standardization and simplification are:

Table 2.5

Basis	*Simplification*	*Standardization*
Meaning	Definition	Definition
Objectives	Refer Ans. 19	Refer Ans. 19
Nature	It is an additive process because higher and better standards are set by organizations	It is a reduction/elimination process
Example	Nokia and Toyota have set high standards for their products and have gained large market share	Men's shirts generally follow size range of 38, 40 and not superfluous sizes like 38.5, 39.75

Q26. What are the objectives of method study?

Q27. Which concept was devised by Taylor by using method study?

Q28. What is the purpose of time study?

Q29. What is the purpose of motion study?

Refer Ans. 19 for answers to the above questions

Q30. What do you mean by mental revolution?

Ans.

- Mental revolution involves a change in the interpersonal attitude of workers and management from competition to cooperation and from suspicion to trust
- Earlier, the management suspected the workers of being lazy and workers suspected the management of exploitation
- Mental revolution proposes that they both should realize the other's importance and aim to increase the size of the surplus rather than quarreling over and dividing it
- Management should be ready to share the gains of the business with the workers who must work hard to ensure gains for the firm
- The positive attitude will benefit both the management and the workers

It is said that sum and substance of Taylor's ideas lie not in the disjointed description of the principles of scientific management but in the change of the mindset which is known as mental revolution

Q31. Give a comparative analysis of Fayol and Taylor.

Ans. The comparative analysis is as follows:

Table 2.6

Basis	*Fayol*	*Taylor*
Perspective	Fayol's study initiated at the top level management and then proceeded downwards. He adopted a top-downward approach	Taylor's study initiated at the shop floor level and then proceeded to higher levels. He adopted a bottom-upward approach

Contd.

Table 2.6 (*Contd.*)

Basis	*Fayol*	*Taylor*
Expression	His study is expressed as 'General Theory of Administration'	His study found expression as 'Scientific Management'
Personality	He was a practitioner	He was a scientist. He used scientific methods to solve management problems
Unity of command	Fayol was a staunch proponent of this concept and he proposed unity of command as one of the principles of management	Taylor didn't feel that this concept was very important as under functional foremanship each worker receives orders from 8 foremen
Applicability	Fayol's principles are universally applicable in all kinds of organizations and departments	Taylor's theory is applicable to specialized situations in factory organization and production departments only
Focus	His focus was on improving overall administration and efficiency	His focus was on increasing worker's productivity and organization's profitability
Formation	Fayol's theory was mainly a result of his personal experience and wisdom	Taylor's theory was a result of observation and experimentation

However, despite these differences their theories are considered to be mutually complementary in nature because:

- They can both co-exist in an organization and go hand in hand
- Both the theories are guided by the same objectives of maximization of efficiency and prosperity
- Both the theories form the basis for managerial decision making and management
- Both the theories suggest mutual cooperation and team spirit

For Example:

Taylor's principle of harmony not discord and Fayol's principle of espirit de corps

- Both the theories advocated division of labor

For Example:

Fayol's principle of division of labor and Taylor's technique of functional foremanship

OTHER IMPORTANT QUESTIONS

Q1. What do you mean by work studies?

Ans.

- Scientific work study was proposed by Taylor as a science based approach to an effective and productive completion of work
- Scientific work study aims to determine fair day's work/standard work (minimum work to be completed in a day). This is done by optimum utilization of the various resources and finding the best way to do a job

Q2. Differentiate between time and motion study.

Ans. The differences between time and motion study are:

Table 2.7

Basis	*Time study*	*Motion study*
Purpose	It is a study of the time taken by an average worker of reasonable skills in performing a job. It helps to determine the standard time for a job	Its purpose is to eliminate unnecessary movements and to save time and energy of the worker. The movements were classified as productive, unproductive and incidental
Sequence of performance	It is performed after the motion study	It is performed before the time study
Devices used	It used time measuring devices like stop watch	Taylor had used different symbols, colors and stop watches to identify different motions
Example	If the time taken to manufacture 1 box is 20 minutes then the standard output per hour is 3 boxes and the standard output per day with 7 working hours is 21 boxes	Taylor was able to reduce the motions in brick layering from 18 to 5 thereby increasing productivity by about 4 times

Q3. The production manager of an automobile company asks the foremen to achieve the target production of 200 scooters per day. However, he did not give him the necessary authority for requisition of tools and materials from the store. Can the production manager blame the foremen if he is not able to achieve the target? Explain the principle of management.

Ans. Explain the principle of authority and responsibility

Q4. Name and explain the technique of Taylor which provides motivation to workers to achieve the standard output.

Ans. Differential piece wage system

Q5. Hari and Heena are working for the same organization, having the same qualification and experience. Hari is getting Rs. 4000 per month and Heena is getting Rs. 3000 per month. Which principle is being violated?

Ans. Equity

Q6. Production manager of Bharat Ltd instructs the salesman to go slow in selling products whereas marketing manager is insisting on fast selling. Which principle is violated?

Ans. Unity of command

Q7. Identify the principles of management

i. **Replace I with We**
ii. **First step with self motivation**
iii. **Principle of kindness and justice**
iv. **Right place for physical and human resources**
v. **Balance between the role of seniors and superiors**

Ans.

i. Espirit de corps
ii. Initiative
iii. Equity
iv. Order
v. Centralization and decentralization

Q8. Explain the contributions of Fayol.

Ans. The following contributions were made by Fayol:

1. ***Fayol was the first to identify the four functions of management:***
   - Planning
   - Organizing
   - Directing
   - Controlling

   Although his version was a bit different:
   - Plan
   - Organize
   - Command
   - Coordinate
   - Control
2. ***According to him, all activities of an industrial undertaking could be divided into:***
   - Technical
   - Commercial
   - Financial
   - Security
   - Accounting
   - Managerial
3. ***He also suggested that qualities a manager must possess should be:***
   - Physical
   - Moral
   - Education
   - Knowledge
   - Experience
4. ***The 14 principles of management were propounded by him which are discussed in detail in his book 'Administration Industrielle et Generale' published in 1917 which was published in english as 'General and Industrial Management' in 1949***

Q9. Differentiate between unity of command and unity of direction.

Ans. The differences between unity of command and unity of direction are:

Table 2.8

Basis	*Unity of command*	*Unity of direction*
Meaning	One subordinate should receive orders from and should be responsible to only one superior	Each group of activities having same objective must have one head and one plan
Aim	It prevents dual subordination	It prevents overlapping activities
Implications	It affects an individual employee	It affects the entire organization

Q10. Management principles are unnecessary guidelines as managers take their decision based on their opinions and emotions. Do you agree? Explain.

or

Explain the importance of principles of management.

Ans. Management principles are important as:

1. ***Providing managers with useful insights into the future***
   - They provide the manager with useful insights into real world situations
   - Adherence to these principles adds to their knowledge, ability and understanding of managerial situations
   - It enables them to learn from past mistakes and conserve time by solving recurring problems quickly. Thus, it increases managerial efficiency

   For Example:

   A manager can leave routine decision taking to his subordinates and deal with exceptional situations which require his expertise following principle of delegation

2. ***Optimum utilization of resources and effective administration***
   - Resources both human and material available with the company are limited and must be put to the optimum use, i.e. they should give maximum benefit with minimum cost

- Principles equip the managers to foresee the cause and effect relationship of their decisions and actions such that wastages associated with trial and error can be overcome
- Effective administration necessitates impersonalization of managerial conduct so that managerial power is used with due discretion
- Principles limit the boundary of managerial discretion so that their decisions are free from personal bias

For Example:

In deciding the annual budgets for different departments, rather than personal preferences managerial discretion should be bounded by the principle of contribution to organizational objectives

3. *Scientific decisions*
   - Decisions must be based on facts, thoughtful and justifiable in terms of intended purpose
   - They must be timely, realistic and subject to evaluation and measurement
   - Principles help in thoughtful decision making. They emphasize logic rather than blind faith. Such decisions are based on the objective of assessment of the situation and are free from bias
4. *Meeting changing environment requirements*
   - Although principles are in the nature of general guidelines but they can be modified and help managers to meet changing requirements of the environment, i.e. they are flexible to adapt to dynamic business environment

For Example:

Management principles emphasize on division of work and specialization. This has been extended to entire business whereby companies are specializing in core competency and divesting non core business.

Hindustan Lever Ltd has divested on core businesses of chemicals and seeds

- Some companies outsource their non core activities like share transfer management and advertising to outside agencies. Even core processes such as research and development, manufacturing and marketing are being outsourced.

5. ***Management training, education and research***
    - Principles of management are at the core of management theory. These are used as a basis for training, education and research
    - The principles provide basic groundwork for the development of management as a discipline
    - These are taught in professional courses like MBA, BBA
    - They ensure refinement of management practices by facilitating development of new management techniques
    - Thus we see that techniques like operating research, cost accounting, just in time inventory, Kaizen, etc. have developed due to further research on these principles
6. ***Fulfilling social responsibility***
    - The increased awareness of public forces businesses especially ltd companies to fulfill their social responsibilities
    - Management theory and principles have evolved as a response to these demands and the interpretation of the principles has assumed newer and contemporary meanings
    - Equity today, does not only pertain to wages but also value to customers, care for environment, dealings with business associates, etc.

For Example:

BHEL has developed Ranipur in Haridwar

Shri Mahila Griha Udyog Lijjat Papad combines business with social responsibility and makes its stakeholders self reliant

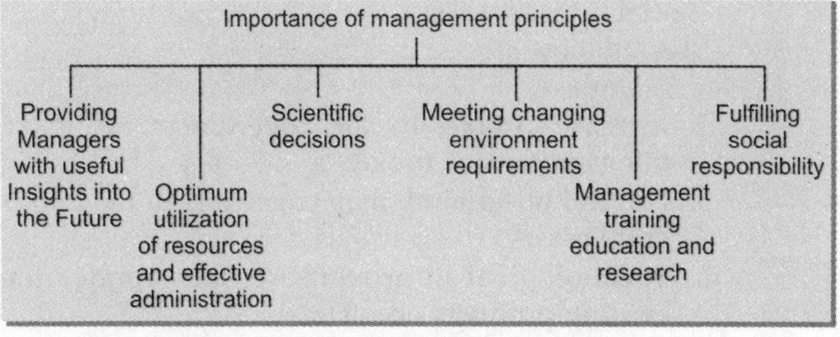

3

Business Environment

Q1. What is meant by *business environment*?

Ans.

- The term 'business environment' refers to the sum total of all individuals, institutions and other forces that are outside the control of a business enterprise but that may affect its performance.
- Individuals may include:
  - Consumers
  - Competitors
- Institutions may include:
  - Government
  - Competitors
  - Consumer groups
  - Courts
  - Media
- Forces may include:
  - Economic
  - Political
  - Social
  - Technology

  For Example:

  i. Increase in taxes by the government can make things expensive to buy

  ii. Political uncertainty may create fear in the minds of investors

  iii. Technological improvements may render the existing products obsolete.

iv. Changes in fashion and tastes of consumers may shift the demand in market from existing to new products

v. Increased competition in market may reduce the profit margins.

Q2. Explain the features of *business environment*.

Ans. The various features of business environment are described below:

1. *Totality of external factors*
   - Business environment is the sum total of all things external to business firms and as such is aggregative in nature.
   - Refer to Ans 1 for components.
2. *Specific and general forces*
   - It includes both specific and general forces.
   - Specific forces include:
     - Investors
     - Customers
     - Suppliers
     - Competitors

     And affect the individual enterprises directly and immediately in their day to day working.
   - General forces include:
     - Social
     - Political
     - Technological
     - Legal

     And have an impact on all business enterprises and thus may affect an individual firm only indirectly.
3. *Inter-relatedness*
   - Different elements or parts of business environment are closely inter related.

   For Example:

   Increased life expectancy of people and increased awareness for healthcare have increased the demand for many health products and services like fat free cooking oil, diet coke, yoga and health resorts.

4. ***Uncertainty***
   - Business environment is largely uncertain as it is very difficult to predict future happenings, especially when environment changes are taking too frequently.

   For Example:

   Ever changing environment of information technology and fashion industries.
5. ***Dynamic nature***
   - Business environment is dynamic in the sense that it keeps on changing whether in terms of technological improvements, shifts in consumer preferences or entry of new competition in the market.
6. ***Complexity***
   - Since business environment consists of numerous inter related and dynamic conditions or forces which arise from different sources, it becomes difficult to comprehend what exactly constitutes a given environment.

   For Example:

   It may be difficult to know the extent of the relative impact of the social, economic, political, technological or legal factors on change in demand of a particular product in a market.
7. ***Relativity***
   - Business environment is a relative term since it differs from country to country and even region to region.

   For Example:

   i. Political conditions in the USA may differ from those in China

   ii. Demand for sarees may be high in India but very low in France

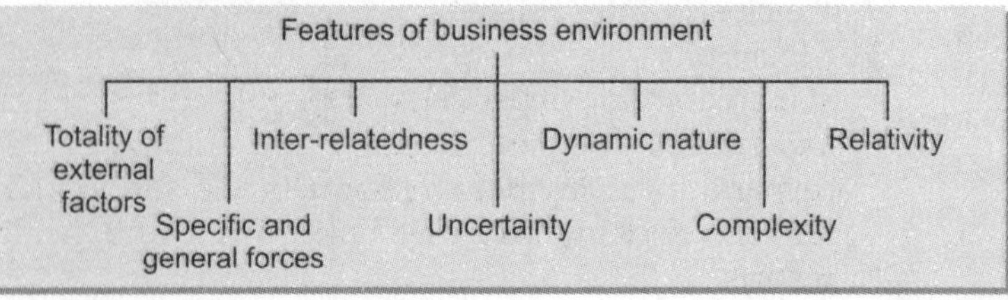

Q3. Political conditions in China differ from that in Pakistan. Which feature of business environment is being highlighted?

Ans. Relativity is being highlighted here.

Q4. Describe the importance of business environment.

or

A good understanding of business environment by the mangers enables the firm to react to various forces. Comment.

Ans. The importance of business environment is described below:

1. *Enables the firm to identify opportunities and getting the first mover advantage*
   - Opportunities refer to the positive external trends or changes that will help a firm to improve its performance
   - Early identification of opportunities helps a firm to be the first to exploit them and not lose them to the competitors.

   For Example:

   Maruti Udyog became the leader in the small car market segment because it was the first to recognize the need for small cars in an environment of rising petrol prices and a large middle class population.
2. *Enables the firm to identify threats and serves as an early warning signal*
   - Threats refer to the external environment trends and changes that will hinder a firm's performance.
   - Environmental awareness can help managers to identify various threats on time and serve as an early warning signal

   For Example:

   If an Indian firm finds that a foreign MNC is entering the Indian market with new substitutes, then this acts as a warning signal. The Indian firm may react by improving quality, reducing price, etc.
3. *Helps in tapping useful resources*
   - Environment is source of various resources for running a business.

- A business enterprise assembles various resources called inputs like:
  - Finance
  - Machinery
  - Power
  - Raw materials
  - Water
  - Labor

  From its environment including financiers, government and suppliers.
- The firm designs policies that allow it to get the resources that it needs so that it can convert those resources into outputs that the environment desires.
- The firm depends on the environment as a source of inputs or resources and as an outlet for outputs.

4. *Helps in coping with rapid changes*
   - Business environment is dynamic and thus it is important to understand the pace of change.
   - The various changes may be:
     - Turbulent market conditions
     - Less brand loyalty
     - Divisions and sub divisions of markets (fragmentation)
     - Rapid changes in technology
     - More demanding customers
     - Intense global competition
   - Managers must understand the environment and develop suitable courses of action.
5. *Helps in assisting in planning and policy formulation*
   - Since environment is a source of both opportunities and threats for a business enterprise, its understanding and analysis can be the basis for deciding the future course of action (planning) or training guidelines for decision making (policy formulation)
   - Entry of new players in the market, means more competition may make an enterprise think afresh about how to deal with the situation.
6. *Helps in improving performance*
   - Business environment makes a difference in performance of an enterprise.

- The future of an enterprise is closely bound up with what is happening in the environment.
- Enterprises that continuously monitor their environment and adopt suitable practices are the ones which improve their current performances.

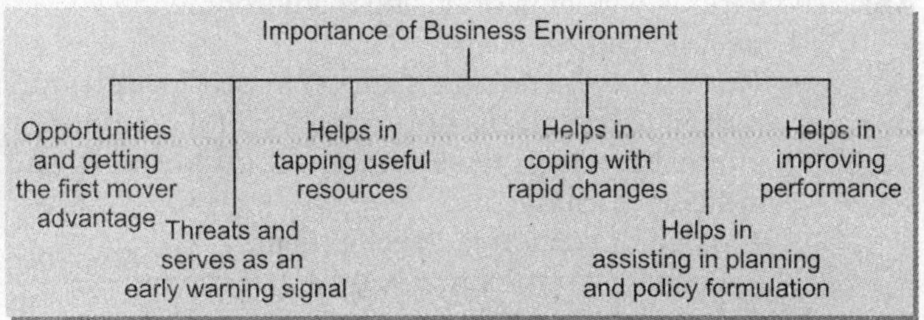

Q5. Name the various factors of Business Environment considered relevant for decision making and improving the performance of an enterprise.

Ans. The various factors relevant to the performance and decision making are:

1. **Economic**
2. **Social**
3. **Technological**
4. **Political**
5. **Legal**

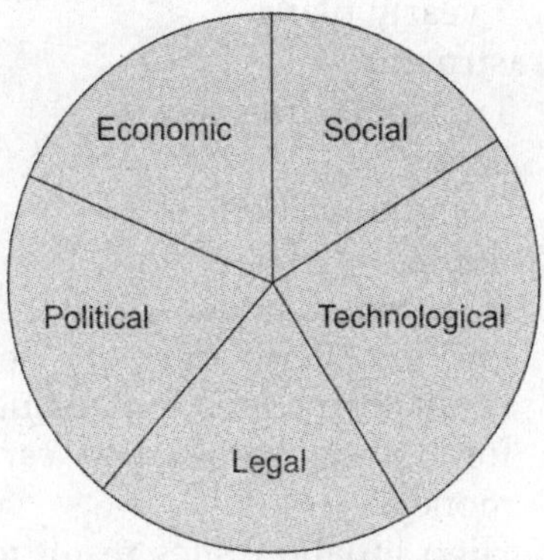

Fig. 3.1: Dimensions of business environment

Q6. Explain the various dimensions/elements of business environment.

or

Explain the various factors constituting the general environment of a business.

Ans. The various elements of business environment:

1. *Economic environment*
   - The various economic factors/macro level factors related to the means of production and distribution of wealth which have an impact on business and industry include:
     - Stage of economic development
     - Economic structure, i.e. mixed economy
       i. Public sector
       ii. Private sector
     - Economic policies of government
       i. Industrial
       ii. Monetary
       iii. Fiscal
     - Economic indices
       i. NNP
       ii. GNP
       iii. PCY
       iv. Personal disposable income
     - Economic planning
       i. Annual budgets
       ii. 5 yearly plans
     - Infrastructure
       i. Transportation
       ii. Banks
       iii. Communication

     For Example:

     i. In automobile and construction companies, low long term rates are beneficial as they result in increased spending by consumers for buying homes and cars on borrowed money.
     ii. High inflation rates result in constraints on business enterprises because they increase the

various costs of business such as the purchase of raw materials or machinery and payment of wages and salaries to employees.

2. *Social environment*
   - The social environment of business includes social force like:
     - Customs and Traditions
     - Values
     - Social Trends
     - Society's expectations from the firm
   - Traditions define social practices that have lasted for decades or even centuries.

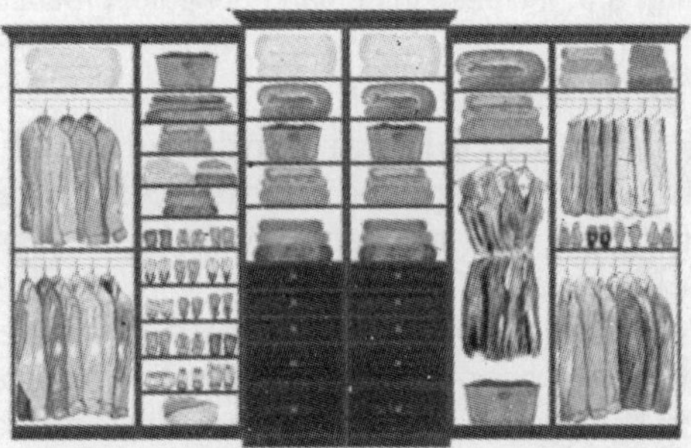

Fig. 3.2: Changes in the fashion industry

For Example:

Celebration of Diwali, Eid, etc. provides significant financial opportunities for greeting card companies, sweets or confectionery manufacturers, tailoring outlets and others.

- Values refer to concepts that a society holds in high regard.

For Example:

Freedom of choice in the market, business' responsibility towards the society and non-discriminating employee practices.

- Social trends present opportunities and threats to business enterprises.

For Example:

Health and fitness trend has become popular among large number of urban dwellers.

Fig. 3.3: Increase in demand of health products

3. *Political environment*
   - It includes political conditions such as general stability and peace in the country and specific attitudes that elected government representatives hold towards business.
   - Political stability builds up confidence among business people to invest in the long term projects for the growth of the economy. Political instability can shake that confidence.

   For Example:

   Even after opening up of our economy in 1991, foreign companies found it extremely difficult to cut through the bureaucratic red tape to get permits for doing business in India
4. *Technological environment*
   - This includes forces relating to scientific improvements and innovation which provide new ways of producing goods and services and new methods and techniques of operating a business.

   For Example:

   i. Airline companies have internet and www. pages where customers can book for flight destinations, check times, fares and book tickets.

   ii. Shifts in demand from vacuum tubes to transistors, from steam locomotives to diesel and electric engines, from fountain pen to ball point pen, etc.

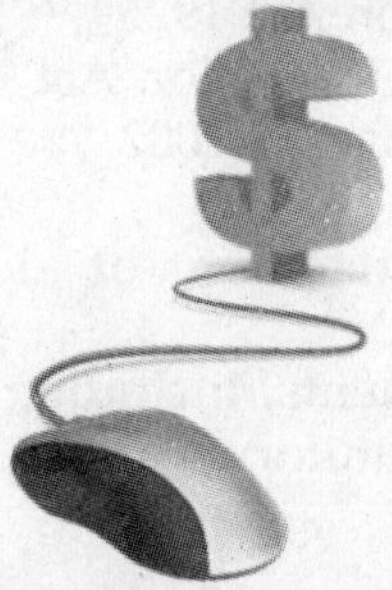

Fig. 3.4: Banking can be done through the internet

Fig. 3.5: Rail and air reservation can be done online

5. *Legal environment*
   - It includes various legislations passed by the government, administrative orders issued by government authorities, court judgments as well as the decisions rendered by various commissions and agencies at every level of the government: state, centre or local.
   - An adequate knowledge of rules and regulations framed by the government is a pre-requisite for better business performance. These include:
     - Companies Act 1956
     - Workmen's Compensation Act 1923
     - Industries (Development and Regulation) Act 1951
     - Exports (Control) Act 1947
     - Factories Act 1948
     - Industrial Disputes Act 1947

- Trade Union Act 1926
- Consumer Protection Act 1986
- Competition Act 2002

For Example:

i. The advertisement of alcoholic beverages is prohibited.
ii. Advertisements, including packets of cigarettes carry the statutory warning, 'smoking is injurious to health'

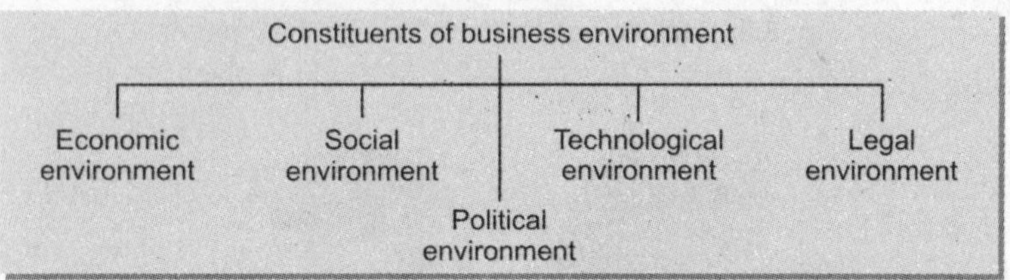

Q7. What were the problems faced by India during independence?

Ans. The various problems faced by India were:

1. The Indian economy was mainly agricultural and rural in character.
2. About 85% of the population was living in the villages.
3. About 70% of working population was in agriculture.
4. Production was carried out using low productivity and irrational technology.
5. There was no good health system and communicable diseases were widespread, mortality rates were high.

Q8. What were the main objectives of India's development plan?

Ans. The main objectives were to:

1. Initiate rapid economic growth to raise the standard of living, reduce unemployment and poverty.
2. Become self-reliant and set up a strong industrial base with emphasis on heavy and basic industries.
3. Reduce inequalities of income and wealth.
4. Adopt a socialistic pattern of development based on equality so as to prevent the exploitation of man by fellow men.

Q9. Mention the important features of the New Industrial Policy of 1991.

Ans. The important features of the NEP of 1991 are:

1. Many of the industries reserved for the public sector under the earlier policy, were de-reserved. The role of the public sector was limited to only four industries of strategic importance.
2. Disinvestment was carried out in case of many public sector industrial enterprises.
3. Policy towards foreign capital was liberalized. The share of foreign equity participation was increased and in many activities 100% FDI was permitted.
4. Automatic permission was now granted for technology agreements with foreign companies.
5. Foreign Investment Promotion Board (FIPB) was set up in order to promote and channelize foreign investment in India.

Q10. What is the essence of the New Economic Policy of 1991?

Ans. The essence of the NEP of 1991 was to:

1. Liberate the industry from the shackles of the licensing system (Liberalization)
2. Tremendously reduce the role of the public sector. (Privatization)
3. Encourage foreign private participation in India's industrial development. (Globalization)

Q11. Liberalization of Indian markets took place w.r.t. certain area. Explain.

or

Explain liberalization which was introduced as an important economic reform.

Ans.

- The economic reforms which were introduced were aimed at liberalizing the Indian business and industry from all unnecessary controls and restrictions.
- They signaled the end of the license-permit-quota raj.

Liberalization in the Indian industry took place with respect to:

1. Abolishing licensing requirement in most of the industries except a short list.
2. Freedom in deciding the scale of the business activities, i.e. no restriction on expansion/ contraction of business activities.
3. Freedom in fixing the prices of goods and services.
4. Removal of restrictions on the movement of goods and services.
5. Reduction in tax rates and lifting of unnecessary controls over the economy.
6. Making it easier to attract foreign capital and technology to India.
7. Simplifying the procedures for imports and exports.

Q12. Write short notes on privatization and globalization.

Ans. Privatization

- The new set of economic reforms aimed at giving greater role to the private sector in the nation building process and a reduced role to the public sector.
- To achieve this, the government redefined the role of the public sector in the New Economic Policy of 1991 as follows:
  - Adopted the policy of planned disinvestments of the public sector.
  - Decided to refer loss making and sick enterprises to the Board of Industrial and Financial Reconstruction (BIFR).
- Disinvestment means transfer in the public sector enterprises to the private sector.
- It results in the dilution of government stake in the public enterprise. If there is a dilution of government ownership beyond 51%, it would result in transfer of ownership and management of the enterprise to the private sector.

Globalization

- It means integration of various economies of the world leading towards the emergence of a cohesive global economy.
- The government of India, till 1991, had followed a policy of strictly regulating imports in value and volume terms. These were with respect to:

  - Licensing of imports
  - Quantitative restrictions
  - Tariff restrictions
- The new economic reforms aimed at trade liberalization directed at import liberalization, export promotion through rationalization of the tariff structure and reforms wrt foreign exchange so that India doesn't remain isolated.
- Globalization involves an increased level of interaction and interdependence among various nations.
- Physical geographical gap or political boundaries no longer remain barriers for a business enterprise.

Q13. Mention certain restriction before the NEP which were imposed on imports.

Ans. Refer to short note on globalization.

Q14. The Indian corporate sector has come far to face with several challenges due to the government policy changes. Explain

or

Briefly discuss the impact of the government policy change on business and industry.

Ans. The impact on the business and industry is described below:

1. *Increased competition*
   - As a result of changes in the rules of industrial licensing and entry of foreign firms, competition for Indian firms has increased.
   - This is notable especially in service industries like:
     - Telecommunication
     - Airlines
     - Insurance
     - Banking

     which were earlier in the public sector.
2. *More demanding customers*
   - Customers today have become more demanding as they are well informed.
   - Increased market competition gives the customer wider choice in purchasing better quality of goods and services.

3. *Rapidly changing technological environment*
    - Increased competition forces the firms to develop new ways to survive and grow in the market.
    - New technologies make it possible to improve machines, products, process and services.
    - The rapidly changing technological environment creates big challenges before small firms.
4. *Necessity for change*
    - In a regulated environment of pre 1991 era, the firms could have relatively stable policies and practices.
    - After 1991, the market forces have become turbulent because of which the enterprises have to continuously modify their operations.
5. *Need for developing human resource*
    - Indian enterprises have long suffered with inadequately trained personnel.
    - New market conditions require people with higher competence and greater commitment.
6. *Market orientation*
    - Earlier firms had product oriented marketing operations. They used to produce first and then go to the market for sale. In a fast changing world, there is a shift to market orientation and the firms have to study and analyze the market first and produce goods accordingly.
7. *Loss of budgetary support to public sector*
    - The central government's budgetary support for financing the public sector outlays has declined over the years.
    - The PSUs have realized that in order to grow and survive, they have to be more efficient and generate their own resources for the purpose.

The impact of the government policy changes particularly in respect of LPG has been positive as the Indian business and industry has shown great resilience in dealing with the new economic order.

OTHER IMPORTANT QUESTIONS

Q1. Identify the business environment.

- **i. Prohibition of advertisements of alcoholic beverages.**
- **ii. Banking sector reforms have led to easier credit terms and better services.**
- **iii. Demand for reservation and jobs for minorities.**
- **iv. Equal pay for equal work for male and female workers.**

Ans.

- i. Legal
- ii. Economic
- iii. Social

Q2. Which process aims at giving greater role to the private sector in the nation building process?

Ans. Privatization

Q3. Which is the process by which government control over the industries is being loosened?

Ans. Liberalization

Q4. Now the firms have to study and analyze the market first and produce goods accordingly. Identify the impact of NEP.

Ans. Market orientation

Q5. Mention some service industries where competition for Indian firms has increased due to the impact of government policy changes.

Ans. The various service industries are:

1. Telecommunications
2. Airlines
3. Banking
4. Insurance

Q6. According to the new economic order what role was assigned to the public and private sector?

Ans. Government gave lead role to public sector for infrastructure industries. The private sector was broadly given the responsibility of developing consumer goods industry.

Q7. What is a truly globalized economy?

Ans. A truly globalized economy implies a boundary less world where there is:

1. Free flow of goods and service across nations
2. Free flow of capital across nations
3. Free movement of people across borders
4. Free flow of information and technology
5. A global governance perspective
6. A common acceptable mechanism for settlement of dispute

4

Planning

Q1. Define *planning*.

Ans.

- Planning can be defined as setting objectives for a certain period of time, formulating various courses of action to achieve these and then selecting the best possible alternative from among the various possibilities available.
- Planning is deciding in advance what to do, where to do, how to do and for whom to do. It is one of the basic managerial functions.
- It seeks to bridge the gap between where we are and where we want to go. It is what managers do at all stages.
- It is concerned with both means and ends i.e. what is to be done and how is it to be done.

Q2. Which resource is limited in planning?

Ans. Time is limited in the functioning of planning.

Q3. Explain the most significant features of planning.

Ans. The various features of planning are:

1. *Planning focuses on achieving objectives*
    - Specific goals are set out in the plans in addition to the activities to be undertaken to achieve these goals.
    - Thus, planning is purposeful since it includes determination of objectives.
    - It has no meaning unless it contributes to the achievement of pre-determined organizational goals.

- Objectives should be clear, exact and realistic in nature.

Fig. 4.1: Planning focuses on achieving objectives

2. ***Planning is a primary function of planning***
   - It lays down the basis for various other functions of management
   - All other managerial functions (OSDC) are performed within the framework of the already drawn plans.
   - Planning precedes other functions.
   - This is also referred to as the primacy of planning.
   - The various functions of management are all inter-related and are equally important.
3. ***Planning is pervasive***
   - Planning is required at all the levels of management, i.e. top, middle and lower.
   - It is required in all departments of organization like production, finance, HR, etc.
     - The top management undertakes planning for the firm as a whole
     - Middle management does departmental planning
     - Lower management does operational planning on day to day basis
   - It is required in all organizations whether small or large, business or non business.
4. ***Planning is an ongoing and never ending process, i.e. planning continues till the organization continues***

- Plans are prepared for a specific period of time, say for a month, quarter or a year.
- At the end of this period there is a need for a new plan based on new requirements and future conditions.
- Continuity of planning is related with the planning cycle.

5. ***Planning is futuristic/forward looking***
   - Planning basically involves looking ahead and preparing for the future.
   - The purpose of planning is to meet future events effectively to the best advantage of the organization.
   - It implies looking into the future, analyzing and predicting it.
   - It is regarded as a forward looking function based on forecasting.
   - Through forecasting, future events are anticipated and plans drawn accordingly.

   For Example:

   Sales forecasting is the basis on which a business prepares its annual plans for production and sales.
6. ***Planning involves decision making***
   - It involves making a choice from among various alternatives and activities.
   - Planning involves:
     - Identifying alternatives
     - Analyzing alternatives
     - Selecting the most viable alternative
7. ***Planning is a mental exercise***
   - It requires:
     - Application of mind with a foresight
     - Intelligent imagination
     - Sound judgment
     - Creativity
   - Planning requires logical and systematic thinking rather than wishful thinking or guess work
   - Thinking for planning must be orderly and based on the analysis of facts (past and present information) and forecasts (future predictions)

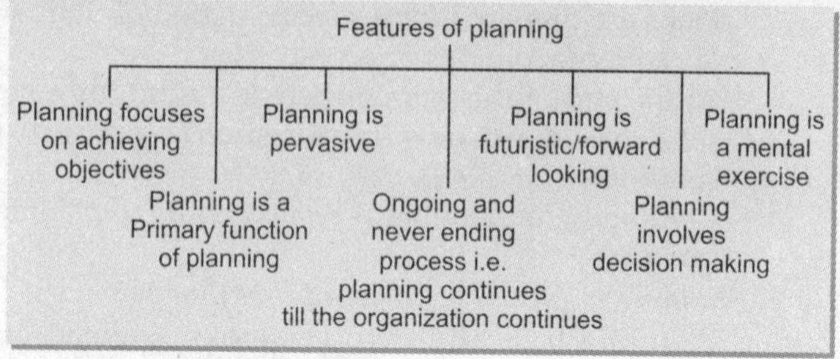

Q4. Explain the planning process.

Ans. The process of planning is as explained below:

1. ***Setting objectives***
   - Objectives are the end results towards which an activity is aimed.
   - Objectives will be set up for the entire organization, based on these, departmental objectives and individual objectives are specified.
   - Objectives should be:
     - Clear
     - Specific
     - Quantitative in terms
     - Realistic
   - The managers must contribute their ideas and participate in the objective deciding process.

   For Example:

   Company's main objective is to increase profits by 15%. The production and sales department would derive their departmental objectives based on this.
   - Objectives give direction to all people in the organization.
2. ***Developing planning premises***
   - Premises are the assumptions about the future.
   - They are the basic material upon which plans are to be drawn.
   - They may be in the form of:
     - Forecasts
     - Existing plans
     - Past information

- All managers involved in planning should be familiar with the premises.
- Various kinds of premises are:
  - *Tangible:* no. of units of production, time available
    Intangible: motivation, goodwill
  - *Internal:* number of workers, capital, machinery
    External: changes in technology, government policy
  - *Controllable:* number of workers, capital, machinery
    Uncontrollable: change in technology, government policy.

  For Example:

  Forecasts being made for demand and interest rates.

3. ***Identifying alternative courses of action***
   - It is important to identify the various ways to act so as to achieve the objectives.
   - The possible alternatives are identified by collecting and analyzing relevant information.
   - It is desirable to confine to those alternatives which are:
     - Strategic
     - Promising
     - Directly related to the situation
   - In order to identify alternatives many people should be involved in sharing of ideas.

   For Example:

   To attain the objective of increasing profits by 15% the following can be done:

   i. Change the production technique
   ii. Explore new markets
   iii. Cut down the cost of production

4. ***Evaluating the alternative courses of action***
   - The pros and cons of each alternative has to be weighed.
   - The positive and negative aspects should be analyzed in the light of the main objective.
   - Sometimes detailed calculations are required like calculation of earning per share, etc.

- The cost benefit analysis or risk return analysis is carried out in order to evaluate each alternative.

5. ***Selecting the best alternative***
   - This step involves decision making.
   - The ideal alternative or plan should be the most:
     - Feasible
     - Profitable
     - With least negative consequences
   - All plans, alternatives may not always be subject to mathematical analysis.
   - The managers' experience and judgment plays a significant role in selecting the best alternative.
   - Sometimes a combination of plans and alternatives may be selected instead of one particular best course of action.

   For Example:

   To increase profits the firm may cut the cost of production and explore new markets.

6. ***Formulating derivative plans and implementation of plans***
   - Derivative plans are derived from the main plan and includes:
     - Policies
     - Procedures
     - Rules

     In order to implement the main plan.

     For Example:

     To explore new markets the derivative plans would be:

     i. Method of production

     ii. Designing and advertising
   - In this step the pans are put into action.
   - For successful implementation of plans, they should be:
     - Communicated to all
     - Cooperation should be sought from all

7. ***Follow up action***
   - The existing plans are reviewed at regular intervals to ensure their relevance and effectiveness.
   - This step involves monitoring the plans so as to ensure that the objectives are achieved.

- Whenever required, the plans must be revised based on new facts and changing environment.

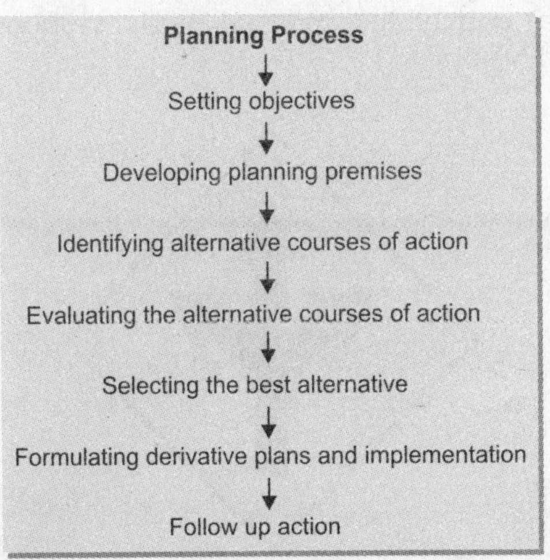

Q5. An organization has set up objectives in the planning process. Explain the other steps in the process that it needs to undertake to complete planning.

Ans. Refer to the planning process.

Q6. Planning is a one step process. Do you agree? Why?

Ans. No, planning is not a one step process. Refer to the planning process.

Q7. Failing to plan is planning to fail. Comment.

or

Planning is beneficial for all. Comment.

Ans. Planning is important because:

1. ***Planning provides directions***
   - Planning focuses on setting objectives. (refer to the features)
   - Planning helps in setting objectives. (refer to the process)
   - If there was no planning, employees would be working without direction and the organization won not be able to achieve the desired goals.

2. *Planning reduces the risk of uncertainty*
   - Planning is forward looking. (refer to the features)
   - Changes or events can't be eliminated but they can be anticipated and managerial responses to them developed.

Fig. 4.2: Planning provides directions

3. *Planning reduces overlapping and wasteful activities*
   - It serves as the basis of coordinating activities and efforts of various divisions, departments and individuals.
   - It helps in avoiding confusion and misunderstanding. Work is carried on smoothly without interruption. Useless activities are eliminated.
   - It is easier to detect inefficiencies and take corrective measures
4. *Planning promotes innovation*
   - Planning is a mental exercise. (refer to the features)
5. *Planning facilitates decision making*
   - Planning helps the manager to look into the future and make a choice from amongst the various courses of action available.
   - The manager has to evaluate each alternative and select the most viable proposition on the basis of cost benefit analysis and his personal judgment and experience.

Fig. 4.3: Planning promotes innovation

6. ***Planning establishes standards for controlling***
   - Planning involves setting of goals/standards which form the yardstick against which the actual performance is measured, i.e. objectives to be achieved.
   - Standards are laid down in planning.
   - This involves a comparison of standard performance with the actual performance.
   - The difference between the standard and the actual is called deviation.

   For Example:

   Standard performance = 100 units
   Actual performance = 75 units
   Deviation = –25

   - Corrective measures are taken to ensure that deviations do not occur again.
   - Thus, planning is a pre-requisite for controlling.

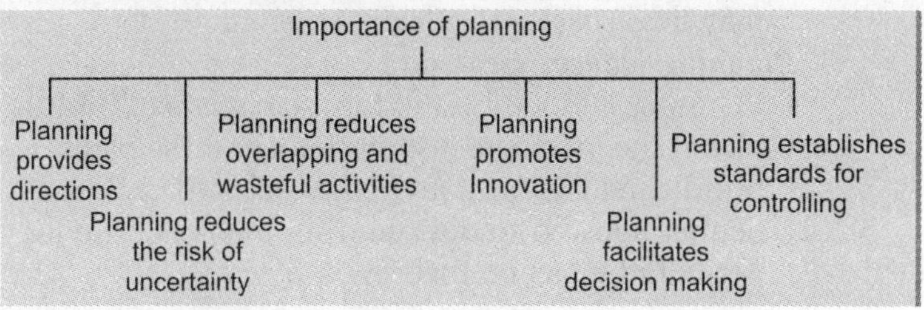

Q8. Planning is a pre-requisite for controlling. Explain.

Ans. Refer to 'Planning establishes standards for controlling'

Q9. Explain the limitation of planning.

Ans. The limitations of planning are as explained below:

1. ***Planning leads to rigidity***
   - In any organization, a well defined plan is drawn up with specific goals to be achieved within a specific time frame.
   - These plans then decide the future course of action and managers may not be in a position to change them.
   - This rigidity in plans creates difficulty. Managers should be given some flexibility so as to be able to cope up with the changed circumstances.
2. ***Planning may not work in a dynamic environment***
   - The business environment is dynamic, and not constant. It consists of various dimensions:
     - Economic
     - Social
     - Technological
     - Political
     - Legal

     And the organization has to constantly adapt itself to changes.
   - It becomes difficult to accurately assess future trends in the environment.

   For Example:

   Natural calamity, unstable economic or political conditions, competition in the market may upset financial plans.
   - Planning can't foresee everything and thus there may be obstacles to effective planning.
3. ***Planning reduces creativity***
   - Planning is done by the top management and the rest of the members just implement these plans.
   - Middle management and other decision makers are neither allowed to deviate from plans nor are they permitted to act on their own.

- Much of the initiative/creativity inherent in them gets reduced totally

4. *Planning involves huge costs*
   - When plans are drawn up huge costs are incurred in their formulation.
   - Detailed plans require scientific calculations to ascertain facts and figures.
   - The costs involved sometimes may not justify the benefits derived from the plans.

Fig. 4.4: Only the top management is at work while the lower management sits idle

5. *Planning is a time-consuming process*
   - Sometimes plans to be drawn up take so much time that there is not much time left for their implementation.
6. *Planning does not guarantee success*
   - The success of a firm is possible only when plans are properly drawn up and implemented. Any plan needs to be translated into action else it is meaningless.
   - Managers tend to rely on previously tried and tested successful plans. The success of the plan again is uncertain as there are several other factors that need to be considered.
   - This kind of complacency and false sense of security may lead to failure instead of success.

Despite its limitations, planning is not a useless exercise. It is a tool to be used with caution. It provides a basis for analyzing future courses of action but is not a solution to all problems.

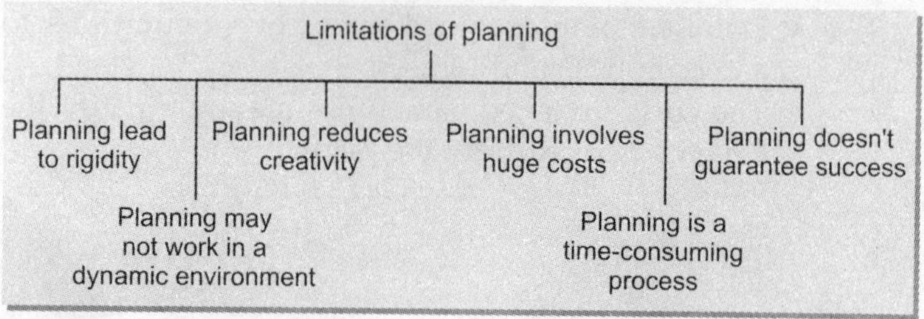

Q10. Planning may not work in a dynamic environment. Comment.

Ans. Refer to the limitations of planning.

Q11. Planning does not guarantee success. Comment

Ans. Refer to the limitations of planning. If for more marks then mention all points.

Table 4.1: Types of plans

Basis	*Objective*	*Strategy*	*Policy*
Meaning	• Desired future position.	• Provides broad contours of an organization's business.	• General statements that guide thinking towards a particular direction.
	• Ends towards which all activities of a firm are directed.	• Future decisions defining organization's directions and scope in the long run.	• Broad parameters within which a manager may function.
	• Future state of affair swhich the organization strives to achieve.	• Comprehensive plans formulated for meeting challenges posed by competitors or other external forces.	
Purpose	• To determine what is to be done.	• Helps organizations to establish an	Guide to managerial action and decision

Contd.

Table 4.1: Types of plans (*Contd.*)

Basis	*Objective*	*Strategy*	*Policy*
		identity in the business environment.	making and in implementation of strategy.
	• Focus on broad and general issues.	• Helps the organizations to cope up with environmental threats and capitalize on opportunities.	
	• End point of planning. • Set up by top management. • Guide for overall business planning.		
Origin	Derived from the philosophy and mission of the organization.	Derived from objectives and comprehensively helps to accomplish them.	Derived from objectives and provides a basis for interpreting strategy.
Nature	They are: • Specific • Measurable in quantitative terms • Basic	General in nature and includes 3 dimensions: • Determining long term objectives. • Adopting a particular course of action· • Allocating resources. External changes will affect an organization's strategy.	General response to a particular problem or situation, may be major (i.e. for customers who are outsiders) or minor (i.e. for insiders)
	• Time bound • Vary from business to business. • In the form of written statements'		
Example	• Increase sales by 12% by March 2012 • Earning 20% of profit for the business	Marketing strategy may include: • Identifying the customers· • Establishing the demand for the goods	• Purchase policy related to nature of manufacturing· • Recruitment policy· • Pricing policy · • Credit policy

Table 4.2

Basis	*Procedure*	*Method*	*Rule*	*Programme*	*Budget*
Meaning	• Steps in a chronological order on how to carry out activities. • They are meant for insiders to follow.	Prescribed/standard ways to perform routine and respective jobs	Specific statement that informs what is to be done or not to be done.	Detailed statements outlining object, policies, procedures, rules and budgets to implement any course of action	Statement of expected results in numerical terms.
Purpose	Helps to enforce policy and attain predecided objectives	Proper method/ways help to save time, money and effort and increase performance efficiency.	To ensure discipline	Help to implement course of action	Functions as a control device to take care of deviations
Origin	Derived from the policies of the enterprise	Deals with performance of one step of the procedure	Derived from (expected behavioral) norms	Derived from entire gamut of activities and policy and includes all minute details	Derived from forecast of expected quantifiable figures
Nature	Specified steps to be taken in a particular situation	Specific in nature and may vary from task to task	Most specific statements which if violated may result in penalty. They apply to all individuals in the organization	General statements	• Specific fundamental planning instruments • Numerical • Time bound
Example	• Procedure for requisitioning of supplies before production • Selection procedure	• Different training methods of management levels. Top management does seminars, lectures and lower levels use work oriented methods • Methods of compensation: Time rate, piece rate	• Rule of no smoking • Rule of no entry	• Programme for development of a new product • Training of new employees • Programme for construction of a new mall	• Cash budget for management of cash inflow and outflow • Sales budget • Advertising budget

OTHER IMPORTANT QUESTIONS

Q1. Planning is the basic function of management. Identify the feature.

Ans. Planning is a primary function of management.

Q2. Planning is an exclusive function of the top level. Comment.

Ans. No. Planning is a pervasive function. (Refer to the features)

Q3. A single course of action does not justify planning. Identify the feature.

Ans. Planning involves decision making.

Q4. Planning eliminates uncertainty. Do you agree? Why?

Ans. No. Planning reduces it. (Refer to the importance)

Q5. Why are rules regarded as plans?

Ans.

- Plans provide future course of action for the achievement of organizational objectives
- Similarly, rules provide desirable course of action/non-action to ensure discipline within the organization.

Q6. Is a planning a solution to all problems?

Ans. No. Explain the limitations of planning.

Q7. Which is the simplest type of plan?

Ans. Rule

5

Organizing

Q1. What has Wipro done to become a contending force among other global giants?

Ans. Wipro organized itself in a way that allowed customer orientation to dominate other goals and diversified on the basis of product lines. It also modified the relationships within the management hierarchy to suit the predetermined goals.

Q2. Name the function of management which involves designing roles to be performed by suitably skilled people and defining the inter-relationships between these goals.

Ans. Organizing.

Q3. Define *organizing*.

Ans.

- According to Louis Allen, organizing is the process of:
  - Identifying and grouping the work to be performed
  - Defining and delegating responsibility and authority
  - Establishing relationships for the purpose of enabling people to work most effectively together in achieving goals
- Organizing is a process which coordinates human efforts, assembles resources and integrates both into a unified whole to be utilized for achieving specified objectives.
- Organizing is defined as a process that initiates implementation of plans by clarifying jobs and working

relationships and effectively deploying resources for attainment of desired and identified results.

Q4. Explain the various steps involved in the process of organizing

Ans. The process of organizing consists of :

1. ***Identification and division of work***
   - The first step in the process of organizing involves identifying and dividing the work that has to be done in accordance with the predetermined plans.
   - The work is divided into manageable activities so that duplication can be avoided and the burden of work can be shared among employees.

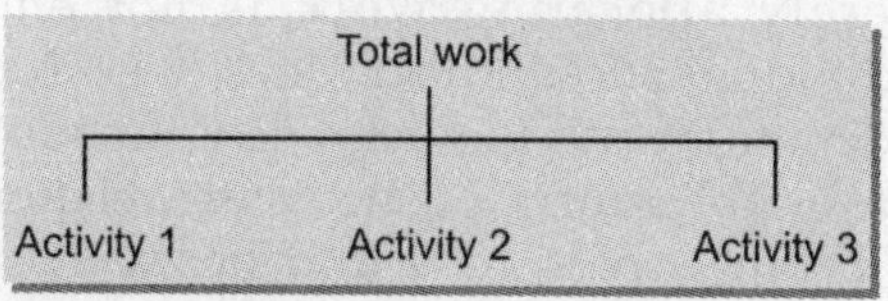

2. ***Departmentalization***
   - Once work has been divided into small and manageable activities then those activities which are similar in nature are grouped together.
   - This grouping process is called departmentalization and such sets facilitate specialization
   - Departments can be created using several criteria as a basis like:
     - Territory (north, south)
     - Products (appliances, clothing)

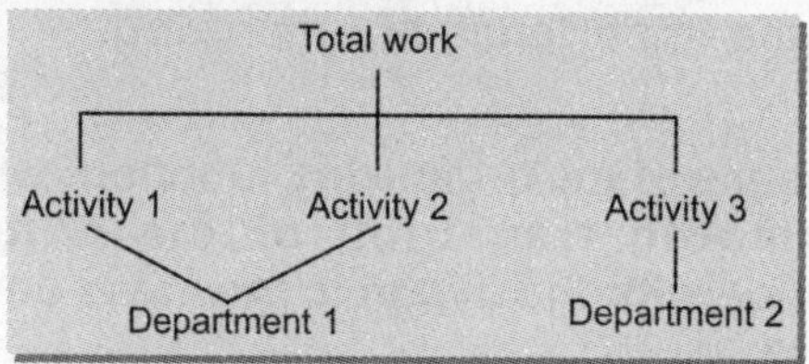

3. ***Assignment of duties to various job positions***
   - It is necessary to define work to various job positions and allocate the work to these positions

- Once departments have been formed, each of them is placed under the charge of one individual
- Jobs are then allocated to the job positions of each department. This is called job description.
- Job description helps to identify the required skills and ability of an individual necessary to perform a job. These skills, experience and ability is defined in a statement called as job specification
- It is essential for effective performance that a proper match is made between the nature of a job and the ability of an individual. The work must be assigned to those who are best fitted to perform it .

4. *Establishing reporting relationships*
   - Merely allocating work is not enough. Each individual should also know who he has to take orders from and to whom he is accountable.
   - The establishment of such clear relationships helps to create a hierarchy and helps in coordination amongst various departments.

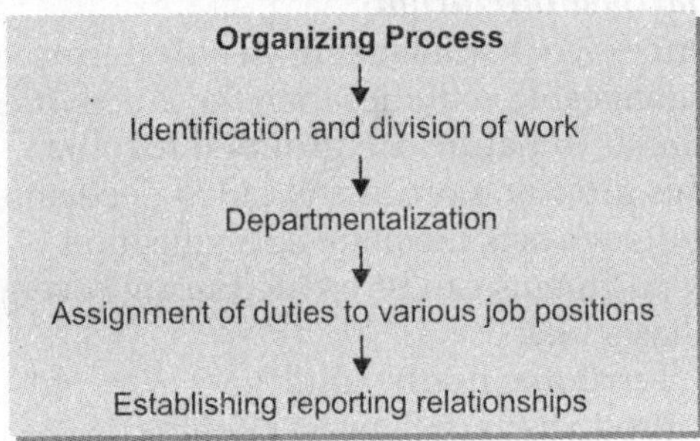

Q5. Explain the importance of organizing.

or

Performance of the organizing function can pave way for a smooth transition of the enterprise in accordance with the dynamic business environment. Comment.

Ans. The importance of organizing is explained below:

1. *Benefits of specialization*
   - It leads to systematic allocation of jobs among the workforce

- This reduces workload and enhances productivity because of specific workers performing a specific job on a regular basis.
- Repetitive performance of a particular task allows a worker to gain experience in that area and leads to specialization

2. *Clarity in working relationships*
   - The establishment of working relationships clarifies lines of communication and specifies who is to report to whom
   - This removes ambiguity in the transfer of information and instructions
   - It helps in creating a hierarchical order thus enabling the fixation of responsibility and the specification of extent of authority to be exercised by an individual
3. *Optimum utilization of resources*
   - Organizing leads to the proper utilization of all materials, financial and human resources.
   - The proper assignment of jobs avoids overlapping of work and also makes possible the best use of resources
   - Avoidance of duplication of work helps in preventing confusion and minimizing the wastage of resources and efforts.
4. *Adaptation to change*
   - The process of organizing allows a business enterprise to accommodate changes in the business environment
   - It allows the organization structure to be suitably modified and the revision of inter-relationships amongst managerial levels to pave way for a smooth transition
   - It also provides stability to the organization as it can then continue to survive and grow in spite of changes.
5. *Effective administration*
   - Organizing provides a clear description of jobs and related duties. This helps to avoid confusion and duplication

- Clarity in working relationships enables proper execution of work. Management of an enterprise becomes easier and this brings effectiveness in administration

6. ***Development of personnel***

   Refer to delegation of authority in the latter part of the chapter

7. ***Expansion and growth***
   - Organizing helps in the growth and diversification of an enterprise by enabling it to deviate from existing norms and taking up new challenges

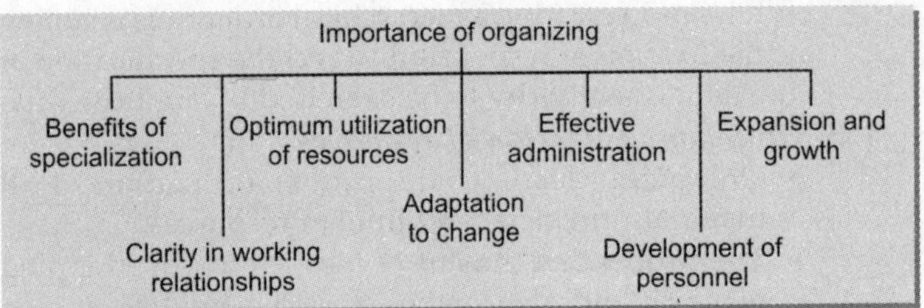

Q6. What is the outcome of the *organization process*?

Ans. Organization structure

Q7. What is the need for an *organization structure*?

Ans. The need for an organization structure is felt by an enterprise whenever it grows in:

1. Size
2. Complexity

Q8. Define organization structure.

Ans.

- It can be defined as the framework within which managerial and operating tasks are performed
- It specifies the relationship between people, work and resources
- It allows correlation and coordination among human, physical and financial resources thus enabling a business enterprise to accomplish desired goals

- The organization of a firm is shown in an organizational chart

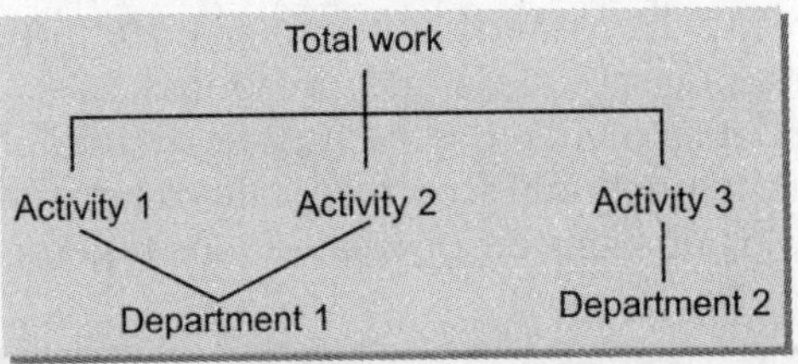

Q9. What is meant by span or control of management?

Ans.

- It refers to the number of subordinates that can be effectively managed by a superior
- It is essential as it:
  - Determines the levels of management in the structure
  - Gives shape to the organizational structure to a large extent

Q10. On what basis can the type of organization structure be adopted?

Ans.

- The type of structure adopted by an organization will vary with:
  - Nature
  - Size

  of activities performed by the organization
- It can be classified under 2 categories:
  - Functional structure (on the basis of functions)
  - Divisional structure (on the basis of products produced)

Q11. What is meant by functional structure? Explain with an example.

Ans.

- Grouping of jobs of similar nature under functional heads and organizing these major functions as separate departments creates a functional structure

- All departments report to a coordinating head.

For Example:

In a manufacturing concern, division of work into key functions will include production, purchase, marketing, accounts and personnel.

- The departments may be further divided into sections.

Thus, a functional structure is an organizational design that groups similar or related jobs together

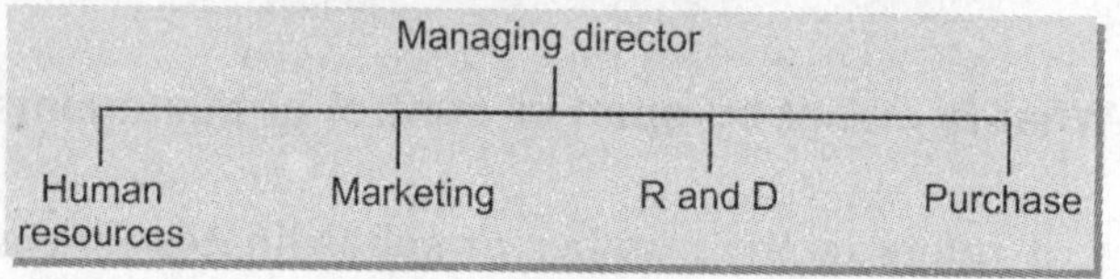

Q12. State the advantages of the functional structure.

Ans. The various advantages of the functional structure are as given below:

1. ***Ensure occupational specialization***
   - It leads to occupational specialization since emphasis is laid on a specific function
   - This promotes efficiency in utilization of manpower as employees perform similar tasks within a department and are able to improve performance
2. ***Promotes control and coordination***
   - It promotes control and coordination within a department because of similarity in the tasks being performed
3. ***Increases operational and managerial efficiency***
   - It helps in increasing managerial and operational efficiency which helps to increase the profits.
4. ***Minimizes duplication of efforts***
   - It minimizes duplication of effort which results in economies of scale and thus lowering cost
5. ***Facilitates training of employees***
   - It makes training of employees easier as the focus is only on a limited range of skills
6. ***Due attention to various functions***
   - It ensures that different functions get due attention

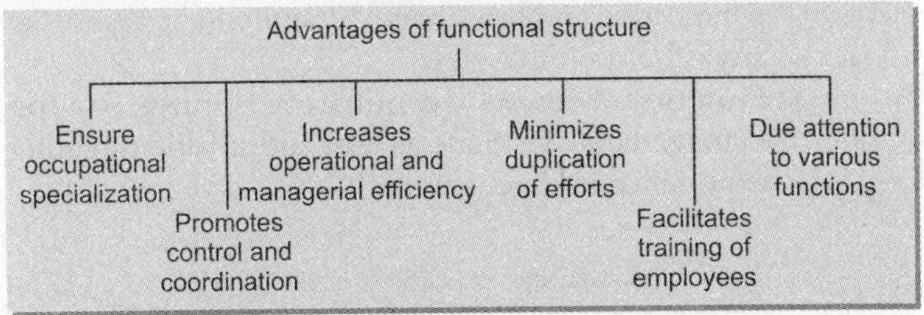

Q13. Functional structure suffers from certain disadvantages. Explain.

Ans. The various disadvantages of a functional structure are:

1. *Less emphasis on overall objectives*
   - It lays less emphasis on overall objectives of the firm than the objectives pursued by a functional head.
   - It may lead to functional empires wherein the importance of a particular function may be over emphasized.
   - Pursuing departmental objectives at the cost organizational objectives can hinder the interaction between two or more departments.
2. *Problems of coordination between departments*
   - It may lead to problems of coordination as information has to be exchanged between functionally differentiated departments.
3. *Conflict of interests*
   - A conflict of interest may arise when the interests of two or more departments are not compatible

   For Example:

   The sales department insisting on a customer friendly design may lead to production difficulties
   - Dissensions may prove to be harmful in terms of fulfillment of organizational interest
   - Inter-departmental conflict can also arise in the absence of clear differentiation of responsibility
4. *Leads to inflexibility/narrow perspective*
   - It may lead to inflexibility as people with same skills and knowledge base may develop a narrow

perspective and thus, have difficulty in appreciating any other point of view
- Functional heads do not get training for top management positions as they are unable to gather experience in diverse areas

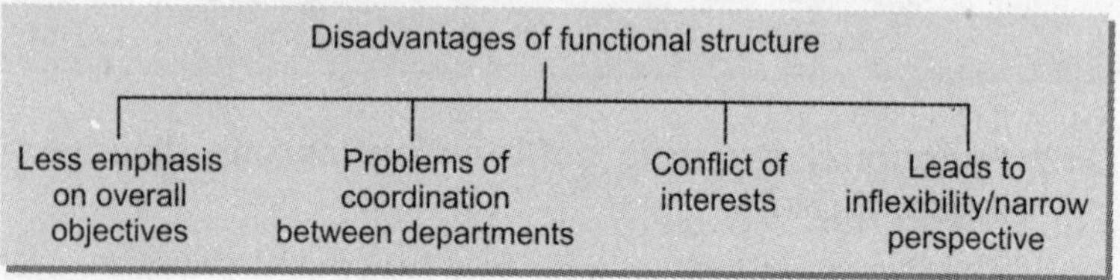

Q14. Mention where a functional structure is more suitable.

Ans. A functional structure is more suitable when:

1. Size of organization is large
2. Diversified activities and operations
3. High degree of specialization
4. Number of products produced is limited to one

Q15. What is meant by divisional structure? Illustrate with the help of an example.

Ans.

- In a divisional structure, the organization structure comprises separate business units or divisions. Each unit has a divisional manager who has the authority over the unit and is responsible for performance.
- Each division is multi functional because within each division functions like production, marketing, finance, purchase, etc. are performed together to achieve a common goal
- Each division is self-contained as it develops expertise in all functions related to a product line
- Each division works as a profit centre where the divisional head is responsible for the profit or loss of his division

For Example:

A large company may have divisions like cosmetics, clothing, etc.

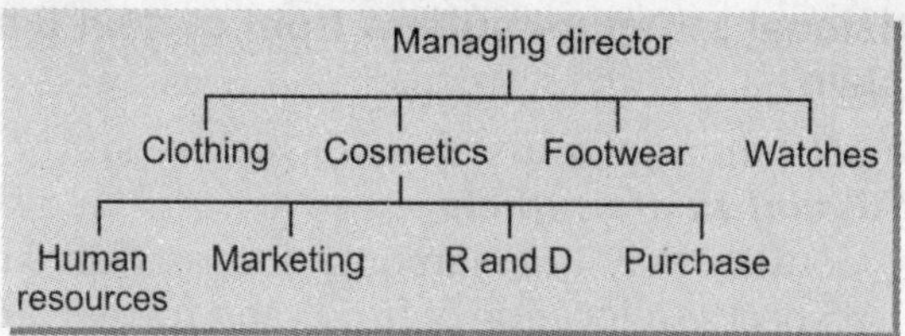

Q16. What are the advantages of division structure?

Ans. The various advantages of a division structure are:

1. ***Product specialization***
   - Product specialization helps in development of varied skills in a divisional head and this prepares him for higher positions as he gains experience in all functions relevant to a particular product
2. ***Helps in fixation of responsibility***
   - Divisional heads are accountable for profit, as revenues and costs related to different departments can be identified and assigned to them
   - This provides a proper basis for performance measurement. It also helps in fixation of responsibility in cases of poor performance of the division and appropriate remedial actions can be taken
3. ***Promotes flexibility and initiative***
   - It promotes flexibility and initiative because each division functions as an autonomous unit which leads to faster decision making
4. ***Facilitates expansion and growth***
   - It facilitates expansion and growth as new divisions can be added without interrupting the existing operations by simply adding another divisional head and staff for the new product line

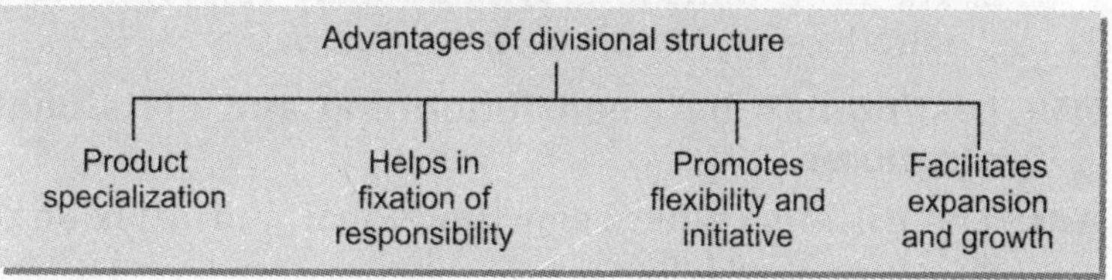

Q17. Divisional structure suffers from certain limitations. Explain.

Ans. The limitations of a divisional structure are:

1. ***Possibility of conflicts***
   - Conflict may arise among different divisions with respect to allocation of funds and further a particular division may seek to maximize profits at the cost of other divisions
2. ***Duplication of efforts***
   - It may lead to increase in costs as there may be a duplication of activities across products.
   - Providing each division with separate set of functions increases expenditure
3. ***May lead to ignorance towards organizational interest***
   - It provides managers with the authority to supervise all activities related to a particular division
   - In course of time, such a manager may gain power and in a bid to assert his independence may ignore organizational interest

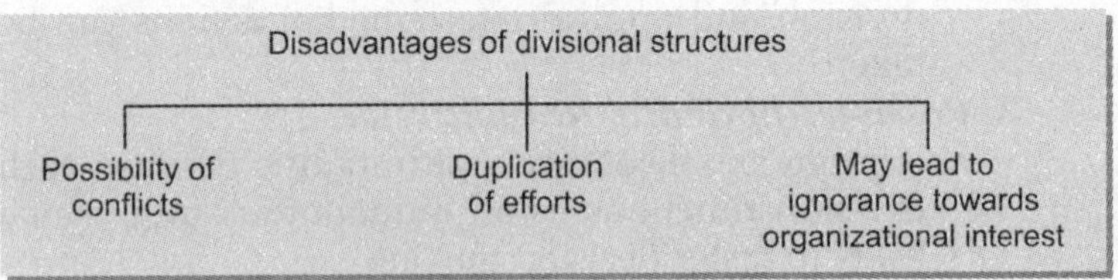

Q18. When is a divisional structure more suitable?

Ans. The divisional structure is more suitable when:

1. A large variety of products are manufactured using different productive resources
2. The firm wants to grow, add more employees and introduce new levels of management

Q19. Distinguish between functional and divisional structures.

Ans. The difference between functional and divisional structures is as follows:

Table 5.1

Basis	*Functional structure*	*Divisional structure*
Formation	Formation is based on functions.	Formation is based on product lines and supported by functions
Specialization	There is functional specialization.	There is product specialization.
Responsibility	Difficult to fix responsibility in a department	Easy to fix responsibility for performance
Managerial development	Difficult, as each functional manager has to report to the top management	Easier, autonomy as well as the chance to perform multiple functions helps in managerial development
Cost	Functions aren't duplicated hence are economical	Duplication of resources is there in various divisions hence costly
Coordination	Difficult for a multi-product company	Easy, because all functions related to a particular product are integrated in one department

Q20. What is meant by formal organization? State its features.

Ans.

- Formal organization refers to the organization structure which is designed by the management to accomplish a particular task
- It specifies clearly the boundaries of authority and responsibility and there is systematic coordination among the various activities to achieve the organizational goals
- The formal organization is a system of well defined jobs, each bearing a definite measure of authority, responsibility and accountability

The various features of a formal organization are:

1. ***Defines official relations***
   - It specifies the relationships among various job positions and the nature of their inter-relationship. This clarifies who has to report to whom

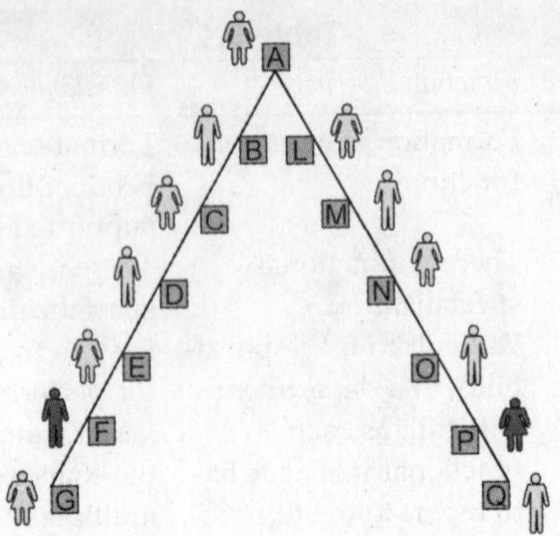

Fig. 5.1: Formal organizations

2. ***Specific rules and regulations***
    - It is a means to achieve the objectives specified in the plan, as it lays down the rules and procedures essential for their achievement
3. ***Basis of coordination***
    - Efforts of various departments are inter-linked, integrated and coordinated through the formal organization
4. ***Deliberate creation***
    - It is deliberately designed by the top management to facilitate the smooth functioning of the organization
5. ***Emphasis on work***
    - It lays more emphasis on the performance than inter-personal communication among the employees

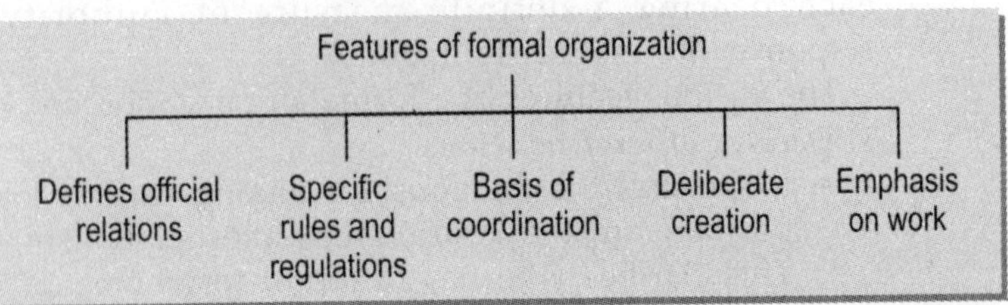

Q21. What are the advantages of formal organization?

Ans. The various advantages of formal organization are:

1. ***Easier to fix responsibility***
   - It is easier to fix responsibility since mutual relationships are clearly defined
2. ***Helps in avoiding duplication of efforts***
   - It avoids duplication of efforts as there is no ambiguity in the role that each member has to perform as duties are specified.
3. ***Establishes unity of command***
   - Unity of command is maintained through an established chain of command
4. ***Helps to accomplish goals***
   - It leads to effective accomplishment of goals by providing a framework for the operations to be performed and ensuring that each employee knows his role
5. ***Provides stability to the organization***
   - It provides stability to the organization. This is because behavior of employees can be fairly predicted since there are specific rules to guide them

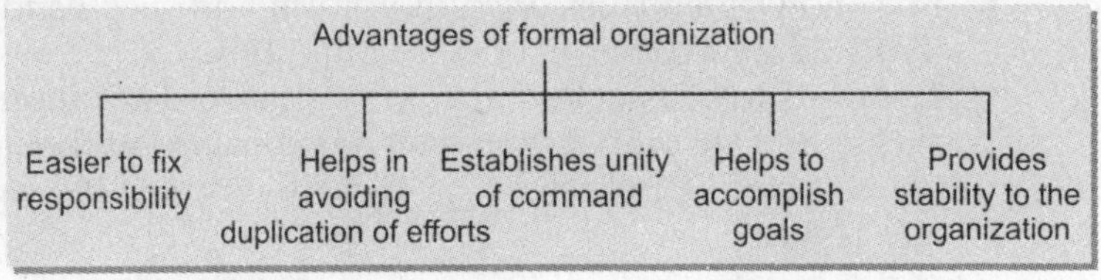

Q22. Discuss the limitations of formal organization.

Ans. The various limitations of a formal organization are:

1. ***Procedural delay***
   - The formal communication may lead to procedural delays as the established chain of command has to be followed which increases the time taken for decision making.
2. ***Rigidity***
   - Poor organization practices may not provide adequate recognition to creative talent, since it does not allow deviations from rigidly laid down policies.

3. ***Incomplete picture of organization***
   - It is difficult to understand all human relationships in an enterprise as it places more emphasis on structure and work
   - Hence, formal organization doesn't provide a complete picture of how an organization works

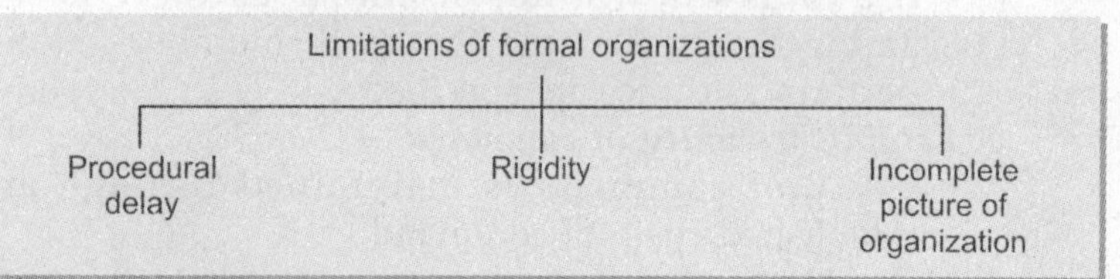

Q23. What is meant by informal *organization*?

Ans.

- Interaction among people at work gives rise to a 'network of social relationships among employees' called the informal organization.
- Informal organization emerges from within the formal organization when people interact beyond their officially defined roles
- It has no written rules, is fluid in form and scope and doesn't have fixed lines of communication
- According to Chester Barnard, an informal organization is an aggregate of inter-personal relationships without any conscious purpose but which may contribute to joint results

Q24. Informal organization emerges from within the formal organization. Comment.

Ans.

- Informal organization is a part of formal organization. It arises when people at work interact socially to fulfill their social needs
- Man is a social animal and he needs to interact beyond officially defined roles.
- When people have frequent contacts they cannot be forced into a rigid formal structure. Rather, based on their interaction and friendship they tend to form groups which show conformity of interest.

For Example:

Groups of people who take part in cricket matches on Sundays, meet in the cafeteria for coffee, are interested in dramatics, poetry, cinema, etc.

Fig. 5.2: Informal organization

Q25. What are the features of informal *organization*?

Ans. The various features of an informal organization are:

1. *Exists within formal organization*
   - It originates from within the formal organization as a result of inter-personal interaction among employees.
2. *Standards of behavior based on group norms*
   - The standards of behavior evolve from group norms rather than officially laid down rules and regulations
3. *Independent channels of communication*
   - Independent channels of communication without specified direction of flow of information are developed by members of the group
4. *Not deliberately created*
   - It emerges spontaneously and is not deliberately created by the management
5. *No definite structure*
   - It has no definite structure or form as it is a complex network of social relationship among employees

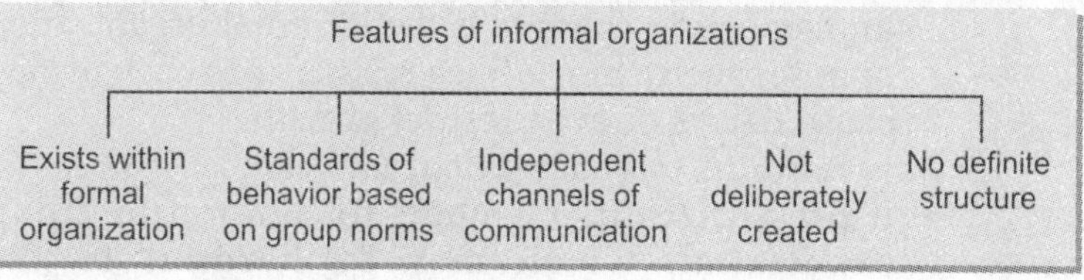

Q26. Discuss the advantages of an informal organization.

Ans. The various advantages of an informal organization are:

1. ***Fast spread of communication***
   - Prescribed lines of communication aren't followed leading to faster spread of information as well as feedback
2. ***Helps to fulfill social needs***
   - It helps to fulfill the social needs of the members and allows them to seek like minded people. This increases their job satisfaction as it gives them a sense of belongingness
3. ***Completes the inadequacies of formal organization***
   - It contributes towards fulfillment of organizational objectives by compensating for inadequacies in the formal organization.

   For Example:

   Employees' reaction towards plans and policies can be tested through informal network

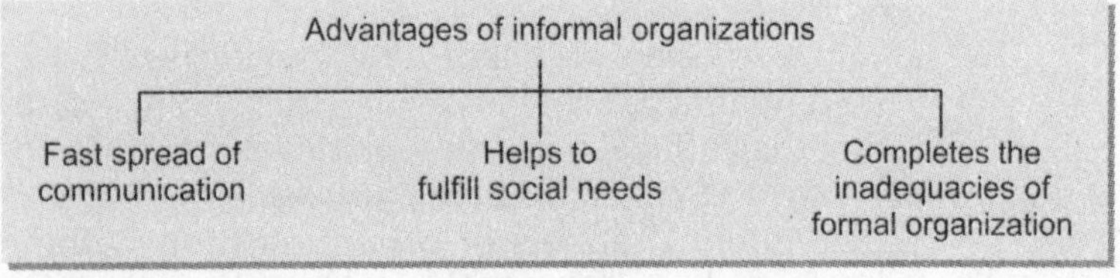

Q27. Discuss the limitations of an informal organization.

Ans. The various limitations of an informal organization are:

1. ***Disruptive force***
   - Informal organizations may become a disruptive force when it spreads rumor. This may work against the interest of the formal organization.
2. ***May cause delays or restrict growth***
   - The management may not be successful in implementing changes if the informal organization opposes such a move. Such resistance to change may cause delays or even restrict growth.
3. ***May harm the organizational interest***
   - It pressurizes its members to conform to group expectation which may be harmful to the

organization if the norms set by the groups are against the organizational interest

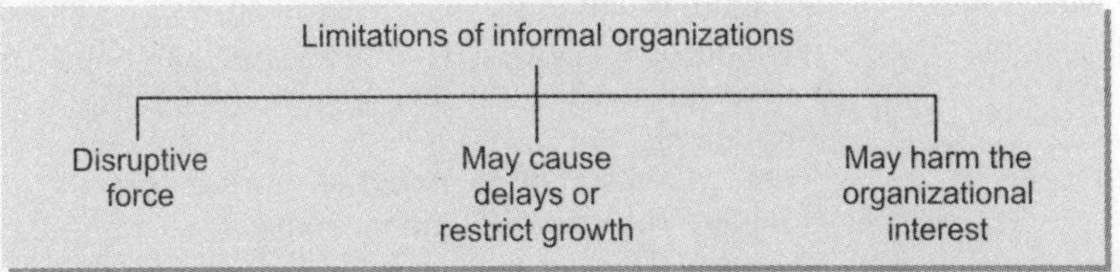

Q28. Informal organizations can be eliminated. Do you agree? Give reasons.

Ans.

- Informal organization can't be eliminated altogether. It would be in the best interest of the organization if the existence of such groups is recognized and the roles played by the members identified
- The knowledge of such groups can be used to gather their support and consequently lead to improved organizational performance
- Such groups can also provide vital communication channels. Instead of confronting them, the management should skillfully take advantage of both the formal and the informal organization so as to let the work continue smoothly. (Take help of Ans. 24 to elaborate further, if needed)

Q29. Formal organization is better than an informal organization. Do you agree? Why?

Ans.

- If YES, then substantiate with the advantages of formal organization and the limitations of informal organization
- If NO, then substantiate with the limitations of formal organization and the advantages of informal organization.

Q30. Distinguish between formal and informal organization.

Ans. The difference between formal and informal organization is as follows:

Table 5.2

Basis	*Formal organization*	*Informal organization*
Meaning	Structure of authority relationships created by management employees	Network of social relationships arising out of interactions among
Origin	Arises as a result of company rules and regulations	Arises as a result of social interaction
Authority	Arises by virtue of management position	Arises out of personal qualities
Behavior	Directed by rules	There is no set behavior pattern
Flow of communication	Communication takes place through scalar chain	Flow of communication is not through a planned route. It can take place in any direction
Nature	Rigid	Flexible
Leadership	Managers are leaders	Leaders may or may not be manager but are chosen by the group

Q31. On which principle of management is the concept of delegation of authority based?

Ans. It is based on the division of labor

Q32. What is meant by delegation?

Ans.

- Delegation refers to the downward transfer of authority from a superior (delegator) to a subordinate (delegatee)
- It is a pre-requisite to the efficient functioning of a firm as it enables a manager to use his time on high priority activities
- It also satisfies the subordinate's need for recognition and provides them with opportunities to develop and exercise initiative
- Delegation does not mean abdication
- According to Louis Allen, delegation is the process a manager follows in dividing the work assigned to him so that he performs that part which only he can perform effectively, because of his unique organizational

placement and so that he can get others to help with what remains.

Q33. Delegation does not mean abdication. Comment.

Ans.

- Delegation refers to sharing or transferring authority from a superior to a subordinate
- Delegation does not imply abdication or escaping from accountability
- A superior/manager will continue to remain accountable for the performance of the task assigned to him
- Authority granted to a person can be taken back and re-delegated to another person
- Thus, irrespective of the extent of authority delegated, the manager still remains accountable as he was, before delegation

Q34. Explain the various elements/steps in the process of delegation of authority.

Ans.

- According to Louis Allen, delegation is the entrustment of responsibility and authority to another and the creation of accountability for performance

  The essential elements of delegation are:

  1. ***Authority***
     - Authority refers to the right of an individual to command his subordinates to take action within the scope of his position
     - The concept of authority arises from the established scalar chain which links the various job positions and levels of an organization
     - In the formal organization, authority originates by virtue of an individual's position and the extent of authority is highest at the top management and reduces successively as we move down the corporate ladder, i.e. authority flows from top to bottom and the superiors have authority over the subordinates.
     - Authority determines the superior-subordinate relationship

- Authority is of 2 types:
  - Official authority (related to position)
  - Personal authority (related to personality)
- Authority is restricted by law and the rules and regulations of the organization.

2. ***Responsibility***
   - Responsibility is the obligation of a subordinate to properly perform the assigned duty
   - It arises from a superior-subordinate relationship as the subordinate is bound to perform the duty assigned to him by his superior
   - Responsibility flows upward, i.e. a subordinate is responsible to his superior
   - Relationship between responsibility and authority is as follows:
     - For effective delegation the authority granted must be commensurate with the assigned responsibility
     - If authority granted is more than the responsibility, it may lead to misuse of authority
     - If responsibility assigned is more than the authority, it makes a person ineffective.
3. ***Accountability***
   - Accountability implies being accountable for the final outcome.
   - Once authority has been delegated and responsibility accepted, on cannot deny accountability. It cannot be delegated and flows upward, i.e. a subordinate will be accountable to a superior for satisfactory performance of work
   - This is the principle of absolute accountability
   - It indicates that the manager has to ensure the proper discharge of duties by his subordinates. It is enforced through regular feedback on the extent of work accomplished

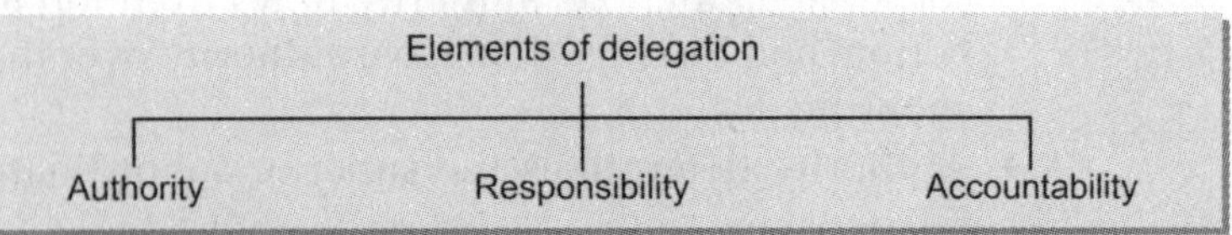

Q35. Distinguish between authority, responsibility and accountability.

Ans. The difference between authority, responsibility and accountability is as follows:

Table 5.3

Basis	*Authority*	*Responsibility*	*Accoutability*
Meaning	Right to command	Obligation to perform task assigned	Answerability for the outcome of assigned task
Delegation	Can be delegated	Can not be totally delegated	Can not be delegated
Origin	Arises from formal position	Arises from delegated authority	Arises from responsibility
Flow	Flows downward from superiors to subordinates	Flows upward from subordinates to superiors	Flows upward from subordinates to superiors

Q36. The directors of Core Ltd. Manufacturing CCTVs have asked their production manager to achieve a target production of 120 TVs per day. The manager has asked his foreman to achieve this target but he did not give him the authority for requisition of tools and materials from stores department. The foreman could not achieve the desired target.

a. Can the directors blame the production manager?

b. Can the production manager blame the foreman?

Ans.

a. Yes. Ultimate accountability for performance rests with the production manager, i.e. accountability can't be delegated. (absolute accountability)

b. No. There is no parity between the responsibility and authority

Elaborate answers with the help of previous answers.

Q37. Explain the principle of absolute accountability.

Ans.

- Accountability refers to answerability of a subordinate to his superior for the performance of the task assigned to him

- Accountability is absolute in nature. It ca not be delegated or transferred.
- The manager remains accountable to his superior for the task assigned to him even when he has delegated the same task to his own subordinate
- The manager can not shift his accountability to his subordinate

For Example:

Production manager sets a target for the foreman. The foreman delegates the same task to the workers. If the targets could not be met due to the fault of the workers, the foreman can't shift his accountability to his workers. He continues to be answerable to the production manager

Q38. Delegation is an essential process. Comment.

or

Effective delegation leads to certain benefits. Explain.

Ans. Delegation is important as described below:

1. *Effective management*
   - By empowering employees, the managers are able to function more efficiently as they get more time to concentrate on important matters
   - Freedom from doing routine work provides them with opportunities to excel in new areas
2. *Employees' development*
   - As a result of delegation, employees get more opportunities to utilize their talent and this may give rise to latent abilities in them
   - It allows them to develop skills which help them to perform complex tasks and assume responsibilities which improve their career path
   - It makes them better leaders and decision makers
   - Delegation helps by preparing better future managers
   - Delegation empowers the employees by providing them with the chance to use their skills, gain experience and develop themselves for higher positions
3. ***Motivation of employees***

- It helps in developing hidden talents of the employees and has psychological benefits
- When a superior entrusts a subordinate with a task, it isn't merely sharing of work but involves trust on the superior's part and commitment on the part of the subordinate
- Responsibility for work builds the self esteem of an employee and improves his confidence. He feels encouraged and tries to improve his performance further.

4. *Facilitating of growth*
   - Delegation helps in the expansion of an organization by providing a ready workforce to take up leading positions in new ventures
   - Trained and experienced employees are able to play significant roles in the launch of new products by replicating the work ethos they have absorbed from the existing units, in the newly set up branches.
5. *Basis of management hierarchy*
   - Delegation of authority establishes superior-subordinate relationships, which are the basis of hierarchy of management
   - It is the degree and flow of activities which determines who has to report to whom
   - The extent of delegated authority also decides the power that each job position enjoys in the organization

Delegation brings efficiency and effectiveness to the organziation

Fig. 5.3: Delegation brings efficiency and effectiveness to the organziation

6. ***Better coordination***
   - The elements of delegation viz. authority, responsibility and accountability help to define the powers, duties and answerability related to various positions in an organization
   - This helps to avoid overlapping of duties and duplication of efforts as it gives a clear picture of the work being done at various levels
   - Such clarity in reporting relationships help in developing and maintaining effective coordination amongst the various departments, levels and functions of management

   Thus, delegation is a key element in effective organizing.

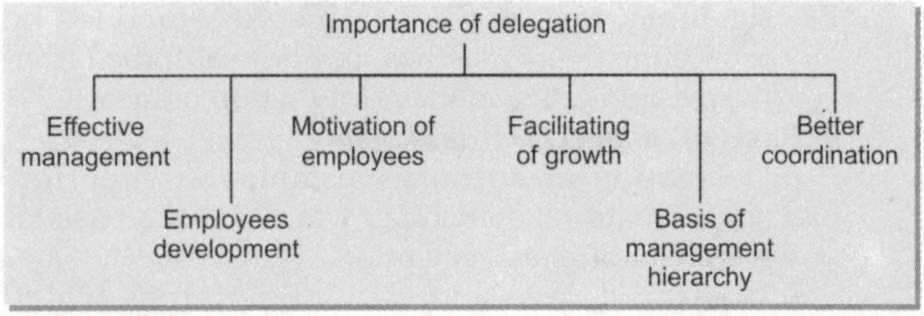

Q39. What do you mean by centralization and decentralization? How are they related to delegation of authority?

Ans.

- Centralization refers to the concentration of decision making authority in the hands of the few at top level management
- Decentralization refers to the distribution of decision making authority to the lowest levels of organization
- Decentralization is a systematic delegation of authority throughout the length and breadth of the organization. It is the end result of delegation
- While centralization increases the role of superiors, decentralization increases the role of subordinates
- Neither complete centralization nor complete decentralization is desirable

- Complete centralization would imply concentration of all decision making functions at the top level of management This would obviate the need for a management hierarchy
- Complete decentralization would imply all decision making in the hands of lower levels of management. This would obviate the need for higher levels of management
- Both scenarios are unrealistic. There should be a balance between centralization and decentralization.
- This balance would depend on various factors like:
  - Size of the organization
  - Ability of the superiors
  - Ability of the subordinates
- Thus in an organization, which grows in size and complexity, there is a tendency towards decentralization because in large organizations the employees who are involved in operations tend to have more knowledge than the top level of management
- Centralization and decentralization are both related to delegation. Since they are relative terms and the relativity is expressed in relation with delegation where delegation refers to downward transfer of authority from superiors to subordinates.

Q40. If we delegate we multiply by 2 but if we decentralize authority, we multiply by many. Explain.

or

Decentralization is the extension of delegation of authority. Explain.

or

Delegation is the process but decentralization is the end result. Explain.

Ans.

- Substantiate with the meaning of delegation
- Substantiate with the meaning of decentralization

For Example:

In an organization, all the leave applications are sanctioned by the General Manger. He feels overburdened and assigns his work and delegates his authority to the HR manager. This is known as delegation

If the HR manager also feels overburdened and he delegates authority for the same task to other departmental managers to sanction leave of members of their respective departments then this is called decentralization

Fig. 5.4: In delegation we multiply by two and in decentralization we multiply by many

Q41. Neither complete centralization nor complete decentralization is desirable. Justify.

Ans. Refer to Ans. 39.

Q42. Distinguish between decentralization and delegation.

Ans. The difference between delegation and decentralization is as follows:

Table 5.4

Basis	*Delegation*	*Decentralization*
Nature	It is a compulsory act as no individual can perform all tasks on his own	It is an optional policy decision. It is done at the discretion of the top management
Freedom of action	There is more control by superiors hence less freedom to take own decisions for subordinates	Less control over executives hence greater freedom of action
Status	It is a process followed to share tasks	It is the result of the policy decision of the top management
Scope	It has a narrow scope as it is limited to a superior and his immediate subordinate	It has a wide scope as it implies extension of delegated authority to the lowest level of management
Purpose	To lessen the burden of the managers	To increase the role of the subordinates by giving them more autonomy

Q43. Decentralization is an optional policy. Explain why an organization would choose to be decentralized?

Ans.

- An organization will choose to be decentralized in order to:
  - Face challenges of its large size
  - Solve organizational problems

  Decentralization becomes of immense importance as mentioned below:

  1. *Develops initiative among subordinates*
     - It helps to promote self reliance and confidence in subordinates as when lower managerial levels are given freedom to take their own decisions they learn to depend on their own judgment
     - It also keeps them in a state wherein they are constantly challenged and have to develop solutions for various problems they encounter
     - A decentralization policy helps to identify those executives who have the necessary potential to become dynamic leaders
  2. *Develops managerial talent for the future*
     - Decentralization gives employees a chance to prove their abilities and creates a reservoir of qualified manpower who can be considered to fill up more challenging positions through promotions
     - It also helps to identify those who may not be successful in assuming greater responsibility
     - Thus, it is a means of management education as well as an opportunity for trained manpower to use its talent in real life situations
  3. *Quick decision making*
     - The managerial hierarchy is a chain of communication in a centralized organization because every decision is taken by the top management; the flow of information is slow as it has to traverse many levels. Response also takes time. Thus, decision making and adaptability to dynamic environments slows down

- In a decentralized organization, decisions are taken at levels which are nearest to the point of action and there is no need for approval from many levels, hence the process is much faster
- There are also less chances of information getting distorted as it doesn't have to go through long channels

4. ***Relief to top management***
   - Decentralization diminishes the amount of direct supervision to be exercised by a supervisor over the activities of a subordinate as they are given freedom to act and decide within the limits set by the superior
   - It also leaves the top management with more time which they can devote to more important policy decisions rather than both policy and operational decisions
5. ***Facilitates growth***
   - It gives greater autonomy to lower levels of management as divisional or departmental heads
   - This allows them to function in a manner best suited to their department and fosters a sense of competition among departments
   - This competition among departments leads to an increase in productivity and the organization is able to generate more returns which may be used for expansion
6. ***Better control***
   - It makes it possible to evaluate performance at each level so that the departments can be individually held responsible for their performance and results.
   - The extent of achievement of organizational objectives and the contribution of each department in meeting the overall objectives can be ascertained. Feedback from all levels helps to analyze variances and improve operations
   - In decentralization, one of the challenges is the accountability of performance

- In response to this challenge, better control systems are being evolved like:
  – Balance score card
  – Management information system
- It compels the management to innovative performance measurement systems

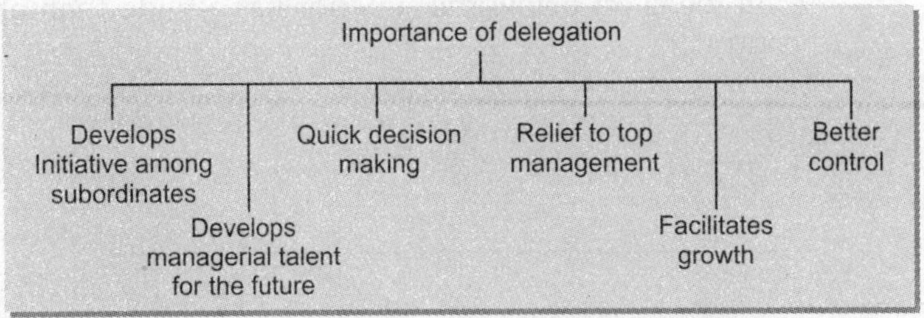

Q44. Name the philosophy that implies selective dispersal of authority as it propagates the belief that people are competent, capable and resourceful.

Ans. Decentralization.

Q45. State a limiting factor of decentralization.

Ans. In spite of all the benefits, decentralization should be applied with caution as it may lead to organizational disintegration if the departments start to operate on their own guidelines which may be contrary to the interest of the firm. Decentralization should essentially be balanced with centralization in all areas of major policy decisions.

OTHER IMPORTANT QUESTIONS

Q1. What is meant by span of control/management? How does it form the basis of management hierarchy?

Ans.

- Span of management refers to the number of subordinates that can be effectively supervised by a superior
- Span of control may be narrow or wide depending on factors like:

– Nature of work
– Ability of superiors
– Ability of subordinates

- Span of control forms the basis of a management hierarchy. It determines the levels of management in the organization structure and gives it shape

For Example:

In the chart below the superior has a wide span of control

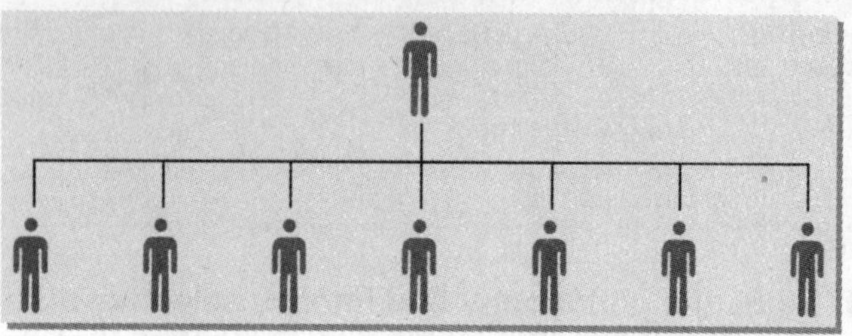

In the above chart, the superior has a narrow span of control

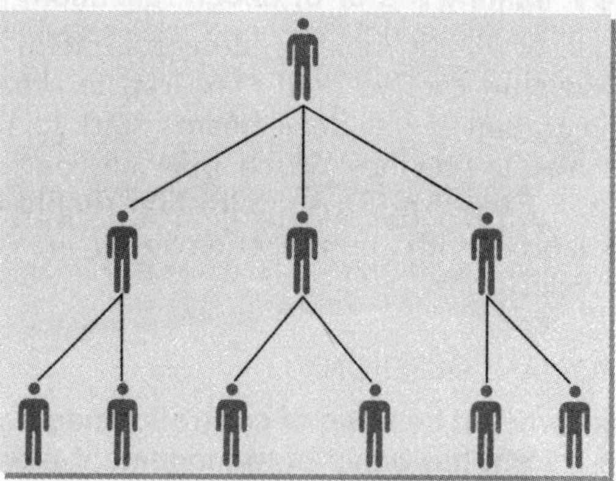

- A small span results in multiple levels and a taller structure whereas a wide span results in fewer levels and a flatter structure
- Thus, span of control is inversely related to number of management levels in the management hierarchy

Q2. Distinguish between centralization and decentralization.

Ans. The difference between centralization and decentralization is as follows:

Table 5.5

Basis	*Centralization*	*Decentralization*
Meaning	Concentration of decision making power in the hands of top management	Distribution of decision making authority across length and breadth of the organization
Decision making authority	Lies with the top level management	Shared with the lower levels of management
Freedom of action	Subordinates have less freedom of action	Subordinates have more freedom of action
Suitability	More suitable in small organizations	More suitable in large and complex organizations

Q3. Reena runs a factory wherein she manufactures footwear. The business has been doing well and she intends to expand by diversifying into leather bags and western formal wear, thereby making her company a complete provider of corporate wear. This will enable her to market her business unit as one stop shop for working women. Which type of structure would you recommend for the expanded organization and why?

Ans. Divisional structure. Substantiate with suitability and advantages.

Q4. In an electrical goods manufacturing company there are 4 main activities: production, marketing, finance and personnel. The general manager is planning to structure the organization. Which type of structure is suitable and why?

Ans. Functional structure. Substantiate with suitability and advantages.

Q4. Rahul Enterprises is manufacturing chemicals and textiles. What type of organization structure would be suitable for it?

Ans. Divisional structure.

Q5. Which term denotes the number of subordinates that can be effectively managed by a superior?

Ans. Span of management

Q6. What type of structure can a formal *organization* have?

Ans.

1. Functional structure
2. Divisional structure

Q7. Which network of interaction facilitates emotional and mutual objectives to be fulfilled in an organization?

Ans. Informal organization

Q8. The employees of Ankur Ltd, a software company, have formed a dramatics group for their recreation. Name the type of organization so formed.

Ans. Informal organization

Q9. Identifying and grouping activities is a step in the process of which function of management?

Ans. Organizing

Q10. What gives shape to the *organization structure*?

Ans. Span of management

6

Staffing

Q1. Identify the function of management which deals with human resources or which deals with principal assets/resources of a firm.

Ans. Staffing

Q2. Identify the function of management which is concerned with 'putting people to jobs' or 'putting the right people to the right positions'

Ans. Staffing

Q3. Define staffing.

Ans.

- Staffing is that part of the process of management which deals with:
  - Obtaining
  - Utilizing
  - Maintaining

  A satisfactory and satisfied workforce.
- It has been described as the management function of filling and keeping filled the positions in the organization structure
- Staffing involves the following elements:
  - Manpower planning
  - Recruitment
  - Selection
  - Placement and orientation
  - Training and development
  - Performance appraisal

Fig. 6.1: Staffing means putting people to jobs

- Promotion and career planning
- Compensation

• Simply said, staffing is putting people to jobs

Q4. Why is staffing considered to be a continuous function?

Ans. In an existing enterprise, staffing is a continuous process because:

1. New jobs may be created
2. Some of the present employees may leave the organization causing vacancies

Q5. Explain the steps in the process of *staffing*.

or

What are the elements of *staffing*?

Ans. The various elements of staffing are:

1. ***Estimating manpower requirements (human resource planning)***
   - Human resource planning refers to a process of estimating the number (quantity) and type (quality) of people needed to perform different jobs and accomplish organizational objectives
   - The manpower requirements are translated into:
     - *Job description:* It refers to describing the profile of job (duties and responsibilities)

  - *Job specification*: It refers to specifying the minimum qualifications, experience, personality, characteristics, etc. required to perform that job
- Understanding the manpower requirements would necessitate two significant analysis:
  - *Workload analysis:* It would enable an assessment of the number and type of human resources necessary for performance of different jobs
  - *Workforce analysis:* It helps to identify number and type of people available in the organization
- Both these analysis help to identify whether an organization is overstaffed, understaffed or optimally staffed.
- Overstaffing results in removing the employee or transferring him
- Understaffing results in re-starting the recruitment process

2. ***Recruitment***
   - Recruitment may be defined as the process of searching for prospective employees and stimulating them to apply for jobs in the organization
   - Job description and job specification may be used for developing the situation vacant advertisement
   - There are 2 sources of recruitment:
     - Internal sources like promotions, transfers
     - External sources like advertisements, casual callers, placement agencies
   - The essential objective is to create a pool of prospective job seeking candidates
   - Internal sources may be used to a restricted extent. For fresh talent and wider choice, external sources are used
   - Recruitment does not involve any elimination/ rejection of candidates. Rather it creates a pool of prospective candidates. Hence, it is called a positive process.
3. ***Selection***
   - Selection is the process of choosing from among the pool of the prospective job candidates developed at the stage of recruitment

- The selection process serves 2 important purpose:
  - It ensures that the organization gets the best among available candidates
  - It enhances the self esteem and the prestige of those selected and conveys to them the seriousness with which things are executed in the firm
- Selection is a negative process since it involves elimination/rejection of unsuitable candidates
- Selection procedure involves steps like:
  - Preliminary screening
  - Selection tests
  - Interviews
  - References and background checks
  - Selection decision
  - Medical examination
  - Job offer
  - Contract of employment

4. *Placement and orientation*
   - Placement means putting the right person on the right job. It refers to the employee occupying the post for which he has been selected.
   - The employee is given a brief presentation about the company and is introduced to his superiors, subordinates and colleagues. This process of familiarization is crucial and may have a lasting impact on his decision to stay and also on his job performance
   - Orientation refers to introducing the selected employee to other employees and familiarizing him with the rules and regulation of the organization
5. *Training and development*
   - Training is any process by which the aptitudes, skills and abilities of employees to perform specific jobs are increased. It is a process of learning new skills and application of knowledge. It attempts to improve their performance on the current job as well as prepare them for any intended job

- Development refers to overall learning and growth of an employee which not only improves his job performance but also helps in his personality development.
- There are various methods of training like:
  - Job rotation
  - Internship
  - Coaching

6. ***Performance appraisal***
   - All organizations have some formal or informal means of appraising their employees' performance
   - Performance appraisal means evaluating an employee's current and/or past performance as against certain predetermined standards
   - The employee is expected to know what these standards are and the superior is to provide the employee, feedback on his performance
   - The performance appraisal process includes:
     - Defining the job
     - Appraising performance
     - Providing feedback
7. ***Promotion and career planning***
   - Promotions are an integral part of people's career. They prefer to being placed in positions of increased responsibility. This usually means more pay, more responsibility and job satisfaction
8. ***Compensation***
   - Compensation refers to all forms of payments or rewards given to employees
   - The financial payments may be of 2 types:
     - Direct financial payments like wages, salaries, incentives, commissions, bonuses
     - Indirect financial payments like employee paid insurance, vacations, medical benefits
   - Direct financial payments are also of 2 types:
     - *Time based plan:* It means salary and wages are paid either daily, weekly, monthly or annually on the basis of number of hours worked

  - *Performance based plan:* It means salary and wages are paid according to piecework, i.e. number of units produced
- Certain pay plans can be created which are a combination of time based plans and performance based plans for higher performance
- Some other factors also influence the design of a pay plan like:
  - Legal (labor laws)
  - Unions
  - Equity
  - Company policy

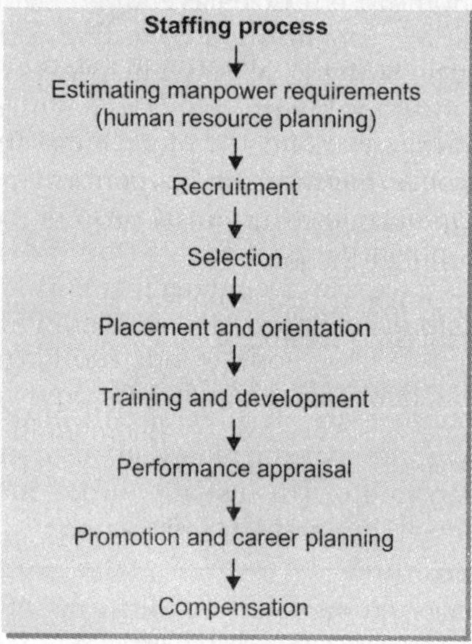

Q6. Explain manpower requirements.

Q7. Identify the 2 analysis which help to understand manpower requirements

Q8. Name the statement which defines duties and responsibilities.

Q9. Name the statement which defines the desirable profile of a job position.

Ans. Job specification

Q10. Why is recruitment considered to be a positive process?

Q11. Explain the meaning of selection as a part of the staffing process

Q12. What are the 2 purposes of selection procedure?

Q13. What does the process of performance appraisal include?

Q14. State the 2 types of financial payments used as compensation to employees.

Q15. State the 2 types of direct financial payments.

Q16. State the factors that influence design of the pay plan.

Ans. All the above questions can be answered with the help of Ans. 5

Q17. Mention certain common factors that influence the recruitment, selection and training process carried out in an organization.

Ans. The various common factors are:

1. Supply and demand of specific skills in the labor market
2. Unemployment rate
3. Labor market conditions
4. Legal and political considerations
5. Company's policy
6. Company's image
7. Technological developments
8. Human resource planning cost
9. General economic conditions

Q18. Explain the 3 aspects of staffing.

Ans. The 3 aspects of staffing are:

1. ***Recruitment***
   - It is a positive step which aims at attracting a number of candidates to apply for the given job
   - The higher the number of people who apply for a job, the higher will be the possibility of getting a suitable employee

2. *Selection*
   - It is a negative process in which a candidate is selected and the others are rejected
   - It aims at selecting the most suitable person out of the candidates who have applied for the job
3. *Training*
   - It is concerned with up gradation of the knowledge and skills of the employees so that their performance can be enhanced

Q19. Name a commonly used component of the recruitment process.

Ans. Advertisement is commonly a part of the recruitment process and can occur through several means like:
1. Newspapers dedicated to job advertisements
2. Professional publications
3. Advertisements placed on windows
4. Campus interviews
5. Job centers

Q20. State the various activities involved in the process of recruitment.

Ans.
- The objective of recruitment is to attract potential employees with the necessary qualifications in adequate numbers for the jobs available
- The various activities involved in the recruitment process are:
  - Identification of the different sources of labor supply
  - Assessment of their validity
  - Inviting application from the prospective candidates for the vacancies
  - Choosing the most suitable sources

Q21. Explain the internal sources of recruitment.

Ans. The various internal sources of recruitment are:
1. *Transfers*
   - It involves shifting of an employee from one job to another, one department to another, or from one shift

to another, without a substantive change in the responsibilities and status of the employee

- It may lead to change in duties and responsibilities, working conditions, etc but not essentially salary
- It is practically a horizontal movement of employees

Advantages

i. Shortage of suitable personnel in one branch may be filled through transfer from other branches.

Fig. 6.2: Transfer

ii. Helps in removal of individual problems and grievances

iii. Training of employees for learning different jobs

2. ***Promotions***
   - It leads to shifting an employee to a higher position, carrying higher responsibilities, with higher status and pay
   - Promotion is a vertical shifting of employees

   Advantages

   i. Improves motivation

   ii. Increases loyalty

   iii. Increases satisfaction level of employees

   iv. It has a psychological impact over the employees as promotion at the top level of the organization may lead to a chain of promotions at the lower levels

Fig. 6.3: Promotion

Q22. The Delhi branch of ABC Ltd has surplus employees. There is a vacancy in the Mumbai office of the same company. The company wishes to recruit employees from within the organization. Suggest a suitable source.

Ans. Transfers

Q23. How do promotions create a psychological impact over the employees?

Ans. Refer Ans. 21

Q24. State the advantages of recruiting employees internally.

Ans. The various advantages of recruiting employees internally are:

1. *Increases motivation and loyalty of employees*
   - Employees are motivated to improve their performance
   - A promotion at a higher level may lead to a chain of promotions at lower levels in the organization
   - This motivates the employees to improve their performance through learning and implementation

- Employees work their commitment and loyalty and remain satisfied within their jobs. Peace prevails in the firm because of promotional avenues

2. *Simple and reliable*
   - Internal recruitment simplifies the process of selection and placement
   - The candidates that are already working in the enterprise can be evaluated more accurately and economically
   - This is a more reliable way of recruitment as the candidates are known to the firm
3. *Reduces the need for training*
   - Transfer is a tool of training the employees to prepare them for higher jobs
   - People recruited from within the organization don't need to undergo induction training
4. *Solves the problem of shortages and surplus*
   - Transfer has the benefit of shifting the workforce from the surplus departments to those where there is a shortage
5. *Cheap and economical*
   - It is cheaper as compared to getting candidates from external sources

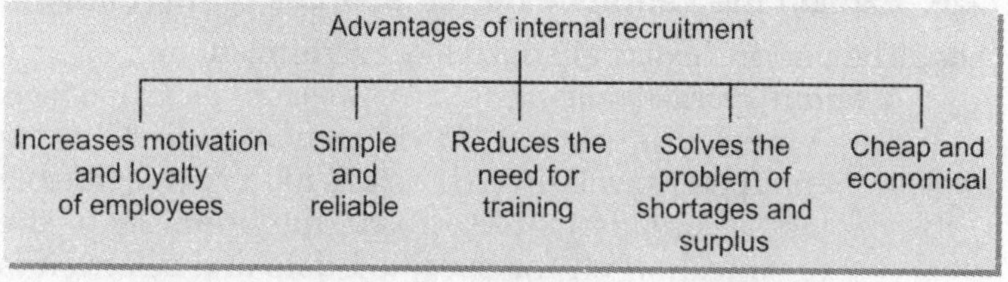

Q25. Internal sources of recruitment suffer from certain limitations. Explain.

Ans. The various limitations of internal sources of recruitment are:

1. *No fresh talent*
   - When vacancies are filled through internal sources the scope for induction of fresh talent is reduced

- Complete reliance on internal recruitment involves danger of inbreeding in the organization by stopping infusion of new blood.

2. *Increases lethargy of employees*
   - The employees may become lethargic if they are sure of time bound promotions
3. *Not suitable for new organizations*
   - A new firm can't have internal sources of recruitment. No firm can fill all its vacancies through internal sources
4. *Reduces the spirit of competition*
   - The spirit of competition among the employees may be hampered as there is no new challenge from outsiders
5. *Reduces productivity*
   - Frequent transfers of employees may often reduce the productivity of the employees

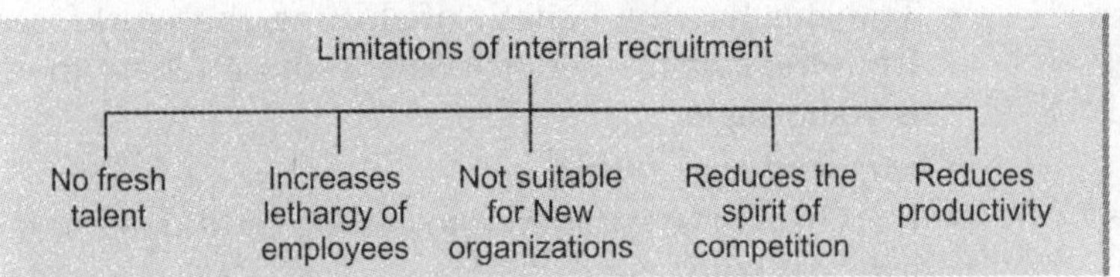

Q26. Explain the various external sources of recruitment.

Ans. The various external sources of recruitment are:

1. *Direct recruitment*
   - A notice is placed on the notice board of the enterprise specifying the details of the jobs available
   - Job seekers assemble outside the premises of the organization on the specified date and selection is done on the spot
   - Suitability
     - Casual vacancies of unskilled or semi skilled jobs
     - Casual vacancies when there is a rush of work or when some permanent worker is absent
   - Such workers are known as casual or badli workers and they are paid remuneration on the basis of daily wages

- Advantages
  - It is absolutely inexpensive as it doesn't involve any cost of advertising vacancies

Fig. 6.4: Notices are placed on the notice board specifying the availability of jobs

2. *Casual callers*
   - Many reputed business organizations keep a database of unsolicited applicants in their offices
   - A list of such job seekers can be prepared and can be screened to fill the vacancies as they arise
   - Advantages: It reduces the cost of recruiting the workforce
   - Suitability: All types of skilled, unskilled and semi skilled job positions
3. *Advertisement*
   - Advertisement in newspapers or trade and professional journals is used when a wider choice is needed
   - Suitability
     - Most of the senior positions of the industry and commerce are filled by this method
   - Advantages
     - More information about the firm and the job can be given on advertisement

   - It gives management a wider range of candidates from which to choose
- Disadvantages
   - It may bring in a flood of response and many times, from quite unsuitable candidates

4. *Employment exchange*
   - Suitability
      - Employment exchanges run by the government are regarded as a good source of recruitment for unskilled and skilled operative jobs
      - In some professions, compulsory notification of vacancies to employment exchange is required by law
   - Advantages
      - They help to match the personnel demand and supply by serving as a link between job seekers and employers
   - Disadvantages
      - The records of employment exchange are often not up to date and many of the candidates referred by them are not found suitable

Fig. 6.5: Employment exchanges are a good source of recruitment

5. *Placement agencies and management consultants*
   - Suitability

  - Placement agencies do substantive work in technical and professional areas (top level executives)
  - Management consultancy firms help the organization to recruit technical, professional and managerial personnel. They specialize in middle and top level executive placements
- Placement agencies provide a nation wide service on matching personnel demand and supply
- Placement agencies compile bio data of a large number of candidates and recommend suitable names
- Placement agencies charge a fee for their services and are of use when extensive screening is required
- Management consultants maintain data bank of persons with different qualifications and skill and even advertise the jobs on behalf of their clients to recruit the right type of personnel

6. *Campus recruitment*
   - Suitability
     - Colleges and institutes of management and technology have become popular source of recruitment for technical, professional and managerial jobs
   - Many big organizations maintain a close liaison with universities, management institutes and vocational schools to recruit qualified personnel for jobs
   - Recruitment from educational institutions is a well established practice of business and is termed campus recruitment

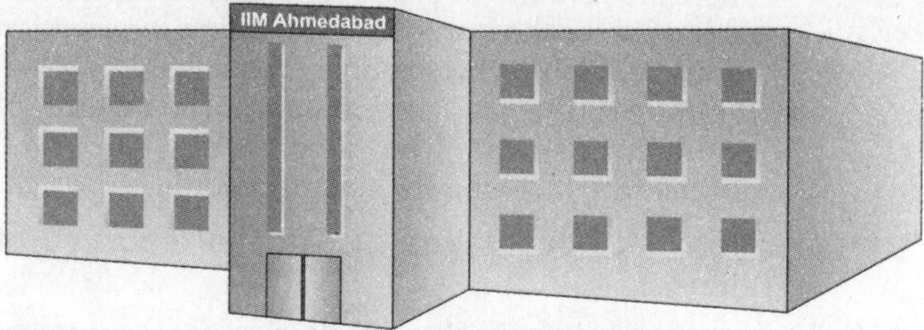

Fig. 6.6: Campus recruitment

7. *Recommendation of employees*
    - Applicants introduced by present employees or their relatives or friends may prove to be a good source of recruitment
    - Such applicants are likely to be good employees because their background is sufficiently known
    - A type of preliminary screening takes place as the present employees know both the company and the candidates and they try to satisfy both
    - Suitability
        - For all types of job positions
8. *Labor contractors*
    - Suitability
        - They maintain close contact with laborers and can provide the required number of unskilled workers at short notice
    - Workers are recruited through labor contractors who are current employees of firms
    - Disadvantages
        - If the contractor himself decides to leave the firm, all the workers employed through him will follow suit
9. *Advertising on Television*
    - The practice of telecasting of vacant posts on TV is gaining importance
    - The detailed requirements of the job and the qualities required to do it are published along with the profile of the firm where the vacancy exists
10. **Web publishing**
    - Internet is becoming a common source of recruitment
    - There are certain websites specifically designed and dedicated for the purpose of providing information about both job seekers and job openings
    - Websites like jobstreet.com, naukri.com are commonly visited both by the prospective employees ant the firms looking for suitable people

Q27. Mention the advantages of external sources of recruitment.

Ans. The various advantages of external sources of recruitment are:

1. *Qualified personnel*
   - By using external sources, the management can attract qualified and trained people to apply for vacant jobs in the organization
2. *Wider choice*
   - When vacancies are advertised widely, a large number of applicants from outside the firm apply which gives the management a wider choice when selecting people
3. *Fresh talent*
   - The present employees may be insufficient or they may not fulfill the specifications of the jobs to be filled
   - External recruitment provides wider choice and brings new blood in the firm
4. *Competitive spirit*
   - The existing staff has to compete with the outsiders and will work harder to show better performance

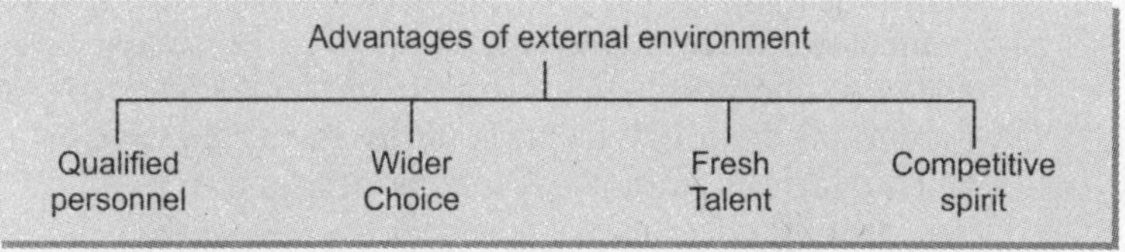

Q28. State the limitations of external sources of recruitment.

Ans. The various limitations of external sources of recruitment are:

1. *Dissatisfaction among esxisting staff*
   - It may lead to dissatisfaction and frustration among existing employees. They might feel that their chances of promotion are reduced
2. *Lengthy process*
   - It takes a long time, the business has to notify the vacancies and wait for applications to initiate the selection process
3. *Costly process*
   - It is costly to recruit staff from external sources. A lot of money has to be spent on advertisement and processing of applications

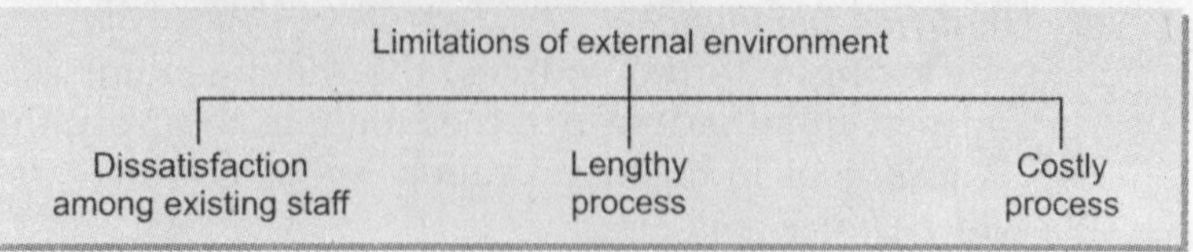

Q29. Explain the various steps involved in the process of selection.

Ans. The various steps in the process of selection are:

1. ***Preliminary screening***
   - It helps the manager to eliminate unqualified or unfit job seekers based on the information supplied in the application forms
   - Preliminary interviews help reject misfits for reasons which did not appear in the application forms
2. ***Selection tests***
   - An employment test is a mechanism (either a paper and pencil test or an exercise) that attempts to measure certain characteristics of individuals
   - These characteristics range from aptitudes such as manual dexterity to personality to intelligence
   - The various important selection tests are:
     - Intelligence tests
       - It is the most important psychological test used to measure the level of intelligence quotient of an individual
       - It is an indicator of a person's learning ability and his ability to make decisions and judgments
     - Aptitude tests
       - It is a measure of individual's potential for learning new skills
       - It indicates the person's capacity to develop. They are good indices of a person's future success score
     - Personality tests
       - It provides clues to a person's emotions, his reactions, maturity and value system
       - These tests probe the overall personality and hence are difficult to design and implement
     - Trade tests
       - They measure the existing skills of the candidates

    - They measure the level of knowledge and proficiency in the area of professions or technical training
  - Interest tests
    - They are used to know the pattern of interests or involvement of a person

3. *Employment interview*
   - Interview is a formal, in-depth conversation conducted to evaluate the applicant's suitability for the job
   - The role of the interviewer is to seek information and that of the interviewee is to provide information. Though, in present times, the interviewee also seeks information from the interviewer
   - The interview helps the employer to check out:
     - Communication skills
     - Personal grooming of the candidate
   - Sometimes interviews may be stressful and subject to personal bias due to which the true personality of the candidate may not be projected
4. *Reference and background checks*
   - Many employers request names, contact address and telephone numbers of references for the purpose of:
     - Verifying information
     - Gaining additional information on an applicant
   - Previous employees, known persons, teachers and university professors can act as references
5. *Selection decision*
   - The final decision has to be made from among the candidates who pass the tests, interview and reference checks
   - The views of the concerned manager will be generally considered in the final selection because it is he who is responsible for the performance of the new employee
6. *Medical examination*
   - After the selection and before the job offer is made, the candidate is required to undergo a fitness test
   - The purpose of the medical examination is:
     - To maintain the health record of the candidate
     - To prevent communicable diseases from entering the organization

- The job offer is given to the candidate declared fit after the exam

7. *Job offer*
   - Job offer is made through a letter of appointment to confirm his acceptance
   - Such a letter generally contains a date by which the appointee must report for joining on duty
   - The appointee must be given reasonable time for reporting
8. *Contract of employment*
   - After the job offer has been made and the candidate accepts the offer certain documents need to be executed by the employer and the candidate
   - These include:
     - An attestation form which contains vital details about the candidate which are authenticated and attested by him. This form is a valid record for future reference
     - A contract of employment which contains basic information like job title, duties, responsibilities, date when continuous employment starts, basis for calculating service, rates of pay, allowances, hours of work, leave rules, sickness, disciplinary procedure, grievance procedure, work rules, termination of employment, etc.

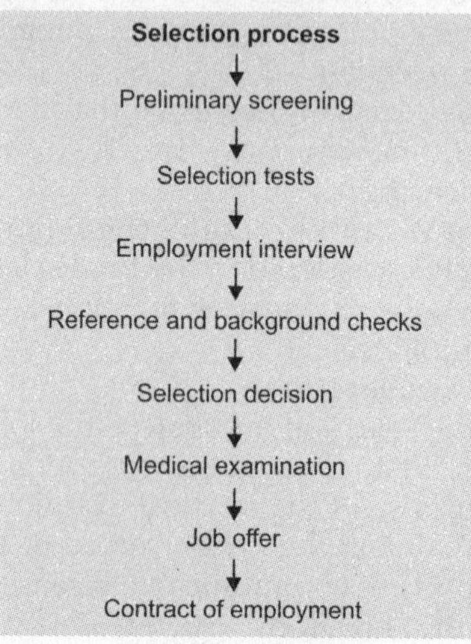

Q30. Explain the different types of selection tests.

Q31. Which selection test is difficult to design and implement?

Q32. How is an aptitude test different from a trade test?

Ans. All the above questions can be answered with the help of Ans.29

Q33. Distinguish between recruitment and selection.

Ans. The differences between recruitment and selection are:

Table 6.1

Basis	*Recruitment*	*Selection*
Meaning	It is a process of stimulating, searching willing and prospective candidates to apply for vacant job positions. It helps to create a pool of applicants	It is a process of choosing the most suitable candidate from the pool of applicants
Nature	It is a positive process since it does not involve any kind of elimination	It is a negative process as it involves rejection of unsuitable candidates
Sequence	It is done before selection	It is done after selection
Complexity	It is a relatively simple process	It is a complex process as it requires the candidates to pass through various hurdles before final selection

Q34. Distinguish between training, development and education.

Ans. The differences between training, development and education are:

Table 6.2

Basis	*Training*	*Development*	*Education*
Meaning	It is a process by which the aptitude, skills and abilities of employees to perform specific jobs are increased.	It refers to the learning opportunities designed to help the employee's growth. It refers to the overall growth of an individual in all	It involves increasing the general knowledge and understanding of employees. It is the understanding and interpretation of

Contd.

Table 6.2 (*Contd.*)

Basis	*Training*	*Development*	*Education*
	It is a process of learning new skills and application of knowledge	respects	knowledge and also developing an overall understanding of the total environment
Purpose	To make the employees proficient in their present jobs thereby improving their performance or preparing them for any intended job. The goals of training are more organization specific than individual specific	To prepare the employees for handling more responsibilities and challenging jobs	To develop an overall understanding and improving the mental capabilities of individuals. It doesn't provide definite answers but develops a logical and rational mind to understand a phenomenon.
Scope	It has a narrow scope as it only enables the employee to do a job	It has broader scope than training but narrower than education. It covers: 1. Improvement in job performance 2. Overall growth of personality. Gives them the maturity to become not only good employees but better men and women and thus actualize their actual potential	The scope of education is wider than that of training and development
Duration	It is time bound and short term	It is an ongoing process and is career bound	It has a long duration
Depth of knowledge	Mainly technical skills are taught. Depth of knowledge provided is according to the job requirement	In depth knowledge is provided for the overall growth of the individual by enhancing their human and conceptual skills	Depth of knowledge is provided according to the level of understanding of individuals. It involves developing mental capabilities
Level of management	Generally for the lower level managers and workers	Generally for middle and top level managers	Managers and workers of all levels
Nature	Practical in nature, mainly technical knowledge and skills are taught	Both theoretical and practical in nature	Mostly theoretical in nature
Payment	Training cost is paid by the employer	Paid by the organization or the employee himself	Paid by the government or the individuals themselves

Q35. Discuss the importance of training to the organization.

Ans. Training is important for an organization as:

1. ***Systematic learning***
   - Training is systematic learning which is better than hit and trial methods which lead to wastage of time, efforts and money
   - Training is much more organized and uniform
2. ***Higher profits***
   - It enhances employee productivity both in terms of quantity and quality, leading to higher profits
   - Since training increases knowledge and skills of employees, they can work better leading to higher benefits to the firm
3. ***Prepares future managers***
   - Training increases knowledge and skills so that employees can handle challenges more effectively and efficiently
   - Training equips the future managers who can take over in case of an emergency
   - Employees have greater chances of promotion
4. ***Increases employee morale***
   - Training increases employee morale and reduces absenteeism and employee turnover
   - This results in higher degree of job satisfaction and loyalty
5. ***Adaptation to changes***
   - It helps in preparing the employees to face challenges of the changing environment as the modern business environment is dynamic
   - Trained employees show a better response to changes and can adapt easily
   - Thus, it helps in obtaining effective response to fast changing environment

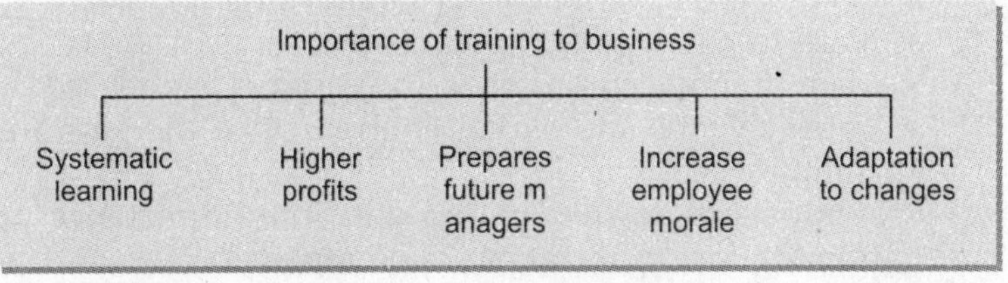

Q36. Discuss the importance of training to employees.

Ans. Training is important to employees as:

1. ***Better career prospects***
    - Improved skills and knowledge due to training lead to better career of the individual
    - There are thus better promotion prospects
2. ***Increased earning potential***
    - Increased performance by the individual helps him to earn more
    - Since productivity and profitability of the firm would increase, he would be in a position to earn more thereby increasing his standard of living
3. ***Reduces accidents***
    - Training makes the employees more efficient to handle machines. Thus, less prone to accidents and more safety
4. ***Higher satisfaction***
    - Training increases satisfaction and morale of the employees
    - Trained employees will have greater knowledge and skills which increases their confidence and morale. Job satisfaction and loyalty increases their contribution to a healthy work environment

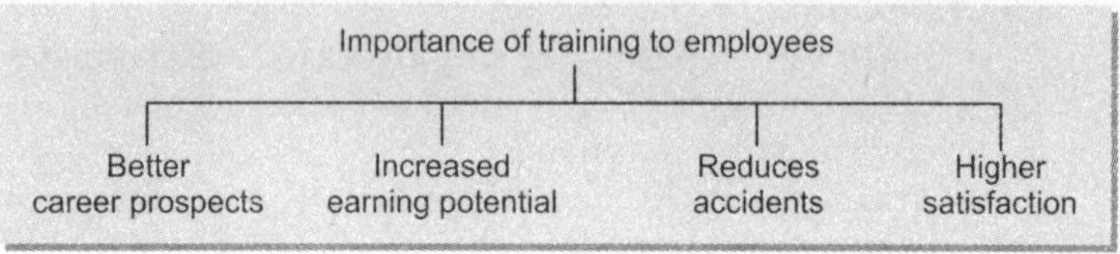

Q37. Explain the importance of training and development.

Ans. The need for training and development arose due to:

- Occurrence of rapid changes in the environment
- Need to re-adapt the products and services
- Manner in which products and services are offered
- Types of jobs and skills required since the jobs are complex

Substantiate the answer with the importance of training for organizations and employees.

Q38. What is the basic difference between on-the-job and off-the-job methods of training?

Ans. On-the-job training means learning while doing and off-the-job training means learning before doing.

Q39. What are the various on the job methods of training?

Ans. The various on the job methods of training are:

1. *Apprenticeship programmes*
   - They put the trainee under guidance of a master worker
   - They are designed to acquire a higher level of skill

   For Example:

   People seeking to enter skilled traits like plumber, electricians and iron workers

   - These apprentices are trainees who spend a prescribed amount of time working with an experienced guide or trainer
   - A uniform period of training is offered to trainees, in which both fast and slow learners are placed together. Slow learners may sometimes require additional training
2. *Coaching*
   - In this method, the superior guides and instructs the trainee as a coach
   - The coach or counselor:
     - Sets mutually agreed upon goals
     - Suggests how to achieve these goals
     - Suggests changes required in behavior and performance
     - Periodically reviews the trainee's progress
   - The trainee works directly with a senior manager and the manager takes full responsibility for the trainee's coaching
   - The trainee is being groomed to replace the senior manager and relieve him from some of his duties. It gives a chance to the trainee to learn the job also
3. *Internship training*
   - It is a joint programme of training in which educational institutions and business firms cooperate
   - Selected candidates carry on regular studies for the prescribed period

- They also work in some factory or office to acquire practical knowledge and skills

For Example:

MBA students after completing their/during the course of their education may be posted for a 3 month internship programme with some organization

4. ***Job rotation***
   - It involves shifting of the trainee from one department to another or from one job to another
   - This enables the trainee to gain a broader understanding of all parts of the business and how the organization as a whole functions
   - The trainee gets fully involved in the departments' operations and also gets a chance to test his own ability and aptitude
   - Job rotation allows trainees to interact with other employees facilitating future cooperation among departments
   - Thus, it helps in promotions, replacements or transfers

For Example:

In banks, an employee may be shifted from collections to loan sanctioning

Q40. Suggest a suitable training method in which the trainee is being groomed to take up senior level position.

Ans. Coaching

Q41. What is the purpose of coaching?

Ans. Refer Ans. 39

Q42. Name the method of training in which a joint programme between an educational institute and business firms takes place.

Ans. Internship programme

Q43. Explain the various types of off the job training methods.

Ans. The various off the job training methods are:

1. ***Classroom lectures/conferences***
   - This approach is well adapted to conveying specific information, procedures methods and rules
   - The use of Audio-Visuals or demonstrations can often make a formal classroom presentation more interesting while increasing retention and offering a way for clarifying difficult points
2. ***Case study***
   - Taken from actual experiences of organizations, cases represent attempts to describe as accurately as possible real problems that managers have faced
   - Trainees study the cases to determine problems, analyze causes, develop alternative solutions and select what they believe to be the best solution and implement it
3. ***Films***
   - They provide information and explicitly demonstrate skills that are not easily represented by other techniques
   - Used in conjunction with conference discussions, it is a very effective method in certain cases
4. ***Vestibule training***
   - Employees learn their jobs on equipments they will be using, but the training is conducted away from the actual work floor
   - Actual work environments are created in a classroom and employees use same equipment , materials and files
   - This is done usually when employees are required to handle sophisticated machinery and equipment

   For Example:

   Sophisticated and expensive cash registers
5. ***Computer modeling***
   - It simulates the work environment by programming a computer to imitate some of the realities of the job and allows learning to happen without the risk or high costs that may be incurred if a mistake is made in real life

   For Example:

   Training given to pilots

6. *Programmed instruction*
    - It incorporates a pre-arranged and proposed acquisition of some specific skills or general knowledge
    - Information is broken into meaningful units which are arranged in a proper way to form a logical and sequential learning package, i.e. from simple to complex
    - The trainee goes through these units by answering questions or filling the blanks

Q44. Discuss the importance of staffing.

Ans.

- Human resources are the most valuable resources and are the foundation of any business
- The ability of an organization to achieve its goals depends on the quality of human resources
- No organization can be successful unless it fills the various posts with the right kind of staff
- The staffing function has gained importance because of:
  - Rapid changes in technology
  - Increasing size of the organization
  - Complicated behavior of human being

  Staffing becomes an essential function of management for the following reasons:

  1. *Helps in discovering and obtaining competent personnel*
      - Through the elements of manpower planning, recruitment and selection it is possible to obtain competent people for the job
  2. *Higher performance*
      - Proper staffing ensures higher performance by putting the right people on the right job
  3. *Continuous survival and growth*
      - Proper staffing ensures survival and growth through succession planning for managers
  4. *Improves job satisfaction*
      - Proper staffing improves job satisfaction and morale of employees through objective

assessment (performance appraisal) and fair rewards for its contribution

5. *Optimum utilization of human resources*
   - Proper staffing helps to avoid over manning, it prevents under utilization of personnel and increasing labor costs
   - It also avoids shortages of human resources by indicating the requirement in advance

Conclusion

Staffing function must be performed by all organizations since if right people aren't available it leads to:

- Wastage of time, money and effort
- Lower productivity
- Lower profitability

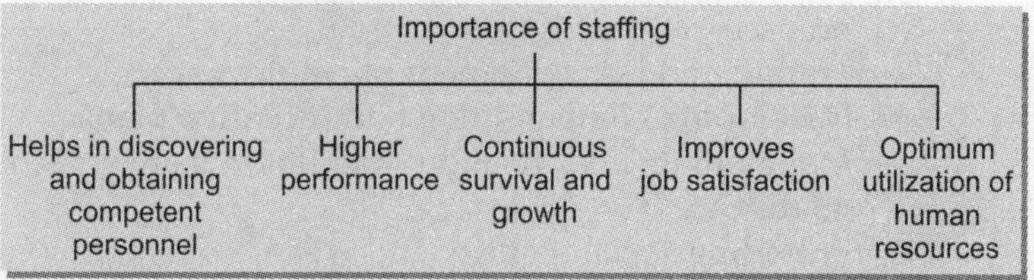

Q45. Staffing is a generic function of management. Explain.

Ans.

- Staffing is an important function which all managers need to perform
- After the organization structure of positions is created it needs to be filled with the right staff
- These people subsequently need to be trained and motivated to work towards attainment of organizational goals
- Staffing function deals with the human element and management of these resources is most important since performance and success of the organization would depend on how well the staffing is done, i.e.
  - Competence
  - Motivation
  - Performance

Q46. Scope of staffing is limited as compared to human resource management. Explain.

Ans.

- In small organizations, it is the responsibility of all managers to deal with and select people to work in the firm
- The managers perform all duties related to employees, salaries, welfare, work conditions, etc.
- The scope of staffing is limited in this case
- In large organizations, as the number of employees increase, a separate department is formed which has specialists in managing people
- Some specialized activities included in human resources management are:
  - Recruitment (search for qualified people)
  - Analyzing jobs, collecting information about jobs, to prepare job description
  - Training and development of employees
  - Developing compensation and incentive plans
  - Maintaining labor relations and union management relations
  - Providing social security and welfare of employees
  - Handling grievances and complaints
  - Defending the company in law suits and avoiding legal complications
- Thus, HRM is a much broader concept

Q47. Discuss the evolution of human resource management.

Ans. Human resource management has replaced the traditional concepts of:

i. Labor welfare

ii. Personnel management

1. *Labor welfare officer*
   - During the industrial revolution trade unions emerged. This led to the need of a labor welfare officer who would be an effective link between owners and workers.
   - His role was limited to bare minimum welfare activities of employees

- He was looked down both by the owners and the workers

2. *Personnel officer/manager*
   - With the introduction of factory system, many were employed under one roof. This job of recruitment, selection and placement was given to one person who was called the personnel officer and was later renamed as the personnel manager
3. *Human resource manager*
   - Human relations approach recognized human factor as the most valuable asset since:
     - Rapid changes in technology
     - Increasing size of organization
     - Complicated behavior of humans
   - As the scope of work increased the personnel manager was replaced by the HR manager

Q48. Staffing is both a line and staff function of management. Do you agree? Why?

Ans. Yes.

- Staffing is a function of management just like planning, organizing, controlling and directing and It is considered to be a distinct functional and specialized area of management like marketing and financial management
- It is an essential function of every manager as well as the main role played by the HR department

OTHER IMPORTANT QUESTIONS

Q1. What is the pre-requisite for conducting the selection process?

Ans. Recruitment

Q2. Name the method of training which facilitates easy promotion, replacements and transfers.

Ans. Job rotation

Q3. What kinds of job are filled through an employment exchange?

Ans. Skilled and unskilled operative jobs

Q4. What is the drawback of recruitment through employment exchange?

Ans. The records of employment exchange are often not up to date and many of the candidates referred by them may not be found suitable

Q5. Why is recommendation of employees a good source of recruitment?

Ans. Background is sufficiently known

Q6. What is the nature of selection tests?

Ans. Negative

Q7. When is a transfer a suitable source of recruitment?

Ans. Refer to the advantages of transfers

Q8. Distinguish between on the job and off the job training methods.

Ans. The differences between on the job and off the job training methods are:

Table 6.3

Basis	*On the job*	*Off the job*
Principle used	Learning while doing a job	Learning before doing a job
Place of working	At the workplace	Away from the workplace
Trainers employed	Generally supervisors and experienced workers	Generally experts from outside
Techniques	1. Apprenticeship 2. Coaching 3. Job rotation 4. Internship	1. Lectures 2. Case study 3. Films 4. Vestibule training 5. Computer modeling 6. Programmed instruction

7

Directing

Q1. Explain the meaning of *directing*.

Ans.

- Directing refers to the process of:
  - Instructing
  - Guiding
  - Motivating
  - Counseling
  - Leading

  People in the organization to achieve its objectives
- Directing is not a mere issue of communication but encompasses many elements like:
  - Supervision
  - Leadership
  - Motivation
- It is one of the key managerial functions performed by every manager. It is a process which takes place throughout the life of an organization

Q2. What are the elements of *directing*?

or

Directing is not a mere issue of communication. Explain.

Ans. Refer to Ans.1

Q3. Explain the important characteristics of directing.

Ans. The important characteristics of directing are:

1. ***Directing initiates action***
   - A manager has to perform this function along with planning, staffing, organizing and controlling while discharging his duties in the organization
   - While other functions prepare a setting for action, directing initiates action in the organization
2. ***Directing takes place at every level of management***
   - Every manager, from top executives to supervisors, performs this function. It takes place wherever superior subordinate relations exist
     - Top level managers issue directions to middle level managers
     - Middle level managers issue directions to their subordinates in the concerned departments
     - Lower level managers issue directions to the workers
3. ***Directing flows from top to bottom***
   - It is initiated at the top level and flows to the bottom through the organizational hierarchy
   - Every manager can direct his immediate subordinate and take the instructions from his immediate boss
4. ***Directing is a continuous process***
   - It is a continuous activity. It takes place throughout the existence of the organization irrespective of people occupying managerial positions
   - Managers may come and go but the directing process goes on as without direction the organizational activities can't continue further

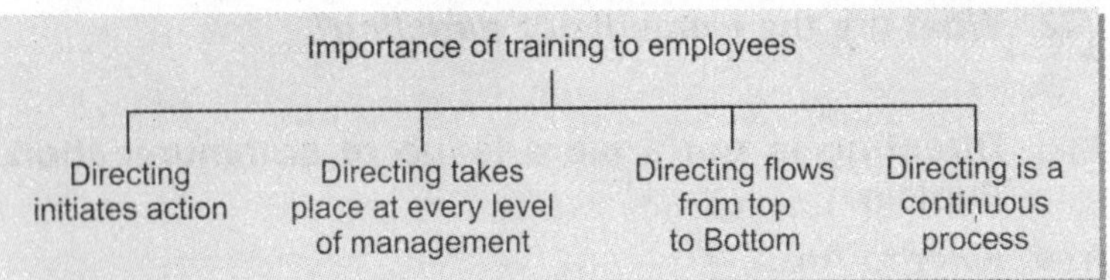

Q4. Which function of management initiates action?

Ans. Directing

Q5. Which functions of management are preparatory in nature?

Ans. Planning, organizing and staffing

Q6. Explain the meaning of supervision.

or

Discuss the 2 meanings of the term supervision.

Ans. Supervision can be understood as follows:

1. ***As an element of directing***
   - The term *'super'* means over and above and the term *'vision'* means the art of seeing
   - Supervision is the process of guiding the efforts of employees and other resources to accomplish the desired goals
   - It means overseeing what is being done by subordinates, giving instructions to ensure optimum utilization of resources and achievement of work goals
2. ***As a function performed by supervisors***
   - Supervision can be defined as the function to be performed by the supervisor, a managerial position in the organizational hierarchy at the operative level, i.e. lower level
   - The functions and performance of the supervisor are vital to any firm as he is directly related with the workers whereas other managers have no direct touch with bottom level workers

Q7. Why is the function of a supervisor at the lower level important?

Ans. Refer to Ans.6

Q8. Discuss the role or importance of a supervisor.

Ans. The importance of a supervisor can be explained as follows:

1. ***Acts as a guide, friend and philosopher***
   - Supervisor maintains day to day contact and friendly relations with the workers
   - A good supervisor acts as a guide, friend and philosopher to the workers

2. *Acts as a link between the workers and the management*
    - He conveys management ideas to the workers and the workers' problems to the management on the other and
    - It helps to avoid misunderstandings and conflict situations between the management and workers/employees
3. *Responsible for task achievement*
    - Supervisor ensures performance of work according to the targets set
    - He takes responsibility for task achievement and motivates his workers effectively
4. *Helps in maintaining unity amongst workers*
    - Supervisor plays a key role in maintaining group unity under his control
    - He sorts out internal differences and maintains harmony within the workers
5. *Acts as a trainer*
    - Supervisor provides good job training to the employees
    - A skilled and knowledgeable supervisor can build efficient team of workers
6. *Provides effective leadership*
    - Supervisory leadership plays a key role in influencing the workers in the organization
    - A supervisor with good leadership qualities can build up high morale among the workers
7. *Provides valuable feedback*
    - A good supervisor analyses the work performed and gives feedback to the workers
    - He suggests ways and means of developing new work skills

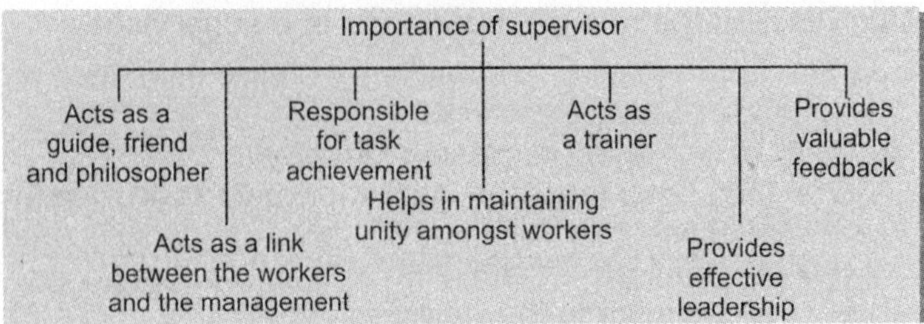

Q9. Define motivation.

Ans.

- According to William G Scout, motivation means a process of stimulating people to action to accomplish desired goals
- Motivation means incitement or inducement to act or move. In the context of an organization, it means the process of making subordinates to act in a desired manner to achieve certain organizational goals

Q10. Explain the following terms with suitable examples.

i. Motive
ii. Motivator

Ans.

i. *Motive*

- A motive is an inner state that:
  - Energizes
  - Activates
  - Directs
  - Moves

  Behavior towards goals
- Realization of a motive causes restlessness in the individual which prompts some action to reduce such restlessness

For Example:

The need for food causes hunger on account of which a man searches for food. Some such motives are hunger, thirst, security, affiliation, need for comfort, etc.

ii. *Motivator*

- It is the technique used to motivate people in a organization
- Motivators can be:
  - Monetary like pay, bonus, retirement benefits, profit sharing, etc.
  - Non monetary like status, recognition, employee participation, etc.

Q11. Discuss the important features of motivation.

Ans. The various features of motivation are:

1. ***Motivation is an internal feeling***
   - They are the urges, desires, aspirations, drives, striving or needs of human beings which are internal and influence human behavior

   For Example:

   People may have the desire for possessing a car, comfortable house, reputation
   - These urges are internal to individuals
2. ***Motivation produces goal directed behavior***

   For Example:

   The promotion in the job may be given to employee with the objective of improving his performance. If the employee is interested in the promotion, it helps to produce improved performance
3. ***Motivation can either be positive or negative***
   - Positive motivation provides positive rewards like increase in pay, promotion, recognition, etc.
   - Negative motivation uses negative means like stopping ,punishments, increments, threatening, etc. which may also induce a person to act in the desired way
4. ***Motivation is a complex process***
   - Individuals are heterogeneous in their expectations, perceptions and reactions
   - Any type of motivation may not have uniform effect on all members

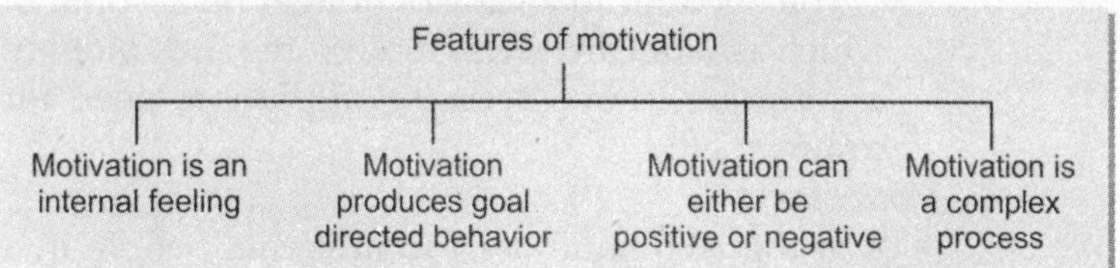

Q12. Motivation is a core element as it helps to identify and satisfy the needs of human resources and thereby improve their performance. Give reasons to support the above statement.

or

Give the importance of motivation.

Ans. Motivation is important for the following reasons:

1. ***Motivation helps to improve employees' performance***
   - It helps to improve performance levels of employees and the organization
   - As proper motivation satisfies the needs of employees, they in turn devote all their energies for optimum performance in work
   - A satisfied employee can always turnout expected performance. Good motivation in the firm helps to achieve higher levels of performance as motivated employees contribute their maximum efforts for organizational goals
2. ***Motivation helps to change negative/indifferent attitudes to positive attitudes***
   - It helps to change negative attitudes of the employees to positive attitudes in order to achieve organizational goals

   For Example:

   A worker may have negative attitudes towards his work if he is not rewarded appropriately
   - If suitable rewards are given and supervisor gives encouragement and praise for the good work done, the worker may develop positive attitude towards the work
3. ***Motivation helps to reduce absenteeism***
   - It reduces absenteeism in the firm. Some of the reasons for absenteeism are:
     - Bad working conditions
     - Inadequate rewards
     - Lack of recognition
     - Poor relations with supervisors and colleagues
   - Through sound motivational system, these deficiencies can be covered. If motivation is adequately provided, work becomes a source of pleasure and workers attend work regularly
4. ***Motivation helps to reduce employee turnover***
   - It reduces employee turnover thus saving cost of new recruitment and training
   - High rate of employee turnover is due to the lack of motivation. If managers identify motivational needs of employees and provide suitable incentives,

employees may not think of changing the organization
- Motivation helps to save costs of recruitment and training. It also helps to retain talented people in the organization

5. ***Motivation helps to introduce changes without resistance***
   - It helps managers to introduce changes smoothly without much resistance from the people
   - Normally, for any change introduced in the firm, there may be resistance for change
   - If the managers can convince the employees that proposed changes will bring additional rewards to employees, they will usually readily accept the change

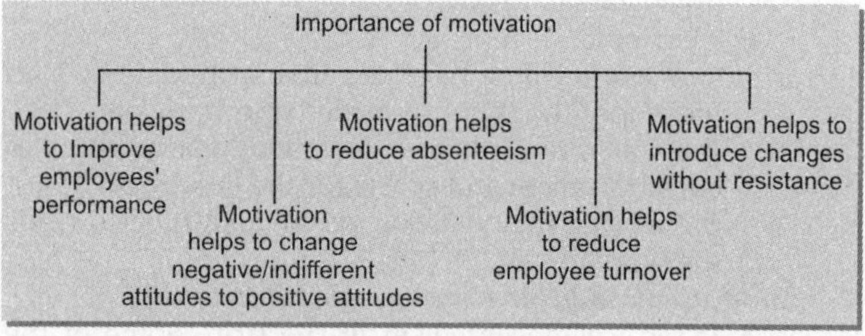

Q13. Explain the process of motivation.

Ans. The process of motivation is as follows:

1. ***Unsatisfied need***
   - The process of motivation begins with awareness of a need or a deficiency

   For Example:

   An employee feels the need for increase in his salary
2. ***Tension/anxiety***
   - This deficiency creates anxiety in the person

   For Example:

   The employee is tensed, restless as he isn't able to maintain a certain standard of living
3. ***Drive***
   - This unsatisfied need and tension stimulates the employee's drive

4. *Search behavior*
   - The drives generate a search behavior to satisfy such need

   For Example:

   The employee may think of either working harder in the same organization or shifting to a new organization

5 *Satisfied need*
   - A specific behavior may lead to the fulfillment of the need

   For Example:

   The employee chooses to work harder in the same organization and gradually experiences an increase in his salary

6. *Reduction of tension*
   - If the need is satisfied the individual is relieved of tension. When one need is satisfied it gives rise to another set of needs

   Thus, motivation is a continuous process since human needs are unlimited whereas the means to satisfy them are limited.

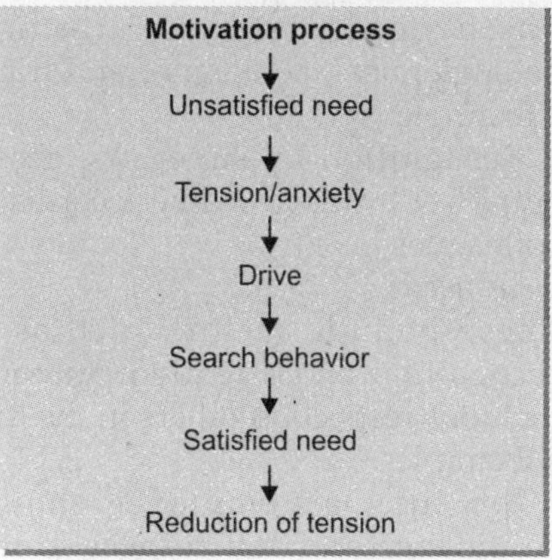

Q14. Explain Maslow's Need Hierarchy.

Ans.

- Maslow's Need Hierarchy Theory is considered fundamental to the understanding of motivation

- Abraham Maslow, a well known psychologist, in a classic paper published in 1943 outlined the elements of an overall theory of motivation
- His theory was based on human needs. He felt that within every human being there exists a hierarchy of 5 needs:

1. ***Basic/physiological needs***
    - These needs are most basic in the hierarchy and correspond to primary needs

    For Example:

    Hunger, thirst, shelter, sleep and sex. In the organizational context, basic salary helps to satisfy these needs
2. ***Safety/security needs***
    - These needs provide security and protection from harms like:
        - Physical
        - Emotional
        - Economic
        - Social

    For Example:

    Job security, stability of income, pension plans
3. ***Affiliation/belonging needs***
    - These needs refer to affection, sense of belongingness, acceptance and friendship

    For Example:

    Recognition by superiors, acceptance of an employee by his co-workers, cordial relations with colleagues
4. ***Esteem needs***
    - These include factors such as self respect, recognition and attention, autonomy status. It includes respecting others in the firm

    For Example:

    Job title, an employee should have self confidence and self respect so that he can be respected by others in the firm
5. ***Self actualization needs***
    - It is the highest level of need in the hierarchy. It refers to the drive to become what one is capable of becoming

For Example:

Growth, self fulfillment, achievement of goals

- Fulfillment of these needs gives psychological satisfaction

Generally monetary incentives like pay, bonus, profit sharing, etc. help in fulfilling the safety and social needs. Non monetary incentives like job security, employee participation, etc. help in satisfying esteem and self actualization needs

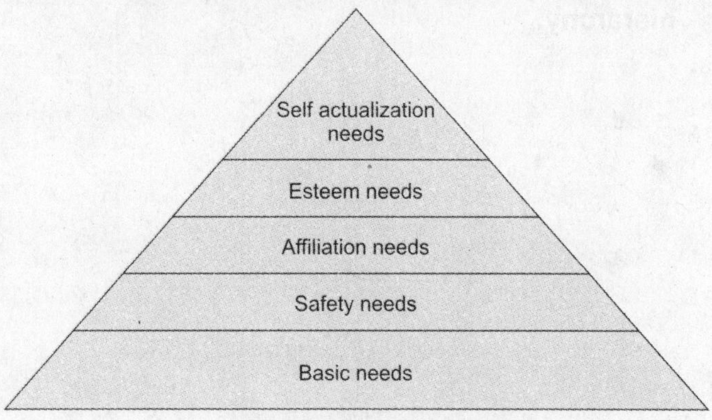

Fig. 7.1: Maslow's need hierarchy

Maslow's theory was based on the following assumptions:

1. People's behavior is based on their needs. Satisfaction of such needs influences their behavior
2. People's needs are in hierarchical order, starting from basic needs to other higher level needs
3. A satisfied need can no longer motivate a person; only next higher level need can motivate him
4. A person moves to the next higher level of the hierarchy only when the lower needs are satisfied

Maslow's theory was questioned on:

1. Classification of needs
2. Hierarchy of needs

But, despite such criticism, the theory is relevant till date as:

1. It helps managers to realize that need level of the employee should be identified to provide motivation to them
2. It is important to understand behavior
3. It is important to identify incentives (financial and non financial) in order to motivate employees working at different levels

Q15. Give an individual example to explain the need hierarchy.

Ans.

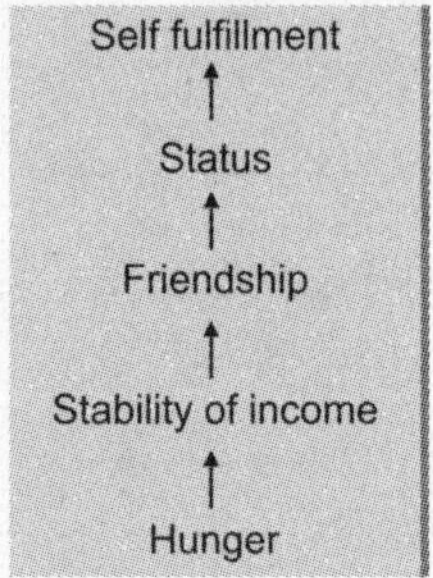

Fig. 7.2

Q16. Give an organizational example to explain Maslow's Need Hierarchy.

Ans.

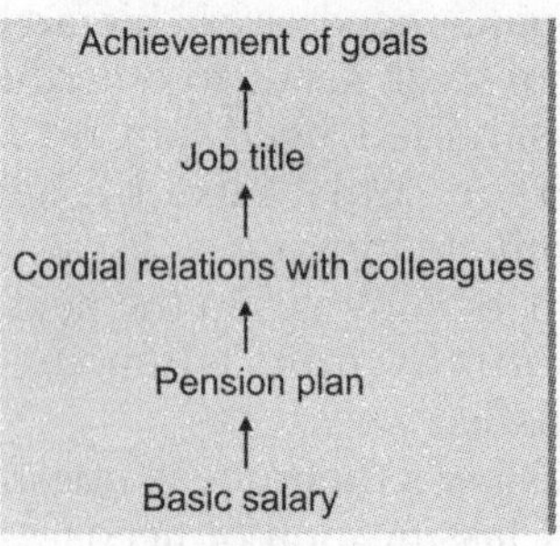

Fig. 7.3

Q17. Give an individual example to explain the need hierarchy.

Ans.

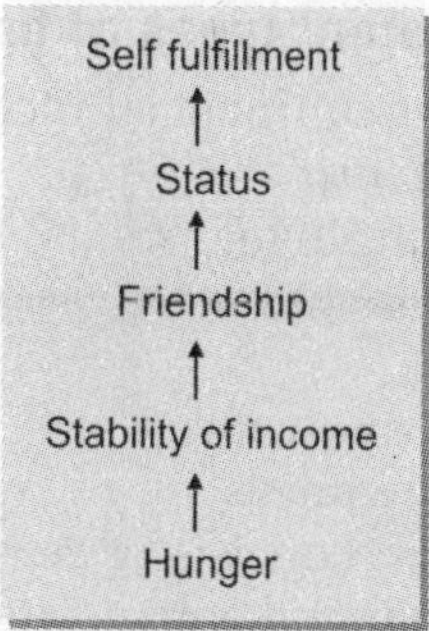

Fig. 7.4

Q18. Identify the highest level of needs.

Q19. Identify the lowest level of needs

Q20. What is the role of Maslow's theory in an organization?

Ans. Refer to Ans.14 for the above questions

Q21. What is meant by incentives?

Ans.

- Incentive means all measures which are used to motivate people to improve performance
- These incentives may be classified as:
  - Financial Incentives like pay, bonus, profit sharing
  - Non Financial Incentives like job security, employee recognition, participation

Q22. Explain financial incentives.

Ans.

- Financial incentives are incentives which are in direct monetary form or measurable in monetary terms and serve to motivate people for better performance
- These incentives may be provided on individual or group basis

- These incentives are more suitable for lower level of employees and help in satisfying lower level of needs

For Example:

Pay, bonus, profit sharing

Q23. Explain the different types of financial incentives.

Ans. The various types of financial incentives are:

1. ***Pay and allowance***
   - For every employee, salary is the basic monetary incentive. It includes:
     - Basic pay
     - Dearness allowance
     - Other allowances
   - Salary system consists of regular increments in the pay every year and enhancement of allowances from time to time. Pay hike and increment may be linked to performance also
2. ***Bonus***
   - It is an incentive offered over and above the wages/salary to the employees
3. ***Productivity linked wage incentives***
   - Several wage incentive plans aim at linking payment of wages to increase in productivity at individual or group level
4. ***Profit sharing***
   - It is meant to provide a share to employees in the profits of the organization
   - This serves to motivate the employees to improve their performance and contribute in increasing profits
5. ***Co-partnership/stock option***
   - Employees are offered company shares at a set price which is lower than the market price
   - Management may allot shares in line of various incentives payable in cash. This creates a feeling of ownership to employees and motivates them contribute for growth of the firm

   For Example:

   Infosys has incorporated this scheme for managerial compensation
6. ***Retirement benefits***

- Several retirement benefits such as:
  - Provident fund
  - Pension
  - Gratuity

  Provide financial security to employees after their retirement
- They act as an incentive when they are in service in the organization

7. *Perquisites*

- Perquisites and fringe benefits are offered such as:
  - Car allowance
  - Housing
  - Medical aid
  - Education to children

  Over and above the salary
- These help to provide motivation to employees

Fig. 7.5: Perquisites include car allowance, housing allowance and educational allowance

Q24. Name the monetary incentive in which employees are offered company's shares at lower prices.

Q25. Give any two types of perquisites.

Q26. Give any two retirement benefits.

Q27. Name the basic monetary benefit.

Ans. Refer Ans.22 for the above questions

Q28. What are non monetary/non financial incentives?

Ans.

- Non monetary incentives are those which are not in money form or measurable in terms of money
- Psychological, social and emotional factors play an important role in providing motivation

- Non financial incentives mainly focus on:
  - Social needs
  - Esteem needs
  - Self actualization needs
- The emphasis is to provide psychological and emotional satisfaction rather than money driven satisfaction

For Example:

If an individual gets promotion in the organization, it satisfies him psychologically as it gives him a feeling of elevation, increase in status, authority, and challenge in the job, etc. Though promotion involves payment of extra money non monetary aspects override monetary aspects.

Q29. Explain the various non monetary incentives.

Ans. The various non monetary benefits are:

1. ***Status***
   - In the organizational context, status means ranking of positions in the organization
   - The authority, responsibility, rewards, recognition, perquisites and prestige of job indicate the status given to a person holding a managerial position
   - Psychological, social and esteem needs of an individual are satisfied by status given to their job
2. ***Organizational climate***
   - It indicates the characteristics which describe the organization and distinguish one from the other.
   - These characteristics influence the behavior of individuals in the organization
   - They include:
     - Individual autonomy
     - Reward orientation
     - Consideration to employees
     - Risk taking
     - General work environment
3. ***Career advancement opportunity***
   - Every individual wants to grow to higher levels in the organization
   - Managers should provide opportunity to employees to improve their skills and be promoted to higher level jobs

- Employees can achieve promotions through:
  - Appropriate skill development programmes
  - Sound promotion policy
- Promotion works as a tonic and encourages employees to exhibit improved performance

4. ***Employee recognition programmes***
   - Most people have a need for evaluation of their work and due recognition
   - They feel that what they should be recognized by others concerned
   - Recognition means acknowledgement with a show of appreciation. When such appreciation is given to the work performed by employees, they feel motivated to perform at higher levels

   For Example:

   i. Congratulating the employee for good performance
   ii. Displaying on the notice board or in the company's news letter about the achievement of the employee
   iii. Installing an award or a certificate for best performance
   iv. Distributing mementos, complementaries like t-shirts, etc. in recognition of employee's services
   v. Rewarding an employee for giving valuable suggestions

Fig. 7.6: Employee recognition programme is an important non monetary incentive

5. *Job enrichment*
   - It is concerned with designing jobs that include:
     - Greater variety of work content
     - Require higher level of knowledge and skills
     - Give workers more autonomy and responsibilities
     - Provide opportunity for personal growth
   - If jobs are enriched and made interesting the job itself becomes a source of motivation to the individual
6. *Job security*
   - Employees want their jobs to be secure. They want certain stability about future income and work so that they don't feel worried on these aspects and work with greater zeal
   - In India, this aspect is more important considering the inadequate job opportunities and too many aspirants for these
   - There is one negative aspect of job security. When people feel that they aren't likely to lose their jobs, they may become complacent
7. *Employee participation*
   - It means involving employees in decision making of the issues related to them
   - These programmes are in practice in the form of:
     - Joint management committees
     - Work committees
     - Canteen committees
8. *Employee empowerment*
   - It means giving more autonomy and powers to subordinates
   - Empowerment makes people feel that their jobs are important
   - This feeling contributes positively to the use of skills and talents in job performance

Q30. Give an example of an incentive which is both in the form of monetary and non monetary incentive.

Ans. Promotion

Q31. Suggest any two methods which will help provide opportunities for career development.

Q32. Displaying on the notice board of a company the achievement of an employee is an example of a non monetary incentive. Identify and give two more examples.

Q33. Give any two ways in which employee participation can be encouraged.

Q34. Give a negative aspect of job security.

Ans. Refer Ans. 29 for the above questions

Q35. Define leadership.

Ans.

- According to George Terry, leadership is the activity of influencing people to strive willingly for group objectives
- Leadership is the process of influencing the behavior of people by making them work voluntarily towards achievement of goals
- It indicates the ability of an individual to maintain good relations with followers and motivate them to contribute for achieving organizational goals

Q36. Explain the features of leadership.

Ans. The various features of leadership are:

1. *Process of influence*
   - Leadership indicates ability of an individual to influence others' behavior to work willingly towards specific goals
2. *Change in behavior of others*
   - It tries to bring change in the behavior of others. It is a process of influencing and bringing about a desirable change in behavior
3. *Interpersonal relations*
   - It indicates interpersonal relations between leaders and followers
4. *Continuous process*

- It is a continuous, ongoing and never ending process which requires continuous communication between the leader and the followers

5. *Common goals*
   - Leadership is exercised to achieve common goals of the organization

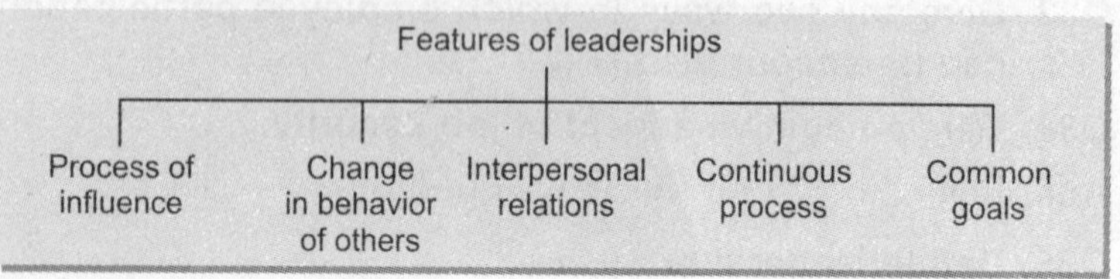

Q37. Who is a leader?

Ans.

- The term leader emerges from leadership
- Leader is an individual possessing attributes of leadership.

Q38. Discuss the role of followers in leader-follower relationship.

or

Why is it important to understand leader follower relationships?

Ans.

- Many times, the success of an organization is attributed to the leader, but due credit is not given to the followers
- Many follower related factors like:
  - Skills
  - Knowledge
  - Team spirit
  - Commitment
  - Willingness to cooperate

  Make a person an effective leader
- It is said that followers make a person a good leader by acceptance of leadership
- Therefore, it is to be recognized that both the leader and the followers play a key role in the leadership process

Q39. Leadership is a key factor in making any organization. Comment.

or

A leader plays a significant role in an organization. Comment.

Ans. According to Stephen Covey, a famous management consultant, managers are important but leaders are vital for lasting organizational success. The importance of leadership/leader is explained below:

1. ***Leadership leads to positive contribution by employees***
   - Leadership influences the behavior of people and makes them contribute their energies for the benefit of the organization in a positive way.
   - Good leaders always produce good results through their followers
2. ***Leadership helps followers in fulfilling their needs***
   - A leader maintains personal relations and helps followers in fulfilling their needs
   - He provides needed confidence, support and encouragement and thereby creates congenial work environment
3. ***Leadership helps in handling conflicts effectively***
   - A leader handles conflicts effectively and doesn't allow adverse effects resulting from conflicts
   - A good leader always allows his followers to ventilate their feelings and disagreement but persuades them by giving suitable clarifications
4. ***Leadership helps in introducing required changes***
   - Leader plays a key role in introducing required changes in the organization
   - He persuades and inspires people to accept changes whole-heartedly
   - He overcomes the problem of resistance to change and introduces it with minimum discontentment
5. ***Leadership provides training to subordinates***
   - Leader provides training to his subordinates
   - A good leader always builds up his successor and helps in smooth succession progress.

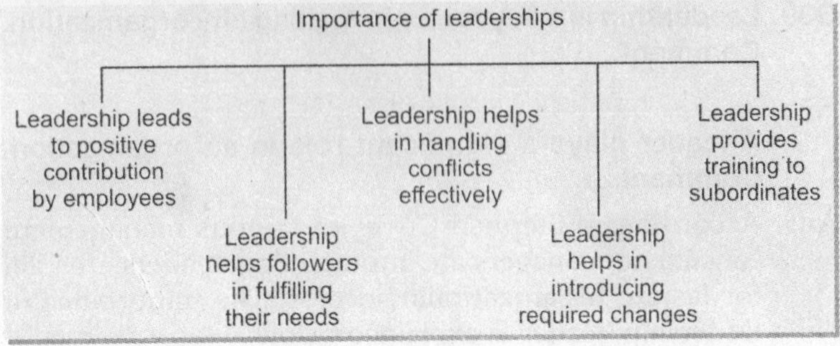

Q40. Explain the unique traits which a good leader should possess.

Ans. The various traits that a good leader must possess are:

1. *Physical features*
   - Physical features like:
     - Height
     - Weight
     - Appearance
     - Health

     Determine the physical personality of an individual
   - It is believed that good physical features attract people. Health and endurance help a leader to work hard which inspires others to work with same tempo
2. *Knowledge*
   - A good leader should have the required knowledge and competence
   - Only such person can instruct and influence subordinates correctly
3. *Integrity*
   - A leader should possess high level of integrity and honesty
   - He should be a role model to others regarding the ethics and values
4. *Initiative*

- A leader should have the courage and initiative.
- He should not wait for opportunities to come to his way rather he should grab the opportunity and use it to the advantage of the organization

5. ***Communication skills***
   - A leader should be a good communicator. He should have the capacity to clearly explain his ideas and make people understand them
   - He should not only be a good speaker but a good listener, teacher, counselor and persuader
6. ***Self confidence***
   - A leader should have high level of self confidence. He should not lose his confidence even in the most difficult times
   - If the leader lacks self confidence, he can't provide confidence to his followers
7. ***Motivation skills***
   - A leader should be an effective motivator
   - He should understand the needs of the people and motivate them through satisfying their needs
8. ***Social skills***
   - A leader should be sociable and friendly with his colleagues and followers
   - He should understand people and maintain good human relations with them
9. ***Decisiveness***
   - Leader should be decisive in managing work
   - Once he is convinced about a fact, he should be firm and should not change opinions frequently

Conclusion

- All good leaders may not necessarily possess all the qualities of a good leader
- It is not possible for any individual to have all the qualities but an understanding about these qualities help the managers to acquire them through training and conscious efforts

Fig 7.7: A good leader must be a good communicator, confident, sociable and decisive

Q41. Explain the relationship between management and leadership.

or

Differentiate between managers and leaders

Ans. The relationship between managers and leaders is as follows:

Table 7.1

Basis	*Management*	*Leadership*
Meaning	It is a set of activities directed towards effective utilization of resources for achievement of organizational goals. It includes planning, organizing, staffing, directing and controlling	It is a process of influencing the behavior of people at work towards realization of specific goals. It is an element of directing which is a function of management.
Scope	It has a broader scope since it is a sum of POSDC	It is narrower in scope since it is a small part of management
Existence	Managers exist only in formal organizations	Leaders may exist in both formal and informal organizations
Purpose	Achievement of organizational goals	Fulfillment of expectations and aspirations of followers in the group
Basis of authority	Manager's authority is based on the position he occupies in the scalar chain	Leader's authority is based upon his personality and qualities he possesses which can influence his followers and seek cooperation from them

Conclusion

We can conclude that:

1. ***All good and successful managers are leaders***
   - All successful managers should possess leadership qualities like:
     - Social skills
     - Integrity
     - Self confidence
     - Decisiveness
     - Communication skills

     Subordinates should treat them as their friends, philosophers and guides
2. ***All leaders aren't necessarily managers***
   - Leaders may not occupy positions of authority in an formal organization
   - They become leaders by virtue of their personality

   For Example:

   Mahatma Gandhi led the nation to freedom without occupying any formal position
3. ***Sometimes managers may not possess leadership qualities. They are not able to win the trust and confidence of subordinates and merely use their position based authority to get work done by the subordinates***

Q42. All managers are leaders but all leaders are not managers. Comment

Ans. Refer Ans. 41

Q43. What is meant by communication?

Ans.

- The word communication has been derived from the latin word 'communis' which means 'common' which consequently implies understanding between the sender and the receiver
- According to Harold Koontz and Heinz Weilhrich, communication is transfer of information from the sender to the receiver with the information being understood by the receiver

- Communication is a process of exchange of:
  - Ideas
  - Views
  - Facts
  - Feelings

  Between or among people to create common understanding

Q44. Which skill is the most important to enhance the abilities of a manager in directing?

Ans. Communication

Q45. Discuss the elements or steps in the process of communication.

Ans.

- According to Harold Koontz and Heinz Weilhrich, communication is transfer of information from the sender to the receiver with the information being understood by the receiver The various steps in the process of communication are:

1. ***Sender***
   - Sender means the person who conveys his thoughts or ideas to the receiver. The sender represents the source of communication
2. ***Message***
   - It is the content of ideas, feelings, suggestions, order, etc. intended to be communicated
3. ***Encoding***
   - It is the process of converting the message into communication symbols like:
     - Words
     - Pictures
     - Gestures
4. ***Media***
   - It is the path through which encoded message is transmitted to the receiver. The channel may be:
     - Written
     - Face to face
     - Phone call
     - Internet

5. ***Decoding***
   - It is the process of converting encoded symbols of the sender
6. ***Receiver***
   - The person who receives the communication of the sender
7. ***Feedback***
   - It includes all those actions of the receiver indicating that he has received and understood the message of the sender
8. ***Noise***
   - It means some obstruction or hindrance to communication, caused to the sender, receiver or message. It can occur at any stage and may lead to a temporary gap in the communication process

   For Example:

   i. Ambiguous symbols that lead to faulty decoding
   ii. A poor telephone connection
   iii. Faulty decoding
   iv. An inattentive receiver
   v. Prejudices obstructing the understanding of the message
   vi. Gestures and postures that may distort the message

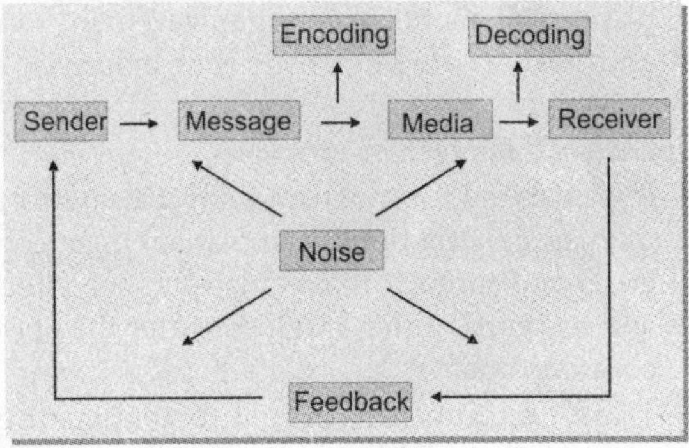

Fig. 7.8: Communication process

Q46. Who is considered to be the source of the communication process?

Ans. Sender

Q47. Does the communication process conclude when the receiver decodes the message? Explain.

Q48. Give an example of communication symbols

Q49. Discuss noise as an element of communication.

Ans. Refer Ans. 44 for the above questions

Q50. Effectiveness of a manager depends significantly on his ability to communicate effectively. In the light of the statement discuss the importance of communication.

Ans. Communication is important for the following reasons:

1. *Acts as basis of coordination*
   - It provides coordination among departments, activities and persons in the organization
   - Such coordination is provided by explaining about organizational goals, the mode of their achievement and inter-relationships between different individuals
2. *Helps in smooth working of an enterprise*
   - It makes possible for the smooth and unrestricted working of the enterprise
   - The job of a manager is to coordinate the human and physical elements of an organization into an efficient and active working unit that achieves common objectives
3. *Increases managerial efficiency*
   - It is essential for quick and effective performance of managerial functions. The management conveys the goals and targets, issues instructions, allocates jobs and responsibilities and looks after the performance of subordinates
   - Thus, communication lubricates the entire organization and keeps it at work with efficiency
4. *Acts as basis of decision making*

- It provides needed information for decision making
- In its absence, it may not be possible for the managers to take any meaningful decision. Only on the basis of communication of relevant information one can take the right decision

5. ***Promotes cooperation and industrial peace***
   - Efficient operation is the aim of all prudent management. It may be possible only when there is industrial peace in the factory and mutual cooperation between the management and the workers
   - The two way communication promotes cooperation and mutual understanding between the management and the workers
6. ***Establishes effective leadership***
   - It is the basis of leadership. Effective communication helps to influence subordinates.
   - While influencing people, leader should possess good communication skills
7. ***Boosts morale and provides motivation***
   - An efficient system of communication enables the management to motivate, influence and satisfy the subordinates
   - Good communication assists the workers in their adjustment with the physical and social aspects of work. It improves human relations in the industry
   - Communication is the basis of participative and democratic pattern of management

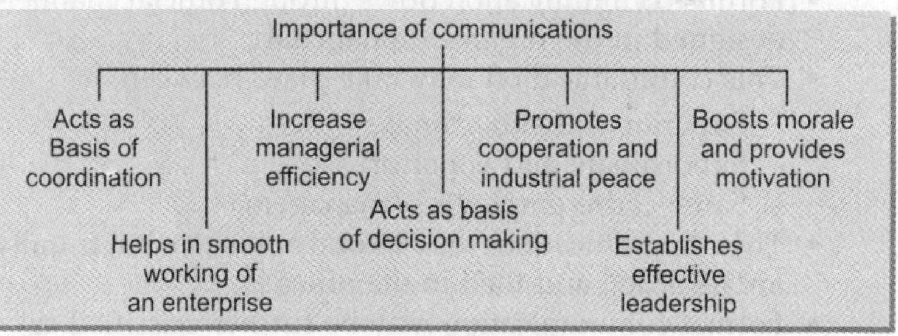

Fig. 7.9: Managers must be effective communicators

Q51. An element of directing has been called the foundation of all group activities by Bernard. Identify.

Ans. Communication

Q52. Identify one management problem observed by an ex-president of American Management Association.

Ans. Communication

Q53. Name the two types of communication that can take place in an organization.

Ans. The two types of communication that can take place in an organization are:

1. Formal
2. Informal

Q54. What is meant by formal communication?

Ans.

- Formal communication flows through official channels designed in the organizational chart
- This communication may take place between :
  - Superior and subordinate
  - Subordinate and superior
  - Same cadre employees/managers
- The communications may be oral or written but usually are recorded and filed in the office
- Formal communication may be further classified as:

- Vertical
- Horizontal/lateral

Q55. Explain the two types of formal communication.

Ans.

1. ***Vertical communication***
   - It flows vertically upwards or downwards through formal channels of communication
   - Upward communication means flow of communication from subordinate to superior
   - Downward communication means communication from superior to subordinate

For example:

Upward communication

a. Request for grants
b. Submission of progress report
c. Application for leave

Downward Communication

a. Ordering employees to complete assigned work
b. Sending notice to employees to attend meetings
c. Passing on guidelines framed by top management to lower and middle management

Fig. 7.10: Vertical communication

2. *Horizontal/lateral communication*
   - It takes place between individuals at the same level and between divisions

   For example:

   A production manager may contact marketing manager to discuss about schedule of product delivery, product design, quality, etc..

Fig. 7.11: Horizontal communication

Q56. What is meant by communication networks?

Ans.

- The pattern through which communication flows within the organization is generally indicated through communication network

Q57. Explain the communication networks in a formal organization

Ans.

1. *Single chain*
   - The network exists between a supervisor and his subordinates
   - Since many levels exist in an organization structure, communication flows from the superior at every level to his subordinate through a single chain

2. ***Wheel***
   - All subordinates under one superior communicate through him only as he acts as a hub of the wheel
   - The subordinates are not allowed to talk among themselves
3. ***Circular***
   - The communication moves in a circle. Each person can communicate with his adjoining two persons
   - In this network flow of communication is slow
4. ***Free flow***
   - Each person can communicate with others freely. The flow of communication is fast in this network
5. ***Inverted V***
   - A subordinate is allowed to communicate with his immediate superior as well as his superior.
   - However, in the latter case, only prescribed communication takes place

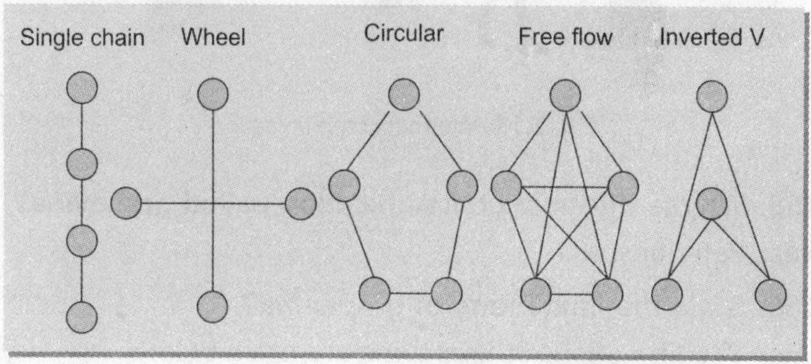

Fig. 7.12: Formal communication networks

Q58. What is meant by informal communication or grapevine?

Ans.

- Communication that takes place without following the formal lines of communication (no prescribed path of communication) is said to be informal communication
- It is generally referred to as the grapevine because it spreads throughout the organization with its branches going out in all directions with no regard to the levels of authority

- Informal communication arises out of the needs of employees to exchange their views, which can't be done through formal channels

For Example:

Workers chit chatting in a canteen about the behavior of the superior, discussing about rumours in the organization that some employees are likely to be transferred.

Fig. 7.13: Informal communication

Q59. Why is informal communication called grapevine?

Ans. Refer ans. 58

Q60. State the limitations of grapevine?

Ans. The limitations of grapevine are listed below:

1. Grapevine may get distorted
2. Leads to unauthentic rumors
3. Hampers work environment
4. Difficult to detect source of communication

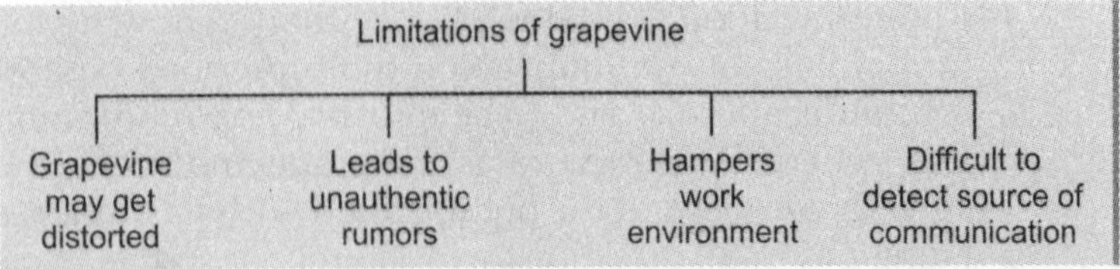

Q61. Grapevine leads to rumors but it may be still helpful. Explain how?

Ans. Grapevine is helpful as it:

1. Carries information rapidly
2. Leads to satisfaction of social needs
3. Allows flexibility
4. Helpful in understanding attitudes and reactions of subordinates
5. Is a suitable channel where formal communication is not possible

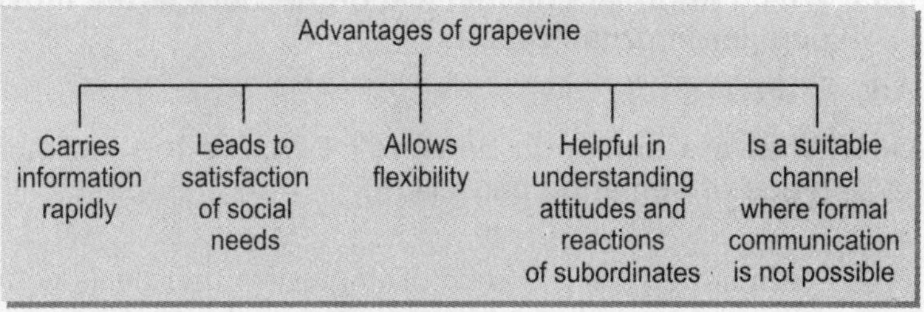

Q62. With the help of diagrams explain grapevine networks in an organization.

Ans. The various grapevine networks in an organization are:

1. ***Single strand network***
   - In this network, each person communicates to the other in sequence
2. ***Probability network***
   - In this network, the individual communicates randomly with other individuals
3. ***Gossip network***
   - In this network, each person communicates with all on a non selective basis
4. ***Cluster network***
   - In this network, the individual communicates with only those people whom he trusts.
   - It is most popular network in organizations

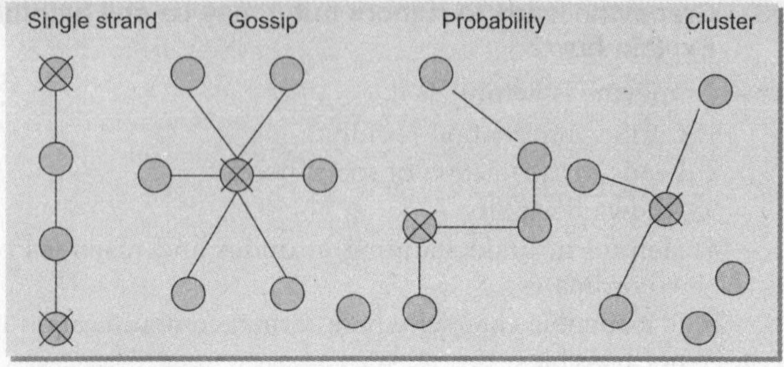

Q63. Which informal communication network is the most popular in organizations?

Ans. Cluster

Q64. What are semantic barriers? Discuss the various types of semantic barriers.

Ans.

- Semantics is the branch of linguistics that deals with the meaning of words and sentences.
- Semantic barriers are concerned with problems and obstructions in the process of encoding and decoding of messages into words or impressions
- Such barriers result on account of use of wrong words, faulty translations, different interpretations, etc.

The various semantic barriers are:

1. ***Badly expressed messages***
   - Sometimes intended meaning may not be conveyed by a manager to his subordinates due to:
     - Inadequate vocabulary
     - Omission of needed words
     - Usage of wrong words
2. ***Symbols with different meanings***
   - A word may have several meanings. The receiver has to perceive one meaning for the word used by the communicator

   For Example:

   Word 'value' can be used as:

i. What is the value of this ring
ii. What is the value of learning computer skills
iii. I value our friendship
   - Wrong perception leads to communication problem

3. ***Faulty translation***
   - Sometimes the communication originally drafted in one language (say English) needs to be translated to the language understandable to workers (say Hindi)
   - If the translator is not proficient in both languages, mistakes may happen rendering a different meaning to the communication
4. ***Technical jargon***
   - It is usually found that specialists use technical jargon while explaining to persons who are not specialists in the concerned field. They may not understand the actual meaning of many technical terms
5. ***Body language and gesture decodings***
   - Every movement of body communicates some meaning
   - The body movement and gestures of the communicator are of essence in conveying the message. If there is no match between what is said and what is expressed in body movements, communication can be incorrectly perceived
6. ***Unclarified assumptions***
   - Some communications may have certain assumptions which are subject to different interpretations

   For Example:

   A boss may instruct his subordinate to take care of a guest. He actually meant that the subordinate should take care of transport, food, accommodation of guest until he leaves. But the subordinate may interpret that the guest should be taken to the hotel with care. The guest suffers due to unclarified assumptions

Q65. What are psychological barriers? Discuss the various types of psychological barriers.

Ans.

- Emotional/psychological factors act as barriers to communication

For Example:

A worried person is unable to communicate properly and an angry receiver can't understand the real meaning of the message

- The state of mind of both the sender and the receiver reflects in the effective communication

The various psychological barriers are:

1. ***Premature evaluation***
   - Sometimes people evaluate the meaning of message before the sender completes his message
   - Such premature evaluation may be due to pre-conceived notions or prejudices against the communication or the sender of the communication
2. ***Loss by transmission and poor retention***
   - When communication passes through multiple levels, repetitive transmission of the message results in loss of or transmission of inaccurate information. It is more prevalent in oral communication
   - Poor retention means that usually people can't retain the information for a long time if they are inattentive or not interested
3. ***Distrust***
   - Distrust between the communicator and communicate acts as a barrier. If the parties don't believe each other, they can't understand each other's message in its original form
4. ***Lack of attention***
   - The pre-occupied mind of receiver and the resultant non listening of message act as major psychological barriers in communication

   For Example:

   An employee explains about his problems to the boss who is pre-occupied with an important report that he is preparing. The boss doesn't grasp the message and the employee is disappointed

Q66. What are organizational barriers? Explain.

Ans.

- Organizational barriers like:
  - Organization structure
  - Rules and regulation
  - Authority relationships can act as barriers to effective communication

  The various organizational barriers are:

  1. *Organizational policy*
     - If the organizational policy, explicit or implicit, isn't supportive of free flow of communication, it may hamper effectiveness of communication

     For Example:

     In an organization with highly centralized pattern, people may not be encouraged to have free communication
  2. *Status*
     - Status of superior may create psychological distance between him and his subordinates
     - A status conscious manager also may not allow his subordinates to express their feelings freely
  3. *Complexity in organizational structure*
     - In an organization where there are number of managerial levels, communication gets delayed and distorted as number of filtering points are more
  4. *Rules and regulations*
     - Rigid rules and cumbersome procedures may be a hurdle to communication. Similarly, communication through prescribed channels may result in delays
  5. *Organizational facilities*
     - If facilities for smooth, clear and timely communications are not provided, communication may be hampered
     - Facilities like:
       - Frequent meetings

- Suggestions box
- Complaint box
- Social and cultural gatherings
- Transparency of operation

Will encourage free flow of communication. Lack of these facilities may create communication problems

Q67. Discuss the personal barriers to communications.

Ans. The various personal barriers to communication are:

1. *Fear of challenge to authority*
   - If a superior perceives that a particular communication may adversely affect his authority, he may attempt to distort, withhold or suppress such communication
2. *Lack of confidence of superior in his subordinates*
   - If superiors donot have confidence in the competence and ability of their subordinates, they may not seek their advice or opinions
3. *Unwillingness to communicate*
   - Sometimes subordinates may not be prepared to communicate with their superior in matters, if they perceive that it may adversely affect their interests
4. *Lack of proper incentives*
   - If there is no motivation or incentive for communication, subordinates may not take initiative to communicate

   For Example:

   If there is no reward, appreciation or recognition for a useful suggestion, the subordinates may not be willing to offer useful suggestions

Q68. Explain with the help of an example how lack of proper incentives can prove to be a personal barrier to communication.

Ans. Refer Ans. 67

Q69. How can the effectiveness of communication be improved?

Ans. The various ways for improving communication effectiveness are:

1. Clarify the ideas before communication

2. Communicate according to the needs of receiver
3. Convey things of help and value to listeners
4. Consult others before communicating
5. Be aware of language, tone and content of message
6. Ensure proper feedback
7. Communicate for present as well as future
8. Follow up communications
9. Be a good listener

Q70. Explain the guiding principles of directing.

Ans. The various guiding principles of directing are:

1. ***Maximum individual contribution***
   - It emphasizes that directing techniques should be such that must help every individual in the organization to contribute to his maximum potential for achievement of organizational objectives
   - It should bring out untapped energies of employees for the greater efficiency of the organization

   For Example:

   A good motivation plan with suitable monetary and non monetary rewards can motivate employees to contribute their utmost efforts for the organization as they feel that their efforts will bring them suitable rewards
2. ***Unity of command***
   - It emphasizes that a person in the organization should receive instructions from one superior only
   - If instructions are received from more than one superior, it creates confusion, conflict, and disorder in the organization. Adherence to this principle ensures effective direction
3. ***Harmony of objectives***
   - Individual objectives of employees and the organizational objectives should not be conflicting or mutually exclusive
   - An employee may expect attractive salary and monetary benefits to fulfill his personal needs and the organization may expect employees to improve productivity to achieve profits

- Good directing should provide harmony by convincing that employee reward and work efficiency are complementary to each other and aren't conflicting

4. *Managerial communication*
   - Effective managerial communication across all the levels in the organization makes direction effective
   - Directing should convey clear instructions to create total understanding to the subordinates. Through proper feedbacks, managers should ensure that subordinates understand their instructions clearly
5. *Appropriateness of direction technique*
   - According to this principle, appropriate motivational and leadership techniques should be used while directing people based on subordinates' needs, capabilities, attitudes and other situational variables

   For Example:

   For some people money can act as an effective powerful motivator while for others promotion may be an effective motivator
6. *Leadership*
   - While directing the subordinates, managers should exercise good leadership as it can influence the subordinates positively without causing dissatisfaction among them
7. *Use of informal organizations*
   - A manager should realize that informal groups or organizations exist within every formal organization
   - He should spot and make use of such organizations for effective direction
8. *Follow through*
   - Merely giving orders is not sufficient
   - Managers should follow it up by reviewing continuously whether orders are being implemented or any problems are being encountered by the subordinates. If necessary, suitable modifications should be made in the directions

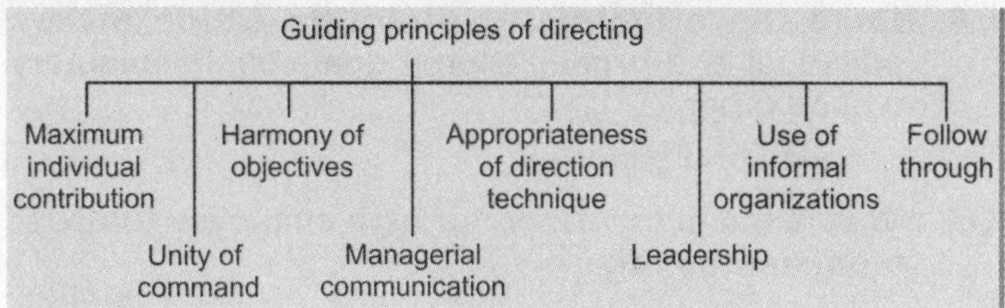

OTHER IMPORTANT QUESTIONS

Q1. You are working in the middle management. Your superior, a top management personnel sent a message to you which you've received and well understood. Is the communication process complete? Explain why?

Ans. No. Explain 'feedback'

Q2. Amit and Micky are working in the same organization but in different departments. One day at lunch time, Micky informed Amit that due to computerization, some people are going to be retrenched. Identify the type of communication.

Ans. Informal

Q3. The workers of an organization complain that their superior Mr. Wadekar does not listen to their suggestions and adopts an autocratic style. Is Mr. Wadekar an effective leader? Give reasons why or why not?

Ans. No. He lacks:

1. Motivation skills
2. Communication skills
3. Does not encourage initiative
4. Social skills

Q4. To create a desire among employees to perform to the utmost of their abilities is an important aspect of directing, Identify and explain how it contributes to the success of an organization.

Ans. Motivation. Give importance

Q5. A supervisor is not required in an organization at all. Do you agree? Give reasons.

Ans. No. Give importance

6. Name the principle of directing which makes individual and organizational goals complementary to each other.

Ans. Harmony of objectives

Q7. What is the main reason for high employee turnover in organizations?

Ans. Lack of motivation

Q8. Discuss why Maslow's Need Hierarchy is important.

Ans. Maslow's Need Hierarchy is important for the following reasons:

1. Helps to understand the classification and arrangement of human needs
2. Helps to identify unfulfilled needs of employees
3. To create satisfied and loyal workforce
4. To provide suitable motivators
5. To improve organizational efficiency, profitability and productivity

Q9. What are the advantages and disadvantages of formal organization.

Ans. The advantages of formal organization are:

1. Provides support to superior subordinate relationships
2. Systematic and orderly
3. Helpful in controlling deviations
4. Less prone to distortions and rumors

The disadvantages of formal organization are:

1. Rigid and rule bound
2. Slow moving process
3. Impersonal and lacks warmth and personal involvement

Q10. Directing is the essence of management. Explain.

Ans. Directing is very important for the following reasons:

1. Directing helps to initiate action
2. Directing integrates employee's efforts
3. Directing guides employees
4. Directing facilitates introduction of changes in organization
5. Directing brings balance and stability in organization

8

Controlling

Q1. What is the meaning of *controlling*?

Ans.

- Controlling means ensuring that activities in an organization are performed as per the plans
- It also ensures that an organization's resources are being used effectively and efficiently for the achievement of predetermined goals
- Controlling refers to the process in which actual performance is compared with standard performance
- According to Koontz and O'Donnel, managerial control implies the measurement of accomplishment against the standard and the correction of deviations to assure attainment of objectives as per plans.
- Deviations are identified and corrective action is taken in order to ensure attainment of objectives according to plans

Q2. 'Controlling is a goal-oriented function.' Explain

Ans.

- Controlling function ensures that the activities conform to the pre-set standards so that organizational goals are achieved. It is a purposeful activity.

Q3. 'Controlling is pervasive in nature.' Explain

Ans.

- Controlling function of a manager is a pervasive function. It is a primary function of every manager.
- Managers at every level of management:

- Top
- Middle
- Lower

Need to perform controlling activities to keep a control over activities in their areas

- Controlling is required in all organizations, be it:
  - Educational
  - Hospital
  - Military
- Controlling is needed in all departments
  - Production
  - Finance
  - Marketing

Q4. Discuss the features/nature of controlling.

Ans.

- Controlling involves action
  - It brings the management cycle back to the planning function. The controlling function finds out how far actual performance deviates from standards, analyses the causes of such deviations and attempts to take corrective actions based on the same.
  - Controlling process helps in the formulation of future plans in the light of the problems that were identified and that helps in better planning in future.
- Controlling is goal oriented
- Controlling is continuous
- Controlling is pervasive
- Controlling is both forward and backward looking.
- Controlling is not the last function of management

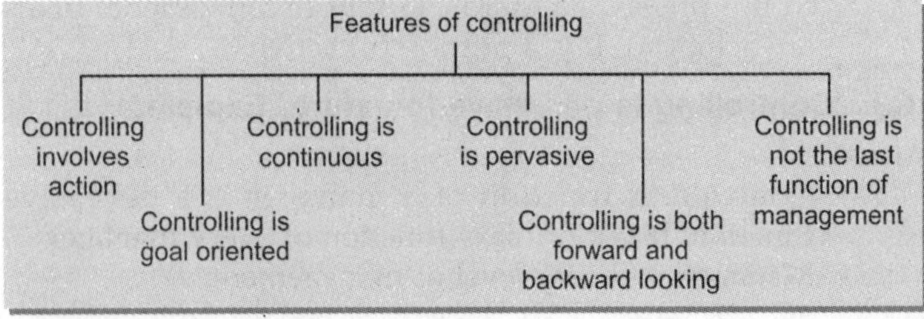

Q5. 'Controlling is an indispensable function of management.' Discuss the Importance of controlling

Ans.

1. *Accomplishing organizational goals*
   - It means progress towards the organizational goals and brings to light deviations, if any. It also indicates corrective actions
   - It guides the organization and keeps it on the right track so that organizational goals might be achieved
2. *Judging accuracy of standards*
   - A good control system enables management to verify whether the standards set are accurate and objective
   - An effective control system keeps a careful check on the changes taking place in the organization and in the environment and helps to review and revise the standards accordingly.
3. *Making efficient use of resources*
   - By exercising control, a manager seeks to reduce wastage and spoilage of resources
   - Each activity is performed in accordance with predetermined standards and norms
   - This ensures that resources are used in the most effective and efficient way
4. *Ensuring order and discipline*
   - It creates an atmosphere of order and discipline in the organization
   - It helps to minimize dishonest behavior of the employees by keeping a close check on their activities
5. *Improving employee motivation*
   - A good control system ensures that employees know well in advance what they are expected to do and what are the standards of performance on the basis of which they will be appraised
   - It thus motivates them for a better performance
6. *Facilitating coordination in action*
   - It provides direction to all activities and efforts for achieving organizational goals
   - Each department and employee is governed by predetermined standards which are well coordinated

with one another. This ensures that overall organizational objectives are accomplished

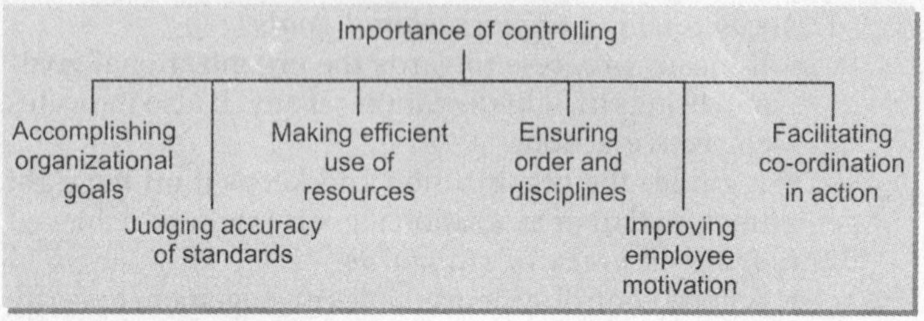

Q7. Explain the relationship between planning and controlling.

Ans.

1. ***Planning is the basis for controlling***
   - A system for control presupposes the existence of certain standards
   - These standards of performance serve as the basis for controlling and are provided by planning function
   - Controlling is blind without planning. If standards are not set in advance, managers have nothing to control
   - If there is no plan, there is no basis for controlling
2. ***Planning without controlling is meaningless***
   - Controlling is necessary to monitor the progress, measure actual performance with the standard performance, identify deviations and take corrective measures to ensure that events conform to plans.
   - Controlling becomes a basis for improving future plans
3. ***Planning is prescriptive whereas controlling is evaluative***
   - Planning is an intellectual process involving:
     - Thinking
     - Analysis
     - Articulation

     To discover and prescribe an appropriate course of action for achieving objectives.

- Controlling checks whether the actual performance or decisions have been translated into desired actions

4. ***Planning and controlling are both forward looking***
   - Planning is forward looking since it is preparing for the future and is based on forecasts about future conditions
   - Controlling is forward looking as corrective action initiated to rectify the deviations helps in improving future plans
5. ***Planning and controlling are both backward looking***
   - Planning is backward looking since it is guided by past experiences
   - Controlling is backward looking as it is like a post mortem of past activities to locate deviations from set standards

Conclusion

1. Planning based on facts makes controlling easier and effective
2. Controlling improves future planning by providing information derived from past experiences

Thus planning and controlling are inseparable twins of management.

Q8. 'Planning and Control are inseparable twins of management.' Explain.

Ans. Refer to Q 7.

Q9. 'Planning is the basis for controlling.' Explain.

Ans. Refer to point 1 of answer for Q 7.

Q10. 'Planning makes Controlling easier and effective.' Explain.

Ans. Refer to point 1 of answer for Q 7.

Q11. ' Planning seeks integrated and articulated programs while controlling seeks to compel events to conform to plans.' Explain

Ans. Explain how planning is prescriptive and controlling is evaluative from above answer.

Q12. 'Although controlling is an important function of management, it suffers from certain limitations.' Explain

Ans.

1. *Difficulty in setting quantitative standards*
   - Control system loses some of its effectiveness when standards can't be defined in quantitative terms
   - This makes management of performance and its comparison with standards a very difficult task. Problems may arise with respect to:
     - Employee morale
     - Human behavior
     - Job satisfaction
2. *Little control on external factors*
   - Generally an enterprise can't control external factors such as government policies, technological changes, competition and natural disasters
3. *Resistance from employees*
   - Control is often resisted by employees. They see it as a restriction on their freedom

   For Example:

   Employees might object when they are kept under a strict watch with help of CCTVs
4. *Costly affair*
   - It is costly as it involves a lot of expenditure, time and effort. A small enterprise can't afford to install an expensive control system. It can't justify the expenses involved
   - Managers must ensure that the cost of installing and operating a control system should not exceed its benefits.

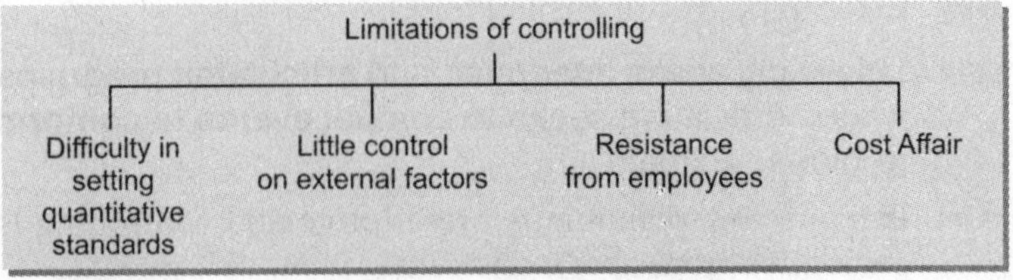

Q13. Explain the steps in the process of controlling

Ans.

1. ***Setting performance standards***
   - Standards are the criteria/benchmark against which the actual performance is measured.
   - Standards can be both:
     - Quantitative – Cost, revenue, time spent, product units
     - Qualitative – Improving goodwill and motivation of employees
   - Qualitative standards should be defined in such a manner so as to make their measurement simpler
   - Example: To improve customer satisfaction in a fast food chain having self service, standards can be in terms of:
     - Time taken by customer to wait for table
     - Time taken to process an order
   - Qualitative Standards are more precise and managers should try to set standards in quantitative terms to make the comparison with actual performance easier.
   - Example: To increase the production units from 10,000 to 12,000 by end of quarter.
   - Standards should be flexible and be able to be modified as and when required due to changes in internal and external business environment
2. ***Measurement of actual performance***
   - Performance should be measured in an objective and reliable manner
   - Performance should be measured in the same units in which standards are set so that comparison is easier
   - Measurement of work should be done during the performance rather than doing it after completion of the task.

     Example: In case of an assembling task(automobile industry), each part produced should be checked before assembling. Some techniques for measuring performance are:

- Performance report of an employee prepared by his superior
- Sample checking: In large organizations certain pieces are checked at random for quality
- Calculation of ratios like gross profit ratio, net profit ratio, return on investment
- Personal observation

3. ***Comparing actual performance with standards***
   - Such a comparison helps to identify the deviation or difference between the actual and standard results.
   - The comparison becomes easier when the standards are set in quantitative terms
   - *Example:* Performance of a worker in terms of units produced in a week can be measured against standard output for the week
4. ***Analyzing deviations***
   - It is important to firstly determine an acceptable range of deviations.
   - Determine acceptable range of deviations

     i. Management by exception was used by managers in this regard. It states that only significant deviations which go beyond the permissible limit should be brought to the notice of the management. It is also called control by exception. If you try to control everything, you will end up controlling nothing.

     - *Example:* Labour cost: Acceptable rate of deviations is 2%; If deviation is 5%, then it must be reported to the management

     ii. Deviations in key result areas (KRAs) should be attended.

     - Control should focus on KRAs which are critical to the success of an organization. KRAs are the critical points. Example: Increase in labour cost by 5% is more critical than 15% increase in postal expenses
   - The causes of deviations should be identified. These could be:
     - Unrealistic standards

  - Defective process
  - Defective materials
  - Defective machinery

5. *Taking corrective action*
   - No corrective action is required when deviations are within acceptable limits
   - Corrective action might involve:
     - Repair of existing machinery
     - Improving physical work condition

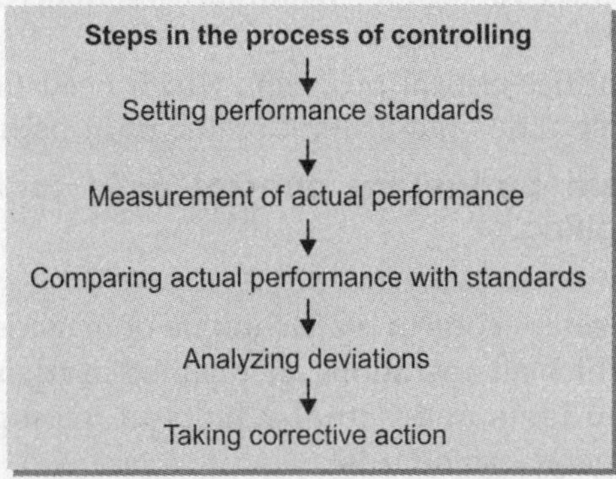

Q12. Give examples to show causes and corrective actions that need to be taken with respect to deviations.

Ans.

Table 8.1

Causes of deviation	*Corrective action*
Defective material	Change the quality specification for the material used
Defective machinery	Repair the existing machine or replace the machine if it is un-repairable
Obsolete machinery	Do technological upgradation of machinery
Defective process	Change the existing process
Defective physical conditions of work	Improve physical working conditions

Q13. State any 4 advantages of critical point control and management by exception.

Ans. The various advantages are:

1. Saves time and effort of managers as they deal with only significant deviations
2. Focuses managerial attention on important areas thus having better utilization of managerial talent
3. The routine problems are left to be dealt by the subordinates. Management by exception, thus, facilitates delegation of authority and increases morale of the employees
4. Identifies critical problems which need timely action to keep the organization on the right path

Q14. Explain budgetary control as a technique of controlling.

Ans.

- Budgetary control is a technique of managerial control in which all operations are planned in advance in form of budgets and actual results are compared with budgetary standards
- A budget is a quantitative statement for a definite future period of time for the purpose of obtaining a given objective
- This comparison reveals the necessary actions to be taken so that organizational objectives are accomplished
- It is also a statement which reflects the policy of that particular period. It will contain figures of forecasts both in terms of time and quantities, for example: sales budget, production budget

Q15. Explain the various types of budgets.

Ans.

1. *Sales budget:* A statement of what an organization expects to sell in terms of quality as well as value
2. *Production budget:* A statement of what an organization plans to produce in the budget period

3. *Cash budget:* Anticipated cash inflows and outflows for the budget period
4. *Capital budget:* Estimated spending on major long term assets like new factory or major equipment
5. *Material budget:* A statement of estimated quantity and cost of materials required for production
6. *Research and development budget:* Estimated spending for the development or refinement of products and processes

Q16. Discuss importance of budgetary control?

Ans.

1. ***Budgeting is a source of motivation*:** It is a source of motivation to the employees who know the standards against which their performance will be appraised and thus enables them to perform better
2. ***Helps in attainment of organizational objectives:*** Budgeting focuses on specific time bound targets and thus helps in attainment of organizational objectives
3. ***Budgeting helps in optimum utilization of resources:*** It helps in optimum utilization of resources by allocating them according to the requirements of different departments
4. ***Budgeting is used for achieving coordination*:** It is used for achieving coordination among different departments of an organization and highlights the interdependence between them.

   For *example:*

   Sales budget can't be prepared without knowing production programs and schedules
5. ***Budgeting facilitates management by exception:*** It facilitates management by exception by stressing on those operations which deviate from budgeted standards in a significant way

Conclusion:

Managers must remember that budgeting shouldn't be viewed as an end but a means to achieve organizational goals

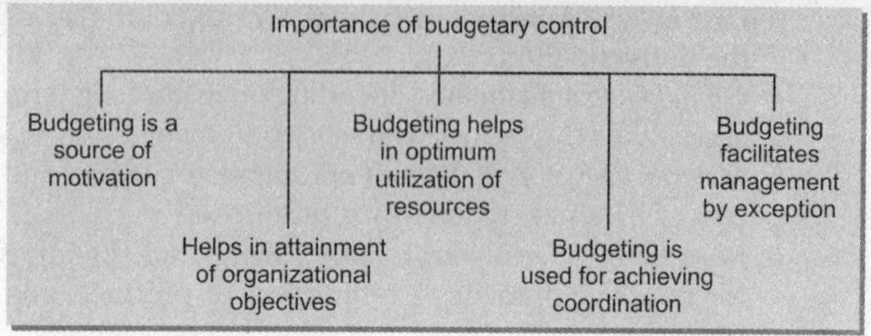

Q17. How is effectiveness of budgetary control ensured?

Ans.

- The effectiveness of budgeting depends on how accurately estimates have been made about the future

Q18. What is the feature of a good budget?

Ans.

- A budget should be flexible so that it can be adopted if forecasts about the future turn out to be different especially in the face of changing forces.

9

Business Finance

Q1. Define *business finance*.

or

'Finance is the lifeblood of every business.' Explain.

Ans.

- It refers to the funds and money required for and available to a business enterprise for carrying out its activities.
- It is regarded as the lifeblood of the business since it is required for:
  - Establishment of a business
  - Operation of a business
  - Expansion
  - Modernization
  - Purchase of tangible assets (e.g. building, machinery)
  - Purchase of intangible assets (e.g. trademark, technical expertise)
  - Diversification

Q2. What do you mean by *financial management*?

Ans.

- It refers to
  - i. Planning
  - ii. Organizing
  - iii. Directing
  - iv. Controlling

Financial activities of any business enterprise.

- It is mainly concerned with
  i. Optimal procurement of funds-This refers to having sufficient funds (nether surplus not deficit) at a minimum cost.
  ii. Optimal utilization of funds- This refers to investment of funds in areas with maximum returns and minimum risks.

Q3. Explain the objectives of financial management.

or

'Wealth maximization of shareholders is the primary objective of financial management.' Explain.

Ans.

- The primary objective of financial management is to maximize the wealth of the shareholders who have contributed to the funds of the business.
- Shareholder's wealth is reflected in the market value of shares.
- The market value increases when the demand for shares rises.
- Demand for shares is seen to rise when high dividend is declared.
- High dividends are declared when the company earns high profit.
- Profits of the business are a result of a manner in which the funds are procured and utilized.
- If the funds are procured at low cost and invested in low risk and high return areas then profits are high.
- Hence, the main objective of wealth maximization can be achieved through the following incidental objectives:
  - Optimal procurement of funds at minimum cost.
  - Optimal utilization of funds in high return areas.
  - Ensuring safety of funds by avoiding misappropriate usage

Fig. 9.2: Financial management aims at maximizing the wealth of shareholders

Q4. Discuss the 3 important decisions areas of financial management.

Ans.

1. *Investment decisions*
   - It refers to the total funds required by a business and investment in different areas.
   - Investment decisions may be long term or short term.

   a. Long term investment decisions are termed capital budgeting decision. It involves investment in fixed assets. These decisions involve huge amount of money and are irreversible except at a huge cost.

   Example:
   - Acquiring a new fixed cost
   - Opening a new office
   - Making investment in a new machine to replace an existing one.

   b. Short term investment decision is known as working capital decisions. It relates to meeting day to day operational expenses of a business.
   - It affects liquidity and profitability of a business.
   - It is concerned with decisions about the current assets like cash levels, debtors, investors.

2. *Financing decision*
   - It relates to sources from where funds may be raised and the proportion in which they may be raised.

- There are 2 major sources of finance
  a. Owner's funds
    - Equity shares
    - Retained earnings
    - Preference shares
  b. Borrowed funds
    - Debentures
    - Public deposits
    - Loans from bank
    - Loans from financial institutions
- This decision determines the debt-equity ratio or capital structure of the firm.
- Debt is cheaper than equity as
  - Interest on debt is tax deductible.
  - Rate of interest on debt is lower
- However, debt is riskier than equity as:
  - Interest has to be paid irrespective of profits.
  - Borrowed fund has to be repaid on the date of maturity.
- On the other hand, equity is more expensive and less risky. (Dividend not compulsory, Equity not to be redeemed)
- After considering various factors like cost and risk, capital structure/financing decision is made.

3. ***Dividend decision***
   - It relates to the allocation of profits earned by the business between
     - Distribution of dividend to shareholders.
     - Retention of profits of the business in the form of retained earnings to meet the future requirements.
   - This decision should be taken in such a manner so that there is a balance between meeting the future requirements of the business and maximizing the shareholder's wealth.

   All the above three decisions should be taken with the single main objective of maximization of wealth of shareholders.

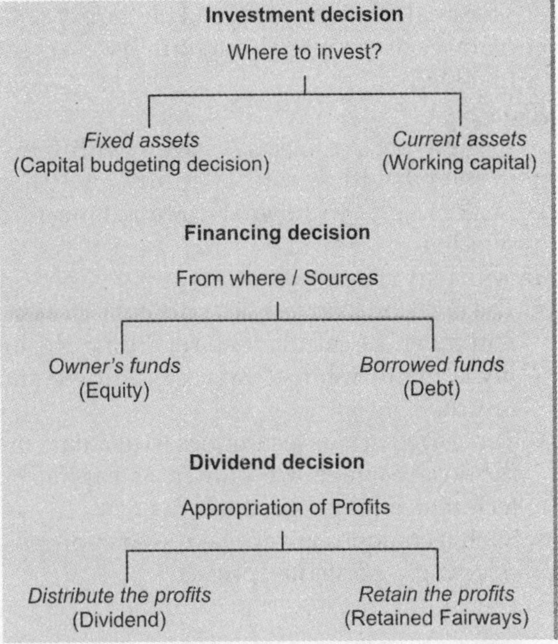

Fig. 9.1: Decision areas of financial management

Q5. Explain the various factors affecting the capital budgeting decision.

Ans. The various factors affecting the capital budgeting decision are:

1. *Cash flows of the project*
   - When a company takes an investment decision involving huge amounts it expects to generate some cash flows over a period.
   - These cash flows are in the form of services of cash receipts and payments over the life of an investment.
   - The amount of these cash flows must be carefully analyzed before considering a capital budgeting decision.
2. *Rate of return*
   - The most important criterion is the rate of return of the project.

- These calculations are based on the expected returns from each proposal and the assessment of risk involved.

Example:

There are 2 projects X and Y with the same risk involved with a rate of return of 10% and 11% respectively. In normal circumstances, Y will be selected.

3. ***Investment criteria involved***
   - The decision to invest in a particular project involves a number. of calculations regarding the amount of investment, interest rate, cash flows and rate of return.
   - There are various techniques to evaluate investment proposals which are known as capital budgeting techniques (like ratio analysis)
   - Such techniques are applied to each proposal before selecting a particular project.

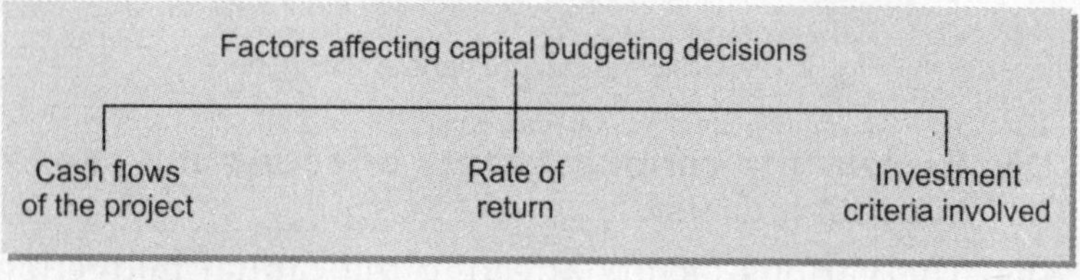

Q6. What needs to be considered if a company has to make a long term investment in a project against which there is no choice?

Ans. If there is only one project then its viability in terms of rate of return viz. investment and its comparability with the industry average is seen.

Q7. What is meant by *financial risk*?

Ans.

- Financial risk is the risk of defaults on payment by a company with respect to fixed obligation, i.e. debt.
- Financial risk is higher for companies which have a high proportion of debt since interest payment and capital repayment is compulsory.

- If a company has high proportion of debt there will be insufficient shareholders to contribute to such payments thereby increasing the element of financial risk.

  Thus, financial risk depends upon the proportion of debt in the capital structure.

Q8. Which is the cheapest source of finance?

Ans. Retained earnings are the cheapest source of finance. However, debt is cheaper than equity.

Q9. Discuss the scope of capital budgeting/management of fixed capital.

or

Capital budgeting decisions are very crucial since it involves management of fixed capital for a long term.

Ans. Capital budgeting decisions are important for:

1. *Long-term growth and effects*
   - These decisions have bearing on the long-term growth.
   - The funds invested in long-term assets are likely to yield in the future.
   - These affect future possibilities and prospects of the business.
2. *Large amount of funds involved*
   - These decisions result is a substantial portion of capital funds being locked in long-term projects.
   - These investment programmes are planned after a detailed analysis is undertaken. This may involve decisions like where to procure funds from and at what rate of interest.
3. *Risk involved*
   - Fixed capital involves investment of huge amounts. It affects the returns of the firm as a whole in the long-term.
   - Investment decisions involving fixed capital influence the overall business risk complexion of the firm.
4. *They are irreversible decisions*
   - Decisions once taken, are not reversible without incurring heavy losses.
   - Abandoning a project after heavy investment is made is quite costly in terms of waste of funds.

- These decisions should be taken only after carefully evaluating each detail otherwise the adverse financial consequences may be very heavy.

Q10. What is meant by *fixed capital* or management of *fixed capital*?

Ans.

- Fixed capital refers to investment in long-term assets. Fixed assets are those which remain in the business for more than 1 year, usually for much longer.

Example: Plant and machinery, land, motor.

- Management of fixed capital revolves around allocation of firm's capital to different projects/assets with long term implications on the business.
- It must be financed through long-term sources of capital such as equity or preference shares, debentures, long-term loan and retained earnings and should never be financed through short term sources.
- These decisions are called investment decisions or capital budgeting decisions and affect growth, profitability and risk of the business in the long run.

Q11. Discuss the factors affecting the fixed capital requirements of the business.

Ans. The various factors are:

1. *Nature of business*
   - The type of business has a bearing upon the fixed capital requirements.
   - There are 2 natures of business:
     - *Manufacturing:* Needs more investment in fixed assets as machinery, etc. have to be purchased.
     - *Trading:* Needs lower investment in fixed assets.
2. *Scale of operations*
   - A larger organization operating at a higher scale needs bigger plant and machinery and thus requires more investment in fixed assets.
   - A small organization requires low investment in fixed assets.
3. *Choice of technique*
   - Some organizations are capital intensive whereas others are labour intensive.

- Labour intensive firms require less investment in fixed assets and hence have low fixed capital.
- A capital intensive firm requires higher investment in plant, as it relies less on manual labour. The requirement for fixed capital is higher.

4. ***Technology up gradation***
   - In certain industries, assets become obsolete sooner and their replacement becomes due faster. Higher investment in fixed assets may be required.

   For example:

   Computers become obsolete faster and are replaced much sooner than furniture.
   - Organizations which use assets prone to obsolescence require higher fixed capital to purchase such assets.
5. ***Diversification***
   - A firm may choose to diversify its operations. With diversification, fixed capital requirements increase.

   Example:

   A textile company diversifying and starting a cement manufacturing plant. Its investment in fixed assets is thus higher.
6. ***Growth prospects***
   - Higher growth of an organization generally requires higher investment in fixed assets. Even if such growth is expected, a business may choose to create higher capacity in order to meet the anticipated higher demand quicker.
   - This entails higher investment in fixed assets and thus higher fixed capital.
7. ***Financing alternatives***
   - A developed financial market may provide leasing facilities as an alternative to outright purchase. When an asset is taken on lease, the firm pays lease rentals and uses it.
   - Hence it avoids huge sums required to purchase it. Availability of leasing facilities, thus, may reduce the funds required to be invested in fixed assets, thereby reducing fixed capital requirements.
   - Such a strategy is especially suitable is high risk lines of business.

8. *Level of collaboration*
   - At times, certain business firms share each other's facilities.

   For example:
   A bank may use another's ATM.
   - This is feasible if the scale of operations of each item isn't sufficient to make full use of the facility.
   - Such collaboration reduces the level of investment in fixed assets for each of the participating firms.

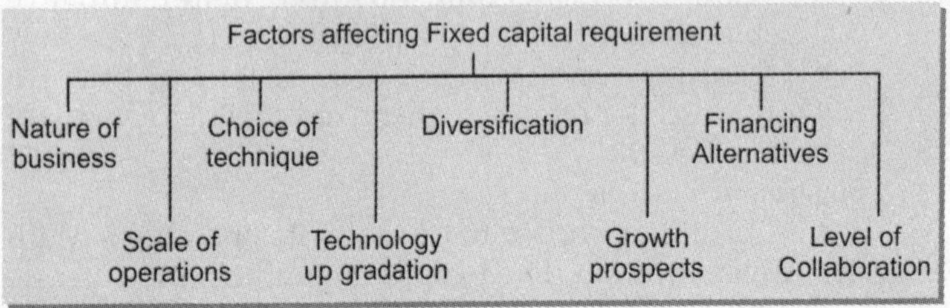

Q12. What is meant by *working capital*?

Ans.

- Apart from the investment in fixed assets, every business organization needs to invest in current assets. Such investment in current assets is known as working capital.
- These investments facilitate smooth day to day operations of the business. Current assets are usually more liquid but contribute less to profits than fixed assets.

For example:

Current assets in order of their liquidity:

- Cash in hand/bank
- Marketable Securities
- B/R
- Debtors
- Raw materials
- Finished goods inventory
- Work in progress
- Prepaid expenses

- These assets are expected to get converted into cash or cash equivalents within a period of one year.

  This decision is crucial and a proper balance needs to be maintained between liquidity and profitability.

Q13. Working capital affects the liquidity and profitability of a business. Discuss the relationship.

Ans.

- Working capital refers to the investment in current assets.
- Current assets are more liquid as they are liable to be converted into cash within a period of one year. Thus these assets provide liquidity to the business.
- Insufficient investment in current assets may make it difficult for a firm to meet its payment obligations.
- However, current assets, provide little or low return as compared to fixed assets.
- For a firm, it is important to strike a balance between liquidity and profitability. Thus, a reasonable share of capital should be contributed towards investment in current assets as it implies more liquidity, less risk and less profitability.

Q14. What is meant by *net working capital*?

Ans.

- Working capital refers to investment in current assets.
- Net working capital refers to the excess of current assets over current liabilities.

Net working assets = Current assets – Current liabilities

- Current liabilities are those payment obligations which are due for payment within one year.

Example: Creditors, bills payable, outstanding expenses

- Current assets are those which can be liquidated by a firm within a period of 1 year

Q15. How are fixed assets and current assets financed?

Ans.

- Fixed assets should be financed only through long term sources of capital like equity and preference shares, debentures, retained earnings, long term loans, etc.

- Current Assets should be financed through short term sources of finance like trade credit, short term loan, etc.

Q16. Discuss the various factors affecting the working capital requirements of a business.

Ans. The various factors affecting the working capital requirements of a business are:

1. ***Nature of business***
   - This influences the amount of working capital required.
   - In a manufacturing concern, raw materials need to be converted into finised goods before any sales are made thus, a manufacturing concern would require more working capital.
   - In a treading concern, there is no distinction between raw materials and finished goods. Sales can be made immediately upon the receipt of materials. Thus, lower amount of working capital is required.
   - In service industry less working capital is required because no inventory needs to be maintained.
2. ***Scale of operations***
   - For large scale business, level of inventory and debtors will be more thus no working capital is required.
   - For a small scale business, level of debtors and inventory will be relatively less, thus working capital is required.
3. ***Business cycle***
   - In case of boom period, demand, production and sales are expected to be higher. Thus, large investment in stock, debtors, etc. is required. Hence, the working capital will be more.
   - During the period of depression, sales and production are low. Thereby, working capital requirements will be lower.
4. ***Seasonal factors***
   - During peak season, there is a high level of activity in terms of demand, production and consumption. Thus, higher amount of working capital is required.
   - During lean season, the level of activity is low thereby, the working capital requirement is also low.

- If certain products are seasonal then the working capital requirement is bound to fluctuate.

5. *Credit allowed*
    - Different businesses allow different credit terms to their customers. This largely depends upon the competition and credit worthiness of the customers.
    - If a business follows a liberal credit policy then it will result in higher amount of debtors thereby increasing the working capital requirement.
    - On the reverse, a strict and tight credit policy will result in lesser amount of debtors, thus reducing the working capital requirements.
6. *Production cycle*
    - This is the time spent between the receipt of raw materials and their conversion into finished goods.
    - Businesses having longer production cycle will have higher working capital requirement in order to meet the various operational expenses till the time sales are made and cash inflow occurs.
    - Businesses with a shorter production cycle will have lower working capital requirement since the time gap between cash outflow (purchase of raw materials) and cash inflow (sale of raw materials) is very small.
7. *Operating efficiency*
    - Businesses manage their operations with varying degrees of efficiency.
    - Businesses which are able to manage its raw materials efficiently (reflected in a higher inventory turnover ratio) and have small amounts tied up in debtors (a higher debtor turnover ratio) are regarded as efficient and will have a lower working capital requirement.
    - Businesses which are not able to manage its raw materials and sales efficiency will need a higher working capital.
8. *Credit availed*
    - Just as a firm allows credit to its customers, it may also get credit from its suppliers.

- If the credit availed is liberal (purchases on credit) the working capital requirement would be lower.
- If the credit availed by a business is on strict terms (purchases on cash) then higher working capital is required.

9. *Availability of raw materials*
   - If raw materials are freely and continuously available then large stocks do not have to be maintained there by reducing the working capital requirement.
   - Also, if the time lag between placement of order and actual receipt of materials (lead time) is long, larger stocks of raw materials need to be maintained thereby increasing the working capital requirement.
10. *Growth prospects*
    - If the growth potential of a particular business is perceived to be higher, higher amount of working capital is required since the level of production and sales will increase.
    - If growth prospects are not very high then the working capital requirement is lesser since production and sales will be limited.
11. *Inflation*
    - High rates of inflation increase the working capital requirement of a business.
    - When prices rise, a larger amount of working capital will get tied up in the stock of raw materials, furnished goods, labor cost, etc.
    - However, an inflation rate of 5% does not mean that every component of working capital will change in the same proportion.
12. *Level of competition*
    - Higher level of competition may:
      i. Require the firm to maintain higher stocks of finised goods to meet demand
      ii. Force the firms to allow credit on libceal turns
    - However, in absence of competition, you need not maintain large stocks and can follow a tight credit policy as it does not result in losing its customers. This will reduce the working capital requirement.

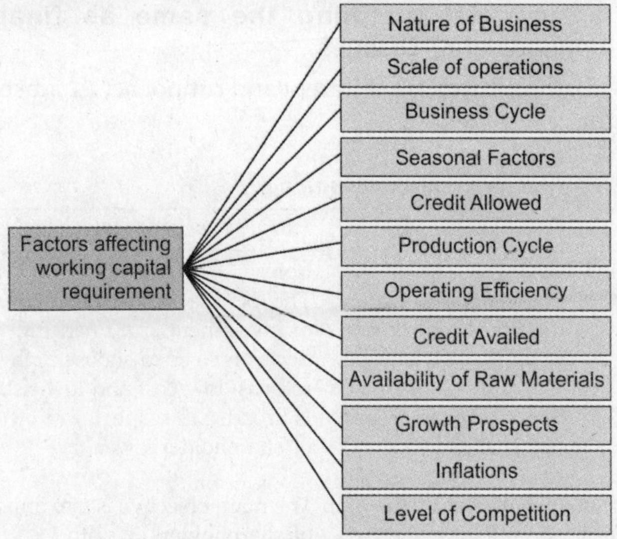

Q17. What do you mean by *financial planning*?

Ans.

- It refers to preparation of a financial blueprint of the firm's future operations.
- It enables the management to decide in advance:
  - Quantum
  - Funds required in the firm in the future in order to avoid shortages and surplus of funds.
- It helps to match the funds required with their availability after taking into consideration
  - Growth
  - Performance
  - Investment for a given period
- It may be
  - Short term
  - Long term
- The objective of financial planning is to ensure that enough funds are available at the right time.
- Ordinarily, financial planning is done for 3–5 years as for longer periods it becomes more difficult and less useful.

Q18. Is financial planning the same as financial management? Discuss.

Ans. No, the 2 terms are different and cannot act as substitutes for each other.

Table 9.1

Basis	*Financial planning*	*Financial management*
Meaning	Refer	Refer
Focus	The focus is to match the funds required with its availability.	The focus is on cost benefit analysis of investment and financing decision so as to choose high returns, low cost and low risk.
Scope	Is narrower in scope and is a part of financial management.	Is broadec in scope of shareholder's wealth.
Objective	It is quided by the twin obective of avoiding shortages and surplus of funds	The main objective is maximization of shareholders' wealth.

Q19. Explain the twin objectives of financial planning.

Ans. The twin objectives are:

1. ***To ensure availability of funds whenever they are required***
   - This includes a proper estimation of the funds required for
     - Purchase of long term assets
     - To meet day to day expenses of business
   - Apart from this, there is a need to estimate the time at which these funds are to be made available.
   - Financial planning also tries to specify possible sources of these funds.
2. ***To see that the firm doesn't raise resource unnecessarily***
   - Excess funding is almost as bad as inadequate funding.
   - Even if there is some surplus money, good financial planning would put it to the best possible use so that the financial resources aren't left idle and don't add to the cost.

Q20. What do you mean by *budgets*?

Ans.
- Short term financial plans are known as budgets.
- Budgets are detailed plan of action.
- They are made for a period of up to 1 year, e.g. advertising budget, cash budget, etc.

Q21. What is meant by long term financial planning? What does it focus on?

Ans. Long term planning refers to long-term growth and investment. It focuses on capital expenditure programs.

Q22. "Financial Planning usually begins with the preparation of sales forecast". Discuss

Ans. The process of financial planning involves:

1. *Preparation of a sales forecast*: If a company makes a financial plan for the next five years, it will have to estimate the likely sales for the next five year.
2. *Preparation of financial statements*
   - Based on sales forecast, financial statements are prepared in order to estimate the funds required for investment in fixed capital and working capital.
3. *Estimation of expected profits*
   - Profits are estimated so as to get an idea as to how much a firm can meet its fund requirement internally in the form of retained earnings.
4. ***Estimation of requirement for external sources of finance.***
5. ***Identifying the various external sources of finance and preparing cash budgets.***

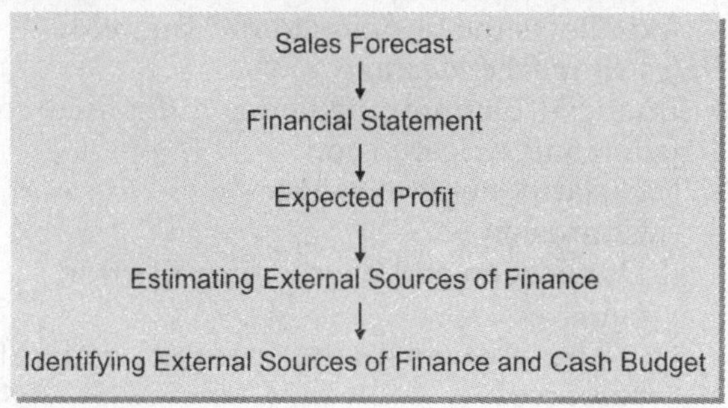

Q23. 'Financial planning is a useless exercise as it is done for the future which is unknown and uncertain'. Do you agree? Give reasons.

or

Discuss the importance of financial planning.

Ans. I disagree with the statement since financial planning is an important part of overall planning of the business. It:

1. ***Helps the business to prepare for the future***
   - Future is uncertain. However, financial planning helps to foresee the future, analyze the problems and find solutions.
   - The blueprint under financial planning offers choices out of which the best may be chosen to tackle the future.

   Example:

   Predicted growth in sales is 21% However, it may happen that the actual growth rate turns out to be 10% or 30%. By preparing the blueprint, the management may decide what must be done in each of the situations in order to run the business smoothly.
2. ***Helps in co-ordination***
   - It helps to integrate various business activities like production, purchase, sale, marketing, etc. and provide them with financial policies and procedures so that they work in coordination and harmony without contradicting each other.
3. ***Helps in avoiding business shocks and surprises***
   - Because of uncertainity, favorable/unfavorable situations may cause business fortunes to fluctuate.
   - Financial planning helps to ease these fluctuations and allows the business to run smoothly.
4. ***Helps to reduce wastage***
   - Financial planning provides a detailed course of action and a clear vision.
   - This clarity helps to reduce
     - Confusion
     - Duplication and overlapping of effort
     - Gaps

     Thereby ensuring proper utilization of resources.

5. ***Provides a link between present and future***
   - Present and future are closely interlinked and can't be isolated from each other.
   - Plans for the future are made in the present on the basis of past experiences, thereby bridging all time gaps.
6. ***Provides a link between investment and financing decisions***
   - These 2 decisions are the pillars of financial management.
   - While investment decision deals with the total amount of funds required, that of financing deals with the sources and the proportion in which these funds may be raised.
   - Financial planning provides a link between these 2 decisions on a continuous basis.
7. ***Facilitates evaluation of actual performance and financial control***
   - Financial plans provide standards which provide the basis for comparing the actual performance so that if there are any deviations (between standard and actual) they can be corrected. Hence, it provides the basis for financial control.

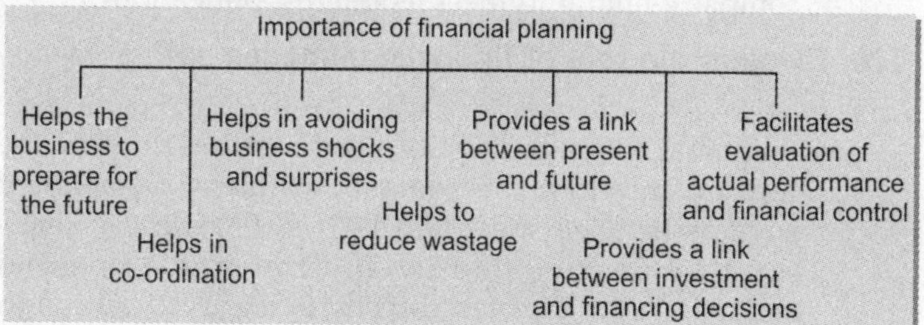

Q24. What is meant by *capital structure*?

Ans.

- It refers to the composition of capital. It relates to the proportion and mix of owner's funds and borrowed funds which are referred to as equity and debt respectively.

Example:

Total funds required : Rs. 10,00,000
Capital structure :
Equity share capital : Rs. 6,00,000
Debentures : Rs. 2,00,000
Loans from bank : Rs. 1,00,000
Retained earnings : Rs. 1,00,000

- It is also referred to as debt-equity ratio.
- Capital structure can be calculated in 2 ways:
  - Debt-equity ratio = Debt/Equity
  - Proportion of debt out of total capital = Debt/(debt + equity)
- A capital structure is considered to be optimum when the proportion of debt and equity is such that it results in an increase in the value of equity shares or simply wealth maximization of shareholders.

Q25. What is meant by interest coverage ratio?

Ans.

- Interest coverage ratio is the no. of times earnings before interest and taxes (EBIT) covers the interest obligations.

  Interest coverage ratio = EBIT/Interest

  Higher the ratio, lower is the risk involved ,of the company failing to meet its interest obligations.

Q26. Discuss the role of financial management.

Ans.

- Financial management has a direct bearing on the financial health of a business. The financial statement such as balance sheet and P/L A/C reflect a firm's financial position. Mostly all items in the financial statements are affected directly or indirectly through some financial management decisions.
- Some prominent examples of the aspects being affected are given below:

  1. ***Size and composition of fixed assets of balance sheet***

Example:

A capital budgeting decision to invest a sum of 100 cr in fixed assets would raise the size of fixed assets shown in financial statements.

2. ***Quantum of current assets and its break up into cash, receivable and inventory***
   - With an increase in investment in fixed asset there is an equal increase in working capital.
   - The quantum of current assets is influenced by financial management decisions.
   - Decisions about credit policy and inventory management affect the amount of debtors and inventory which in turn affects the total current assets of the firm.
3. ***Amount of long-term and short-term financing to be used***
   - Financial management involves decisions about the proportion of short and long term finance.
   - An organization wanting to remain more liquid would raise comparatively more amount on long term basis.
   - There is a choice between liquidity and profitability.
   - It is assured that current liabilities cost less than long term liabilities.
4. ***Break-up of long-term financing into debt and equity***
   - The proportion of debt and equity to be raised is an important financial management decision.
   - The amount of debt, preference share capital, equity share capital, etc. are affected by the financing decision which is a part of financial management.
5. ***All items in the profit/loss a/c viz. interest, depreciation, etc.***
   - Higher amount of debt means higher interest expense.
   - Higher use of equity entails higher payment of dividend.
   - Similarly, an expansion of business which is a result of capital budgeting decisions is likely to affect all items in the P/L A/C of the business.
   - The future financial statements depend upon the past as well as the present financial decisions determined by the quality of its financial management.

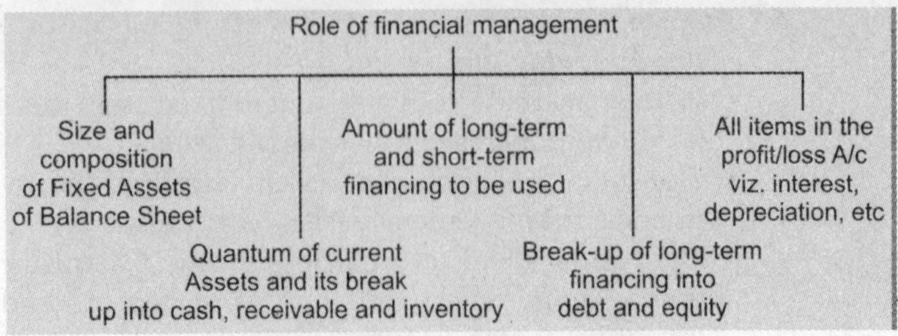

Q27. 'The total risk of a business depends upon the financial risk as well as business risk.' Explain.

Ans.

- Financial risk refers to a position when a company is unable to meet its fixed financial charges or obligations namely interest payment, preference dividend and repayment obligations.
- Apart from financial risk, every business has some operating risk, also known as business risk.
- Business risk depends upon the fixed operating costs. Higher the fixed operating cost, higher is the business risk involved.
- Thereby, the total risk of the business depends both on financial and business risk.

Q28. Explain the relationship between operating cycle and working capital.

Ans. Explain the following three:

- Meaning of operations cycle
- Meaning of working capital
- *Relationship:* Longer the operating cycle, higher the working capital need, shorter the cycle, lesser the need for working capital
  Draw diagram

Q29. How are shareholders likely to gain with a loan component/debt in the capital employed/investment? Explain favorable financial leverage.

or

What is meant by financial leverage? Explain with the help of an example.

Ans. Financial leverage

- Is the proportion of debt to equity (debt/equity) or the proportion of debt to total capital [debt/(debt + equity)]
- An increase in financial leverage implies an increase in the proportion of debt. Debt is cheaper, i.e. the cost of funds will decrease but the financial risk will increase due to fixed obligations with respect to interest payments.
- The positive impact of financial leverage on earning per share (EPS) can be seen with the help of the following example under 2 assumptions viz:
  1. Rate of return on capital employed/investment is greater than the rate of interest on debt.
  2. Interest paid is tax deductible.

	Situation I	*Situation II*	*Situation III*
Total Funds	30,00,000	30,00,000	30,00,000
Equity shares @ 10 each	30,00,000	20,00,000	10,00,000
Debt	Nil	10,00,000	20,00,000

Example:

Assuming :

i. Interest on debt 10%

ii. Tax rate 30%

EBIT - EPS Analysis (Favorable)

Particulars	*I*	*II*	*III*
EBIT	4,00,000	4,00,000	4,00,000
Less: Interest on debt	Nil	1,00,000	2,00,000
EBT	4,00,000	3,00,000	2,00,000
Less: Tax @ 30%	1,20,000	90,000	40,000
EAT	2,80,000	2,10,000	1,40,000
No. of equity shares	3,00,000	2,00,000	1,00,000
EPS = EAT/No. of shares	2,80,000 / 3,00,000 = Rs. 0.93	2,10,000 / 2,00,000 = Rs. 1.05	1,40,000 / 1,00,000 = Rs. 1.4

iii. EBIT: 4 lacs

Note: Explanation

Rate of return = 4,00,000/30,00,000 × 100 = 13.33 %
Conclusion

- The increasing use of debt in the capital structure increases the earning per share as long as the rate of return on investment of a firm, i.e. 13.33% is greater than interest on debt which is 10%.
- Also known as trading on equity, this is a situation of favorable financial leverage in which the company employs more of debt to increase the EPS.

Q30. Explain with the help of an example the condition of unfavorable financial leverage.

Ans.

- Unfavorable financial leverage is a situation when the increased use of debt in the capital structure reduces the earning per share (EPS). This happens because:
  - Rate of return on investment/capital employed is less than rate of interest on debt

	Situation I	*Situation II*	*Situation III*
Total funds	30,00,000	30,00,000	30,00,000
Equity shares @ Rs.10 each	30,00,000	20,00,000	10,00,000
Debt	Nil	30,00,000	20,00,000

Example:
Interest on Debt = 10 %
Tax Rate = 30 %

EBIT – EPS analysis (unfavorable)

Particulars	*I*	*II*	*III*
EBIT	2,00,000	2,00,000	2,00,000
Less: Interest in debt @10%	Nil	1,00,000	2,00,000
EBT	2,00,000	1,00,000	0
Less: Tax rate @ 30%	60,000	30,000	0
EAT	1,40,000	70,000	0
No. of equity shares	3,00,000	2,00,000	1,00,000
EPS = EAT/No. of shares	1,40,000/3,00,000	70,000/2,00,000	01,00,000
EPS	= Rs. 0.46	= Rs. 0.35	0

EBIT = Rs. 2 Lac

Conclusion:

- In the above situation, the increased use of debt and reduced EPS from 0.46 to 0.35 to nil since the rate of return on investment {EBIT/Total Funds X 100 = 6.66%} is 6.66% which is less than the rate of interest on debt which is 10%.
- A company should use debt carefully and must aim for a debt-equity mix which maximizes the return of the shareholders and at the same time keeps the risk factor in mind as well.

Q31. What do you mean by trading on equity?

Ans.

- Trading on equity refers to the increase in profit earned by the equity shareholders due to the presence of debt in the capital structure without any increase in the operating income of the business provided the following 2 conditions are satisfied:
  1. Rate of return on capital employed/investment is greater than rate of interest on debt.
  2. Interest paid is tax deductible.

Q32. What are the factors affecting the financing decision?

or

What are the factors affecting the choice of capital structure?

Ans. The various factors affecting financing decisions are:

1. *Cash flow position*
   - Size of projected cash flows must be considered before issuing debt. Cash flows must not only cover fixed cash payment obligations but there must be sufficient buffer also.
   - It must be kept in mind that a company has cash payment obligations for:
     - Normal business operations
     - Investment in fixed assets
     - For meeting the debt service commitments, i.e. payment of interest and repayment of capital.

2. ***Interest coverage ratio (ICR)***
   - ICR refers to the no. of times earnings before interest and taxes of a company covers the interest obligation.

     ICR = EBIT/Interest
   - The higher the ratio, lower is the risk of the company failing to meet its interest payment obligations.
   - However, the ratio is not an adequate measure as:
     - A firm may have a high EBIT but low cash balance.
     - Apart from interest, payment of preference dividend and repayment obligations are also relevant which aren't included in ICR.
3. ***Debt service coverage ratio (DSCR)***
   - The cash profits generated by the operations are compared with the total cash required for the service of the debt and preference share capital.

$$\text{DSCR} = \frac{\text{Profit after tax} + \text{Depreciation} + \text{Interest} + \text{Non cash exp}}{\text{Preference dividend} + \text{Interest} + \text{Repayment obligation}}$$

   - DSCR takes care of the deficiencies referred to in the Interest Coverage Ratio (ICR).
   - A higher DSCR indicates better ability to meet cash commitments and resultantly, the company's potential to increase debt in its capital structure.
4. ***Return on investment (ROI)***
   - If ROI of the company is more than the rate of interest it can employ debt in its capital structure as it helps in increasing the earnings per share (EPS).
   - If ROI is lower than the cost of debt then the company should not use debt in the capital structure as it would reduce EPS.
5. ***Cost of debt***
   - A firm's ability to borrow at a lower rate increases its capacity to employ higher debt. Hence, more debt can be used if debt can be raised at a lower rate.
6. ***Tax rate***
   - Since interest paid on debt is tax deductible, cost of debt is affected by the tax rate.
   - A higher tax rate makes debt cheaper and increases its attraction in comparison to equity.

Example	*Situation I*	*Situation II*
Total funds	30,00,000	30,00,000
Equity shares (@ Rs. 10 each)	30,00,000	20,00,000
Debt	Nil	10,00,000
Tax rate @ 30%		
Interest on debt @ 10%		
EBIT = Rs. 4 Lacs		

EBIT - EPS analysis (favorable)

Particulars	*I*	*II*
EBIT	4,00,000	4,00,000
Less: Interest on debt @ 10%	0	1,00,000
EBT	4,00,000	3,00,000
Less: Tax @ 30%	1,20,000	90,000
EAT	2,80,000	2,10,000

A comparison of situation I, II in case of favorable financial leverage shows:

1. Loan has increased by Rs. 10,00,000
2. Thereby, interest has increased by Rs. 10,00,000
3. Tax has decreased by 30,000. As interest increases by 1,00,000 and tax reduces by 30,000 the effective interest paid is only Rs.70,000 on a loan of Rs. 10,00,000, i.e. cost of debt/interest becomes cheaper, i.e. only 7% thereby making debt cheaper.

7. ***Cost of equity***
   - Stock owners expect a rate of return from the equity which is commensurate with the risk they are assuming.
   - When a company increases debt, the financial risk faced by the equity holders increases, thereby their desired rate of return may increase. It is for this reason that a company can't use debt beyond a point.
   - If debt is used beyond that point, cost of equity may go up sharply and share price may decrease in spite of increased EPS.

- Therefore, for maximization of shareholder's wealth, debt can be used only up to a level.

8. ***Risks considerations***
   - Use of debt increases financial risk of a business. Financial risk refers to a situation when a company is unable to meet its fixed financial obligations viz interest payment, preference dividend and repayment obligations.
   - In addition, every business has some operating risk also, which is called business risk.
   - Business risk depends upon fixed operating costs. Higher fixed operation costs result in higher business risk and vice-versa.
   - The total risk depends upon both business risk and financial risk.
   - If a firm's business risk is lower, its capacity to use debt is higher and vice-versa.
9. ***Floatation costs***
   - Process of raising resources also involves some cost. Public issue of shares and debentures requires considerable expenditure.
   - Getting a loan from a financial institution may not cost so much.
   - These considerations may also affect the choice between debt and equity and hence the capital structure.
10. ***Flexibility***
    - If a firm uses its debt potential to the full, it loses flexibility to issue further debt.
    - To maintain flexibility, it must maintain some borrowing power to take care of unforeseen circumstances.
11. ***Control***
    - Equity shareholders are the owners of the company who have complete control due to the voting rights they enjoy.
    - Debt does not carry voting rights. If the existing owners of the company wish to retain their control they should opt for raising additional funds through debt.

- If a large amount of debt is raised then the debentures holders may start putting certain terms and conditions on the company thereby making it valuable to takeovers.
- Hence, control is a crucial factor specially in a company in which current holding of management is on a lower side.

12. *Stock market conditions*
    - If the stock markets are bullish, equity shares are more easily sold even at a higher price as use of equity is preferred in such situations.
    - During a bearish phase, a company may find raising of equity capital more difficult and has to opt for debt. During this period, business is slow, investors hesitate to take risk and prefer safe investment in debt because debt ensures fixed payment of interest and repayment of capital.
    - Hence, the stock market conditions affect the choice between the two.
13. *Regulatory framework*
    - Every company operates within a regulatory framework provided by the law.

    For Example:

    Public issue of shares, debentures have to be made under SEBI guidelines (securities and Exchange Based of India)
    - Raising funds from banks and other financial institutions require fulfillment of other norms.
    - The comparative ease with which norms can be met or completed may have a bearing upon the choice of the source of finance.
14. *Capital structure of other companies*
    - In some industries, a useful guideline in the capital structure planning is the debt equity ratio of other companies.
    - There are usually some industry norms which may help. Precaution however must be taken that these are norms are not followed blindly.

    For example:

    If the business risk of a firm is higher, it cannot afford the same financial risk and should go for low debt.

- The management must know what the industry norms are: whether they are following them or deviating from them and adequate justification must be there in both cases.

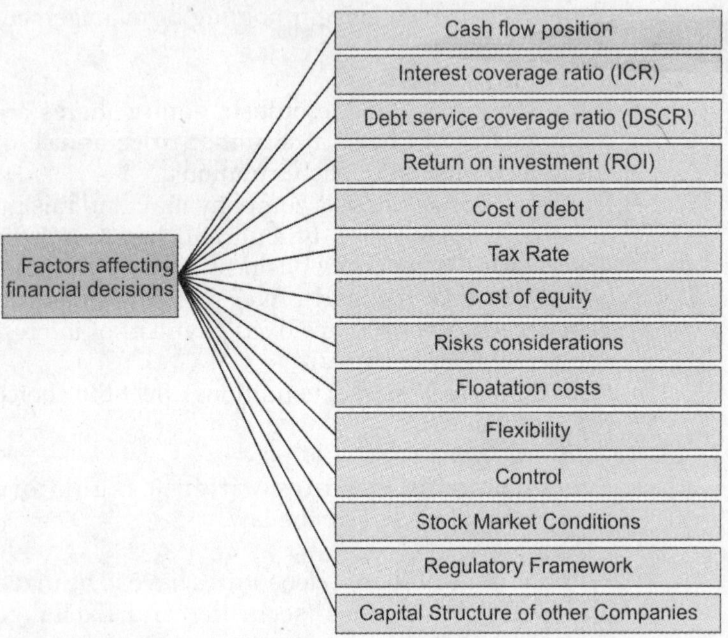

Q33. State any 2 situations where a cash inflow is required.

Ans. To meet

- Normal business operations
- Investment in fixed assets

Q34. Why is ICR not an adequate measure?

or

State the limitations of Interest Coverage Ratio.

Ans. Refer to Ans. 32

Q35. Identify and explain the ratio which takes care of the deficiencies referred to in ICR.

Ans. Debt service coverage ratio (DSCR) covers the deficiencies of ICR. Explain.

Q36. What are the factors affecting dividend decisions?

Ans. The various factors affecting the divided decision are:

1. ***Earning***
   - Earnings is a major determinant of the decision about dividend
   - Dividends are paid out of current and past earnings
2. ***Stability of earnings***
   - Other things remaining the same, a company having stable earnings is in a position to declare higher dividends
   - On the other hand, a company having unstable earnings is likely to pay smaller dividend
3. ***Stability of dividends***
   - Companies generally follow a policy of stabilizing the dividend per share
   - The increase in dividends is generally made when there is confidence that their earning potential has gone up and not just the earnings of the current year
4. ***Growth opportunities***
   - Companies having good growth opportunities retain more money out of their earnings so as to finance the required investment
   - The dividend in growing companies is therefore smaller.
5. ***Cash flow position***
   - Dividends involve outflow of cash
   - Availability of enough cash is necessary for declaration of dividends. A company may be profitable but short on cash.
6. ***Shareholder preference***
   - While declaring dividends, managements keep in mind the preferences of the shareholders in this regard
   - If the shareholders desire that at least a certain amount is paid as dividend, the companies are likely to declare the same
7. ***Taxation policy***
   - If tax on dividend is higher than that on earnings, it would be better to pay less dividends
   - Higher dividends may be declared if the tax on dividend is lower than that on earnings

8. *Stock market reaction*
   - In general, investors view an increase in dividend as a good news and stock prices react positively to it.
   - Similarly, a decrease in dividend may have a negative impact on the share prices in the stock market
9. *Access to capital market*
   - Large and reputed companies generally have easy access to the capital markets and therefore may depend less on retained earnings to finance their growth.
   - These companies tend to pay higher dividends than smaller companies which have relatively low access to the market
10. *Legal constraints*
    - Certain provisions of the Companies Act 1956 place restrictions on payouts as dividend. Such provisions must be adhered to.
11. *Contractual constraints*
    - While granting loans to a company, sometimes the lender may impose certain restrictions on the payment of dividends in the future
    - The companies are required to ensure that the dividends do not violate the terms of the loan agreement

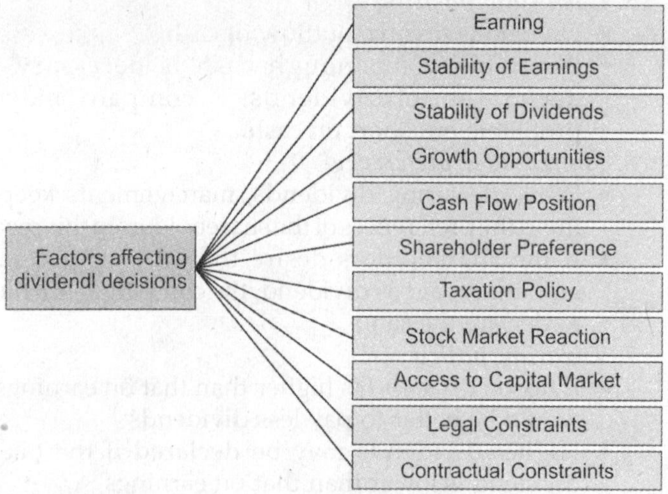

Q37. Discuss whether the working capital requirements of a business dealing with the following products is low or high and give reasons.

Ans.

Table 9.2

Product	*Working capital requirements*	*Reasons*
Bread	Low	• Operating cycle is small • Perishable item, daily sale • Sale price is low • Sold mostly on cash basis
Newspaper	Low	• Life cycle is small as newspaper of one day is discarded on the other day • Sale value is low • Sold mostly on cash basis
Sugar	High	• Ratio of cost of raw materials to the total cost is high • Availability of raw materials is seasonal (sugarcane) so inventory needs to be maintained
Cotton textiles	High	• Same as above
Ice	Low	• Ratio of cost of raw materials to the total cost is low • Sale price is low • Sold mainly on cash basis
Gold jewellery	High	• Ratio of cost of raw materials to the total cost is high • Life span may be large as some pieces of jewellery may not be sold for long periods
Coolers/woolens/ AC/heaters	Fluctuates	• It is high during peak seasons as high demand means higher production which in turn implies higher stock of raw materials and finished goods as well as high operating expenses • Low during off season due to low levels of activity
Cars	Low	• As production is automated, machine oriented and capital intensive, the need for labor and operating expenditure is reduced
Furniture	Low	• No stock needs to be maintained as pieces are made on order • Advance payments are collected thereby reducing working capital needs
Services	Low	• Services are mostly provided on payment of cash or against a small credit period.

10

Financial Markets

Q1. Name the two important sectors of an economic system.

Ans. The 2 important sectors are:

1. Households (savers)
2. Business firms (investors)

Q2. Explain the allocative function performed by financial markets.

Ans.

- A financial market helps to link the savers and investors by mobilizing funds between them. In doing so, it performs what is known as an allocative function.
- It allocates/directs funds available for investment into the most productive investment opportunity. When the allocative function is performed well, 2 consequences follow:
  - The rate of return offered to households would be higher.
  - Scarce resources are allocated to those firms which have the highest productivity for the economy.
- There are 2 major alternative mechanisms by which allocation of funds can be done
  - Banks
  - Financial markets
- Households can deposit their surplus funds with banks, which in turn could lend these to business firms or households can buy shares or debentures offered by business firms.

Q3. Identify the 2 major alternative mechanisms through which allocation of funds can be done?

or

Banks and financial markets are competing intermediaries. Comment.

or

What is meant by *financial intermediaries*?

Ans.

- There are 2 major alternative mechanisms through which allocation of funds can be done via
  - Banks
  - Financial Markets
- Households can deposit surplus money with banks, who in turn could lend it to business firms or households can buy shares and debentures offered by a business firm using financial markets.
- The process by which allocation of funds is done is known as financial intermediation.
- Banks and financial markets are competing intermediaries in the financial system, and give households a choice of where they want to place their savings.

Q4. Explain the meaning of *financial markets*.

Ans.

- A financial market is a market for creation and exchange of financial assets
- They exist wherever a financial transaction occurs.
- Financial transactions could be in the form of creation of financial assets such as the initial issue of shares and debentures by a firm or the purchase and sale of existing financial assets like equity shares, bonds and debentures.

Q5. Name any 2 financial assets.

Ans. Financial assets can be:

1. Shares
2. Debentures

Q6. Explain the concept of financial system.

Ans.

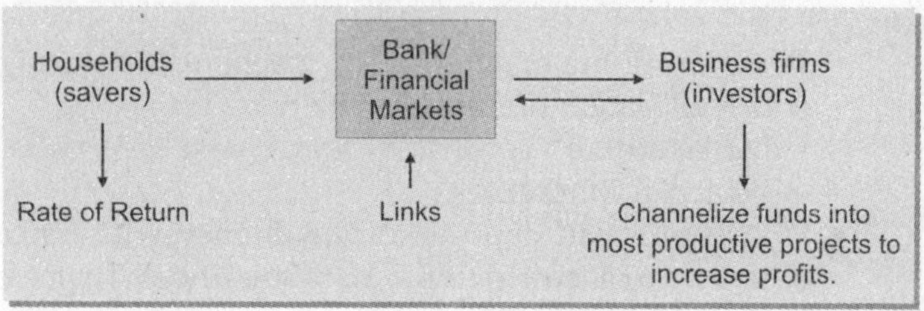

Q7. Discuss the important functions of financial markets.

or

Financial markets play an important role in the allocation of scarce resources in an economy.

Ans. The various functions of financial market are:

1. ***Mobilization of savings and channeling them into the most productive uses***
   - It facilitates the transfer of savings from savers to investors.
   - It gives savers the choice of different investments and thus helps to channelize surplus funds into the most productive use.
2. ***Facilitate price discovery***
   - Forces of supply and demand help to establish a price for a commodity/service in the market.
   - In financial markets, the households are suppliers of funds and business firms represent the demand.
   - This interaction between them helps to establish a price for the financial asset which is being traded in that particular market.
3. ***Provides liquidity to financial assets***
   - They facilitate easy purchase and sale of financial assets.

- Hence they provide liquidity to financial assets, so that they can be easily converted into cash as and when required.
- Holders of assets can readily sell their financial assets through the mechanism of the financial market.

4. *Reduce the cost of transaction*
   - They provide valuable information about securities being traded in the market.
   - It helps save time, money and effort that both buyers and sellers of a financial asset would have to otherwise spend to try and find each other.
   - It is thus, a common platform where buyers and sellers can meet for fulfillment of their individual needs

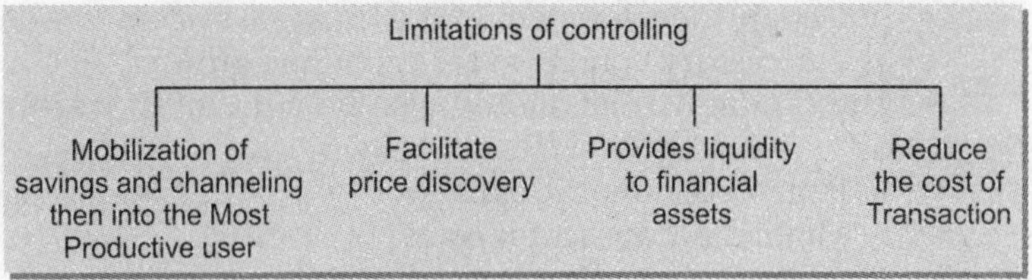

Q8. Identify the supply and demand of funds in financial markets.

Ans. Households are the suppliers of funds and business firms represent demand in a financial market.

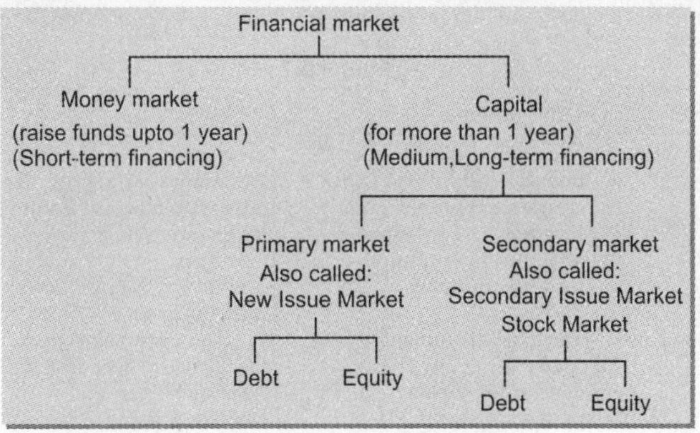

Fig.10.1: Classification of financial markets

Q9. Explain the concept of capital market.

Ans. Capital market refers to facilities and institutional arrangements through which long-term funds both debt and equity are raised and invested.

Q10. What is an ideal *capital market*?

Ans. An ideal capital market is one where finance is available at reasonable cost.

Q11. Development of a financial system is a necessary condition for economic growth. Comment.

Ans.

- The process of economic development is facilitated by the existence of a well functioning capital market
- In fact, the development of the financial system is seen as a necessary condition for economic growth
- The capital market should also be efficient in respect of:
  - Information that it delivers
  - Minimize transaction costs
  - Allocate capital most productively
- It is essential that financial institutions are:
  - Sufficiently developed
  - Market operations are free, fair, competitive and transparent

Q12. Differentiate between capital and money markets.

Ans.

Table 10.1

Basis	*Capital markets*	*Money markets*
Participants	The participants include financial institutions, banks, corporate entities, foreign investors and ordinary retail investors from members of public.	Participation is undertaken by institutional participants like RBI, banks, financial institutions and finance companies. Individual investors although permitted to transact, don't normally do so.
Instruments	The main instruments traded are equity shares, debentures, bonds, preference shares, etc.	The main instruments traded are short-term debt, instruments like trade bill reports, commercial paper, treasury

Contd.

Table 10.1 (*Contd.*)

Basis	*Capital markets*	*Money markets*
		bills, certificates of deposit and call money.
Investment outlay	Investment in securities does not necessarily require huge financial outlay. The value of units of securities is low, i.e. Rs.10 or Rs.100 and minimum trading lot is small, i.e. 10, 50 or 100.	Transactions entail huge sums of money as the instruments are very expensive. For Example: T-bills are available for a minimum amount of Rs.25,000/-
Duration	It deals in medium and long term securities such as equity shares and debentures.	Money market instrument have a maximum tenure of one year and may be even issued for a single day.
Liquidity	These securities are considered liquid investments because they are marketable on the stock exchange but a share may not be actively traded, i.e. it may not easily find a buyer.	These instruments enjoy a higher degree of liquidity as there is a formal arrangement for this. The Discount Finance House of India (DFHI) has been established for the specific objective of providing a ready market for money market instruments.
Safety	These instruments are riskier both with respect to return and principal repayment. Issuing companies may fail to perform as per projections and promoter may defraud investors.	It is much safer with minimum risk of default because of: 1. Shorter duration of investing. 2. Financial soundness of issuers which primarily are the govt. banks and highly rated companies.
Expected returns	The investments generally yield a higher return for investors than money 1. Securities are held for longer duration then there is scope for capital gains in equity shares. 2. In long term, the prosperity of a company is shared by shareholders by way of high dividends and bonus shares.	In money market, the returns are lesser since the securities are held for a shorter period markets. The possibility of time. of returns is higher if:

Q12. Why are money market instruments safer than capital market instruments?

Q13. Why is there a scope of higher earning in capital market instruments?

or

Why are high returns expected in capital markets?

Ans. Refer to the differences for the answers to the above questions

Q14. Explain the meaning/nature/concept of money markets.

Ans.

- The money market is a market for short term funds which deals in monetary assets whose period of maturity is up to one year
- These assets are close substitutes for money
- It is a market where low risk, unsecured and short term debt instruments that are highly liquid are issued and actively traded everyday

Q15. Discuss the nature/concept of primary market.

Ans.

- Primary market is also known as new issue market.
- It deals with new securities being issued for the first time.
- The essential function of a primary market is to facilitate the transfer of investible funds from savers to entrepreneurs, seeking to establish new enterprises or to expand existing ones through the issue of securities for the first time:

Participants:

The investors in this market are banks, insurance companies financial institutions, mutual funds and individuals.

Instruments:

A company can raise capital through the primary market in the form of equity shares, preference shares, debentures, deposits ,loans.

Purpose:

Funds raised may be for setting up new projects, expansion, diversification, modernization of existing projects, mergers and takeovers.

Q16. Discuss the various methods of floating new issues in the primary market

Ans. The various methods of floating new issues in primary markets are:

1. *Offer through prospectus*
   - It is the most popular method of raising funds by public companies in primary market.
   - This involves inviting subscriptions from the public through issue of prospectus.
   - It makes a direct appeal to investors to raise capital, through an advertisement in newspapers and magazines.
   - The issue may be underwritten and is required to be listed on at least one stock exchange.
   - The contents of the prospectus must be in accordance with the provisions of the Companies Act and SEBI disclosure and investor protection guidelines.

   Company ⟶ Prospectus ⟶ Public

2. *Offer for sale*
   - Under this method, securities aren't issued directly to the public but are offered for sale through intermediates like issuing houses or stock brokers.
   - In this case, a company sells securities enbloc at an agreed price to brokers who in turn resell them to the investing public at a higher price to earn profits.

   Company ⟶ Intermediaries/brokers ⟶ General
   (Face value) (Higher value)

3. *Private placement*
   - It is the allotment of securities by a company to institutional investors and some selected individuals.
   - It helps to raise capital more quickly than a public issue
   - Access to the primary market can be expensive on account of mandatory and non mandatory expenses. Thus, it is cost effective

- Some companies which can't afford a public issue, choose to use private placement.

Company selected ⟶ Selected/institutional investor like LIC, UTI, general insurance.

4. ***Rights issue***
   - This is a privilege given to existing shareholders to subscribe to a new issue of shares according to the terms and conditions of the company.
   - The shareholders are offered the 'right' to buy new shares in proportion to the number of share they already possess.

   Company ⟶ Existing shareholders
5. ***e-IPOs***
   - A company proposing to issue capital to the public through the online system of the stock exchange has to:
     - Enter into an agreement with stock exchange which is called Initial Public Offer (IPO).
     - SEBI registered brokers have to be appointed for the purpose of accepting applications and placing orders with the company.
     - The issuer company should also appoint a registrar to the issue having electronic connectivity with the exchange.
     - The issuer company can apply for listing of its securities on any exchange other than the exchange through which it has offered its securities.
   - The lead manager coordinates all activities amongst intermediaries connected with the issue.

Q17. A company wishes to raise money from general public. Explain various methods it can use for floating new issue in the primary market

Ans.

1. Offer for prospectus
2. Offer for sale
3. e-IPOs

Q18. Define a secondary market/stock exchange.

Ans.

- A stock exchange is an institution which provides a platform for buying and selling of existing securities.
- As a market, it facilitates the exchange of a security (share, debentures, etc.) into money and vice-versa.
- According to Securities Contract (Regulation) Act 1956 (SCRA), stock exchange means any body of individuals, whether incorporated or not, constituted for the purpose of assisting, regulating, or controlling the business of buying and selling or dealing in securities.
- It helps companies raise finance, provide liquidity and safety of investment to the investors and enhances the credit worthiness of individual companies.

Q19. What are the functions of a stock exchange?

Ans. The various functions of a stock exchange are:

1. ***Providing liquidity and marketability to existing securities***
   - The basic function of a stock exchange is the creation of a continuous market where securities are bought and sold.
   - It gives investors the chance to disinvest and reinvest.
   - This provides both liquidity and easy marketability to already existing securities in the market.
2. ***Pricing of securities***
   - Share price on a stock exchange is determined by various forces of demand and supply.
   - A stock exchange is a mechanism of constant valuation through which the prices of securities are determined.
   - Such a valuation provides important and instant information to buyers as well as sellers in the market.
3. ***Contributes to economic growth***
   - A stock exchange is a market in which existing securities are resold and traded
   - Through the process of disinvestment and reinvestment savings get channelized into their most productive investment avenues.
   - This leads to capital formation and economic growth.

4. *Safety of transaction*
   - The membership of a stock exchange is well regulated and its dealings are well defined according to the existing legal framework.
   - This ensures that the investing public gets a safe and fair deal on the market.
   - SEBI was established in order to promote a healthy growth of securities market and protection to investors.
5. *Spreading of equity cult*
   - The stock exchange can play a vital role in ensuring wide share ownership by regulating new issues, better trading practices and taking effective steps in educating the public about investments.
6. *Providing scope for speculation*
   - The stock exchange provides sufficient scope within the provisions of law for speculative activity in a restricted and controlled manner.
   - It is generally accepted that a certain degree of healthy speculation is necessary to ensure liquidity and price continuity in the stock market.

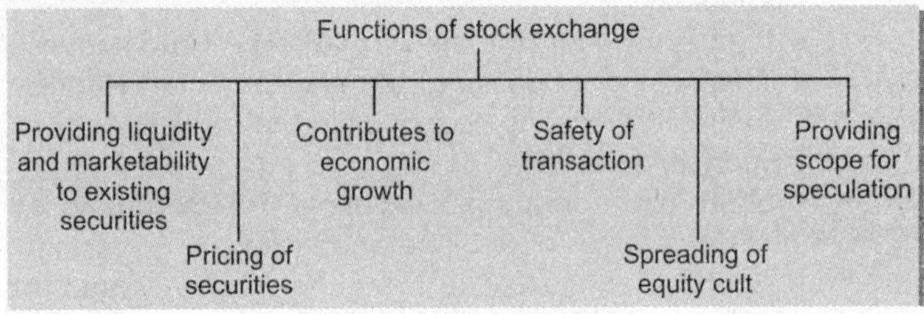

Q20. Explain the trading procedure on a stock exchange.

Ans. Trading procedure involves the following steps:

1. *Selection of a broker*
   - A person intending to buy/sell securities must select a broker who is a member of the stock exchange.
   - Brokers may be individuals, partnership firms or corporate bodies.
   - Earlier, the member brokers owned and managed the stock exchange which led to a conflict of interest between the brokers and their clients.

- Nowadays, the stock exchanges have been demutualized, i.e. ownership rights have been separated from the trading rights of the members.
- The brokers/members are no longer the owners of stock exchange.

2. *Placing the order*
   - After making the choice of a broker, the order is communicated to him personally or through phone, e-mail, etc.
   - The instructions to the broker should specify the name of the securities to be bought/sold and price range within which the order is to be executed.
   - Only securities of listed companies on a stock exchange can be traded.
3. *Executing the order*
   - After the order is received by the broker it needs to be executed.
   - A copy of the transaction containing the name and price of securities along with a brokerage charge by the broker is sent to the client.
   - Initially, trading on a stock exchange was done by auction system but now this method has been replaced by on-line screen based electronic trading system.
4. *Settlement*
   - The mode of settlement depends upon the nature of contract.
   - The mode of settlement may be:
     - Spot/ready deliverycontracts
     - Forward delivery contract
   - Spot delivery is a contract in which actual payment of price by the buyer in cash and delivery of securities by the seller takes place. Such a contract is to be settled either on same day or within a maximum period of a fortnight.
   - Under forward delivery, if a particular share has been put on the forward list on the stock exchange, it means that the contract can be postponed and settled in the next settlement period if both parties agree. Such a postponement is called a badla and it is a unique feature of the Indian stock market. It is

also known as a carryover and certain charges have to be paid called badla charges

- Recently, an electronic book entry form of holding and transferring securities has been introduced. This is known as dematerialization of securities for which buyers and sellers have to open a demat a/c with the designated banks so as to facilitate the transfers from seller to buyer. Dematerialization of securities has helped to eliminate problems of:
  - Theft
  - Forgery
  - Delays
  - Paperwork problems

  All of which were associated with issuing of share certificates which were traditionally regarded as proof of ownership of securities.

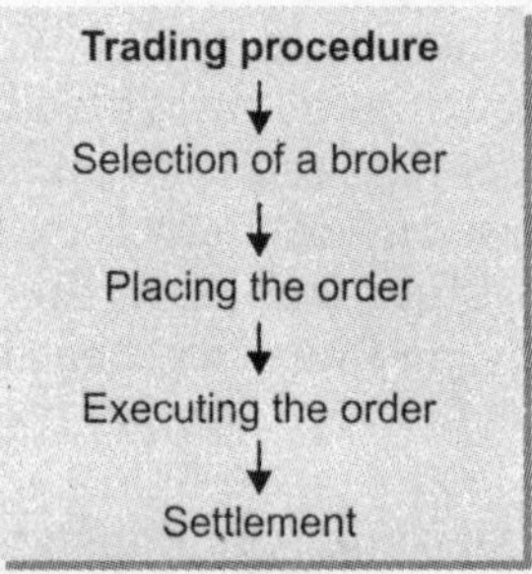

Q21. What is *dematerialization*?

Q22. What is meant by dematerialization of securities?

Ans. Refer Ans.20 for the above questions

Q23. What is meant by accounts w.r.t a stock exchange?

Ans. A stock exchange year is divided into periods which vary from a fortnight to a month. These periods are called accounts.

Q24. How was NSE established and managed?

Ans. NSE (national stock exchange of India)

- Incorporated in 1992
- Recognized as a stock exchange in April 1993

- Started operations in November 1994 (Wholesale Debt Market Segment)
- Started operations in November 1994 (Capital Market Segment)
- Futures and options in June 2000 (Derivatives)
- NSE has set up a nation wide fully automated screen based trading system
- NSE was set up by leading financial institutions, banks, insurance companies and other financial intermediaries. It is managed by professionals, who don't directly/indirectly trade on the exchange.
- The trading rights are with the trading members who offer their services to the investors.
- The board of NSE comprises senior executives from promoter institutions and eminent professionals without having representation from trading members.

Q25. Why was NSE established?

or

NSE has been playing a leading role as a change agent in transforming the Indian capital market. Discuss.

or

NSE was set up with certain specific objectives. Identify and explain these.

Ans. The various objectives of NSE are:

1. *Nationwide trading:* Establishing a nationwide trading facility for all types of securities.
2. *Equal access:* Ensuring equal access to investors all over the country through an appropriate communication network.
3. *Shorter settlement cycles:* Enabling shorter settlement cycles and book entry settlements.
4. *Fair, transparent and efficient market:* Providing a'fair, transparent and efficient securities market using electronic trading system.
5. *Meeting international standards:* Meeting international standards and benchmarks.

Conclusion

1. Within a span of 10 years, NSE has been able to achieve its objectives .
2. NSE has succeeded in taking the stock market to the doorstep of the investors.
3. It has ensured that technology has been harvested to deliver the services to the investors across the country at the lowest cost.
4. It has provided a nation wide screen based automated trading system with a high degree of transparency and equal access to investors irrespective of geographical location.

Q26. Explain the 2 market segments of NSE.

Ans. The 2 market segments of NSE are:

1. *Whole sale debt market segment*
   - This segment provides a trading platform for a wide range of fixed income securities like:
     - Central Govt. securities
     - Treasury Bills
     - State development loans
     - Bonds issued by PSUs
     - Floating rate bonds
     - Commercial paper
     - Zero coupon bonds
     - Index bonds
     - Certificate of deposit
     - Corporate debentures
     - Mutual funds
2. *Capital market segment*
   - This segment of NSE provides an efficient and transparent platform for trading in:
     - Equity shares
     - Preference shares
     - Exchange traded funds
     - Debentures
     - Retail Govt. securities

Q27. Distinguish between NSE and OTCEI (over the counter exchange of India).

Ans.

Table 10.2

Basis	NSE	OTCEI
Size of limited companies	Paid up capital of Rs. 3 cr and above required.	Paid up capital of the company should be Rs. 30 lacs and above.
Establishment	Was established in 1992 and started operations in 1994.	It was established in 1990 and started its operations in 1992.
Objective	Is a nationwide transparent market for providing equal access to investors irrespective of their geographic location.	Is a nationwide transparent exchange for trading in securities of small companies
Securities traded	Capital market as well as money market securities are traded like equity shares, debentures, treasury bills, etc.	Only capital market securities are traded like equity shares and debentures.
Settlement	Payment is made within 15 days of transaction	Payment is made within 7 days of transactions.

Q28. Define the meaning of OTC Markets. State its features.

Ans.

- Over the counter market may be defined as a place where buyers seek sellers and vice-versa and then attempt to arrange terms and conditions for purchase/sale acceptable to both the parties.
- It was set up to provide small and medium companies an access to the capital market for raising finance in a cost effective manner. Example OTCEI, NASDAQ
- It is a negotiated market place that exists anywhere as opposed to the auction market place, represented by the activity on securities exchange.

Q29. Explain the nature/features of NSE.

Ans. Refer Ans. 24
Refer table for features

Q30. What is the purpose of Over the Counter Exchange of India (OTCEI)?

Ans.

- The OTCEI is a company incorporated under the Companies Act 1956. It was set up with the idea to provide small and medium companies an access to the capital market for raising finance in a cost effective manner.
- It is fully computerized, transparent, single window exchange which commenced trading in 1992.
- It was also meant to provide investors with a convenient, transparent and efficient avenue for capital market investment.

Q31. What is the full form of *NASDAQ*?

Ans. NASDAQ stands for National Association of Securities Dealers Automated Quotations. It is the OTC exchange in the USA

Q32. How does trading take place in *OTCEI*?

Ans.

- In the OTC Exchange, trading takes place when a buyer/seller walks up to an OTCEI counter, taps on the computer screen, finds quotes and effects a purchase/sale depending on whether the prices meet the targets. There is no particular market in the geographical sense.
- The OTCEI aims to provide quicker liquidity to securities at a fixed and fair price, liquidity for less traded securities or that of small companies, a simplified process of buying and selling and easy and cheaper means of making public sale of new issues.

Q33. What are the advantages of OTC Market?

Ans. The various advantages of the OTC Market are:

1. ***Trading platform for small and less liquid companies*:** It provides a trading platform to smaller and less liquid companies as they aren't eligible for listing on a regular exchange. Family concern and closely held companies can go public through OTC market.

2. ***Cost effective method***: It is a cost effective method for corporates as there is lower cost of new issues and lower expenses of serving the investors.
3. ***Transparent system:*** It is a transparent system of trading with no problem of bad or short deliveries
4. ***Freedom to dealers:*** Dealers can operate both in new issues and secondary market at their option.
5. ***Freedom of choice to investors***: It gives greater freedom of choice to investors to choose stocks by dealers for market making in both primary and secondary markets.
6. ***Free flow of information:*** Information flow is free and more direct from market makers to customers since there is close contact between them.

Q34. Differentiate between Primary and Secondary Markets.

Ans.

Table 10.3

Basis	*Primary markets*	*Secondary markets*
Nature of securities	There is sale of securities by new companies or further new issues of securities by existing companies to inventors.	There is trading of existing shares only.
Role of company	Securities are sold by the company to the investor directly (or through intermediaries)	Ownership of existing securities is exchanged between investors. The company is not involved at all.
Capital formation	The flow of funds is from savers to investors, i.e. primary market directly promotes capital formation.	It enhances liquidity of shares, i.e. the secondary market indirectly promotes capital formation as the funds don not flow to the company.
Trading (investor's point of view)	Securities can't be sold here, only buying of securities takes place in the primary market,	Both buying and selling of securities can take place on stock exchange.
Price determination	Prices are determined and decided by the management of the company.	Prices are determined by the demand and supply of security.
Geographical	There is no fixed location	It is located at specified places. geographical location.

Q35. What is the full form of *SEBI*?

Ans. SEBI stands for Securities and Exchange Board of India.

Q36. When was SEBI established?

Ans.

- SEBI was established by the Govt. of India on 12 April, 1988 as an interim administrative body to promote orderly and healthy growth of securities market and for investor protection.
- It was to function under the overall administrative control of the Ministry of Finance, Govt. of India.
- It was given a statutory status on 30 January 1992 through an ordinance. The ordinance was later replaced by an act of parliament known as the Securities and Exchange Board of India Act 1992.

Q37. Identify a regulatory body which was setup by the Govt. of India to protect the interest of the investors and regulate the securities market. State the role, purpose and objectives of this body.

Ans. SEBI is the regulatory body which is being talked about:

- It aims at meeting the needs of 3 groups which basically constitute the market viz.
  - Issuers of securities (companies)
  - Investors
  - Market intermediaries

  The objectives of SEBI include:
  1. To regulate stock exchanges and the securities industry to promote their orderly functioning.
  2. To protect the rights and interests of investors, particularly individual investors and to guide and educate them.
  3. To regulate and develop a code of conduct and fair practices by intermediaries like brokers, merchant, bankers, etc. with a view to making them competitive and professional.
  4. To prevent trading malpractices and achieve a balance between self regulation by securities industry and its statutory regulation

Q38. Name the 3 groups which basically constitute the stock markets and how does the environment created by SEBI aims at meeting their needs?

Ans. The 3 groups which constitute the stock markets.

1. ***Issuers of securities (companies)*:** To the issuers it aims to provide a market place in which they can confidently look forward to raising finances they need in an easy, fair and efficient manner.
2. ***Investors:*** To the investors, it should provide protection of their rights and interest through adequate, accurate and authentic information and disclosure of information on a continuous basis.
3. ***Market intermediaries:*** To intermediaries, it should offer a conducive, professionalized and expanding market with adequate and efficient infrastructure so that they're able to render better service to the issuers and investors.

Q39. What is the basic purpose of *SEBI*?

Ans. The basic purpose of SEBI is to create an environmental to facilitate efficient mobilization and allocation of resources through the securities market.

Q40. What were the reasons for establishment of *SEBI*?

Ans.

- The capital market has witnessed a tremendous growth during 1980's characterized particularly by the increasing participation of public. The ever expanding investor populations and market capitalizations led to malpractices on the part of:
  - Companies
  - Brokers
  - Merchant bankers
  - Investment consultants
- Some examples of malpractices include
  - Existence of self styled merchant bankers in official private placement.
  - Rigging of prices.

- Violation of rules of stock exchange
- Unofficial premium on new issues
- Non-adherence of the provisions of Companies Act
- Delay in delivery of shares.

- These malpractices and unfair trading practices have eroded investor confidence and multiplied their grievances.
- The Govt. and stock exchanges were rather helpless in redressing the investors' problem because of lack of proper penal provisions in the existing legislation.
- Govt. of India decided to set up a separate regulatory body known as SEBI.

Q41. Give examples of the malpractices in stock markets.

Ans. Refer Ans. 40.

Q42. State the regulatory functions of SEBI.

Ans. The various regulatory functions of SEBI are:

1. Registration of brokers and sub brokers and other players in the market.
2. Registration of collective investment schemes and mutual funds.
3. Regulation of stock brokers, portfolio exchanges, underwriters and merchant bankers and the business in stock exchanges and any other securities market.
4. Calling for information by undertaking inspection, conducting enquiries and audits of stock exchanges and intermediaries.
5. Regulation of takeover bids by companies.
6. Levying fee or other charges for carrying out the purposes of the act.
7. Performing and exercising such powers under Securities Contract (Regulation) Act 1956, as may be delegated by the Govt. of India.

Q43. State the development functions of SEBI.

Ans. The various development functions of SEBI are

1. Training of intermediaries of the securities market.

2. Undertaking measures to develop the capital markets by adopting a flexible approach.
3. Conducting research and publishing information useful to all market participants.

Q44. State the protective functions of SEBI

Ans. The various protective functions of SEBI are:

1. Prohibition of fraudulent and unfair trade practices viz. misleading statements, manipulations, price rigging
2. Undertaking steps for investor protection.
3. Controlling insider trading and imposing penalties for such practices.
4. Promotion of fair practices and code of conduct in securities market.

Q45. Give the common features of the NSE and OTC markets.

Ans.

Table 10.4

Basis	*NSE*	*OTC*
Institution	Company	Company
Nature	Ringless and fully automated screen based stock exchange	Ringless and fully automated screen based stock exchange
Dealings	Transparent	Transparent
Reach	Nationwide	Nationwide
Promoters	Consortium of financial institutions	Consortium of financial institutions
Place of dealings	Office of NSE member/dealer	Office of OTCEI member/dealer

Q46. Explain the various money market instruments.

Ans.

Table 10.5: Mony market instruments

Basis	*Treasury bills*	*Commercial papers*	*Call money*	*Certificate of deposit*	*Commercial bills*
Issued by	RBI on behalf of the central govt.	Large and credit worthy companies	Commercial Banks	Commercial banks, development financial institutions	Drawer/maker/seller
Issued to	1. Insurance companies 2. Commercial banks	1. Commercial Banks 2. Mutual funds	1. Commercial banks 2. Mutual funds 3. Insurance companies	1. Individuals 2. Corporations 3. Companies	Buyer/payee/drawee
Nature	1. Also called zero coupon bonds 2. Negotiable 3. Freely transferable 4. Promissory note 5. Highly liquid 6. Available for minimum amount of Rs. 25000	1. Unsecured promissory note 2. Negotiable 3. Transferable by endorsement 4. Delivery with a definite fixed maturity period	1. Short term finance repayable on demand 2. Used for inter bank transactions	1. Unsecured 2. Negotiable 3. Short term instruments in bearer form	1. Short term 2. Negotiable 3. Self liquidating instruments
Duration	14 days to 1 year	15 days to 1 year	1 to 15 days	91 days to 1 year	Till maturity
Issued at	Discount for example: Face value = 100000 Issued at a discount at 96000, i.e. 4000 is interest	Discount	Highly volatile interest rate paid on call money known as call rate	Discount	Issued by the seller and accepted by the buyer. Such bills can be discounted with the bank before the maturity date
Purpose	Short term financial needs of the government	1. Seasonal requirements 2. Working capital needs 3. Bridge financing, i.e. floatation costs	Meet the requirements of banks with: 1. Temporary shortage of cash 2. Wants to maintain the cash reserve ratio	Issued during periods of tight liquidity when growth of deposits is slow and demand for credit is high	1. Used to finance the working capital requirements of business firms 2. Facilitate and finance credit sales of firms

Q47. Differentiate between certificate of deposits and fixed deposits.

Ans.

Table 10.6

Basis	*Certificate of deposit*	*Fixed deposit*
Nature	Freely negotiable	Not freely negotiable although they can be pledged
Duration	They can be issued for a period of 91 days to 1 year	They may be issued for a minimum period of 14 days but they may be issued up to any period
Issued at	They are issued at a discount on the actual amount of deposit held	They are issued for the actual amount of deposit

Q48. SEBI is a watchdog of the securities market. Give reasons to support your answer.

Ans. Yes, I agree. Explain protective functions and regulatory functions

Q49. The directors of a newly established company having a paid up share capital of 2.75 cr desire to get its shares traded at an all India level stock exchange. As a finance manager suggest the name of the stock exchange for the purpose. Give 3 reasons in support of your answer.

Ans. They should approach the OTCEI because:

1. The company has a paid up share capital of less than 3 crores
2. In the OTCEI, there is an existence of compulsory market makers (banks, financial institutions) to buy securities for those companies which cannot otherwise find buyers thereby improving their liquidity
3. Less stringent conditions are applicable for listing of securities on the OTCEI as compared to NSE

Q50. The directors of a company want to modernize its plant and machinery by making a public issue of shares. They wish to approach the stock exchange while the finance manager prefers to approach a consultant for a new public issue of shares. Advise the directors whether to approach stock exchange or a consultant for a new public issue of shares and the different methods with which the company may adopt the new public issue of shares.

Ans. The company must approach the consultant because:

1. Stock exchanges are meant for subsequent sale/ purchase of securities
2. The consultant will be able to give their expert advice to the directors

The various methods that the company may adopt for the new public issue of shares are:

1. Offer through prospectus
2. Offer for sale
3. e-IPOs

Q51. What is meant by *bridge financing*?

Ans.

- If a company needs long term finance to buy some machinery then in order to raise the long term funds in the capital market the company will have to incur floatation costs (viz. brokerage, commission, printing of application and advertising)
- Funds raised through commercial paper are used to meet the floatation costs. This is termed as bridge financing.

Q52. What is the relationship between call rate and other short term money market instruments?

Ans. There is an inverse relationship between call rates and other short term money market instruments such as certificates of deposit and commercial paper. A rise in call money rates makes other sources of finance cheaper in comparison for banks.

Q53. What is meant by *SENSEX* ?

Ans.

- SENSEX (Sensitive Index) is the benchmark index of the BSE. As the BSE is the leading exchange of the Indian secondary market, the SENSEX has been an important indicator of the Indian stock market
- An index has just one job, to capture price movement. So a stock index will reflect the price movements of shares
- If SENSEX rises, it indicates the market is doing well. Since stocks are supposed to reflect what companies expect to earn in the future, a rising index indicates that investors expect better earnings from companies
- The SENSEX, launched in 1986 is made up of 30 of the most actively traded stocks representing 13 sectors of the economy. NIFTY comprises 50 stocks representing 21 sectors

Q54. What is a *stock market* index?

Ans.

- A stock market index is a barometer of market behavior.
- It measures overall market sentiment through a set of stocks that are representative of the market
- It reflects the market direction and the day to day fluctuations in the stock prices.
- An ideal stock market index must represent changes in prices of securities and reflect price movement of shares for better market representation

11

Marketing

Q1. What is a *market*?

Ans.

- In the traditional sense, the term 'market' refers to the place where buyers and sellers gather to enter into transactions involving exchange of goods and services.
- This term is also used in the context of:
  - Product market (cotton, gold or share market).
  - Geographical market (national and international).
  - Quantity of goods transacted (retail and wholesale market).
  - Type of buyers (consumer and industrial market).
- In the modern sense, the term has a broader meaning. It refers to a set of actual and potential buyers of a product or service.

For Example:

When a fashion designer designs a new dress and offers it for exchange, all the people who are willing to buy and offer some value for it can be stated to be the market for that dress.

Q2. What is meant by *marketing*?

Ans.

- Traditionally marketing has been described in terms of its functions or activities that direct the flow of goods and services from producers to consumers like:
  - Shopping
  - Selling
  - Designing
  - Merchandising

- In the modern sense, marketing begins even before production (market research) and continues even after selling (customer care)

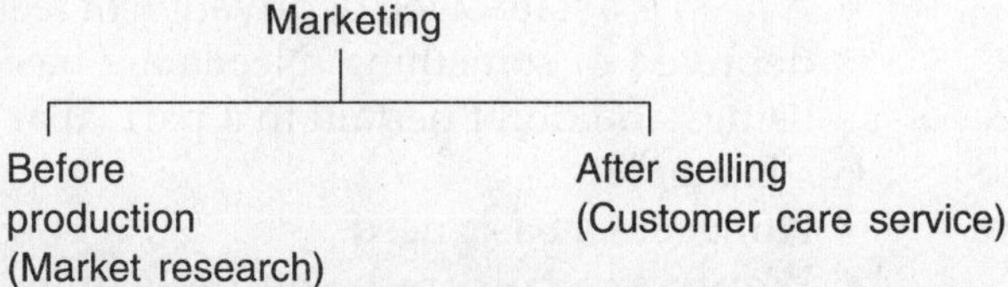

- In modern terms, emphasis is placed on describing marketing as a social process. It is a process whereby people exchange goods and services for money or for something of value to them. Taking the social perspective, Phillip Kotler has defined marketing as, "a social process by which individual groups obtain what they need and want through creating offerings and freely exchanging products and services of value with others. "

Q3. "Marketing is not merely a post-production activity". Do you agree?

Ans. I agree with the above statement as:

- It includes many activities that are performed before production of goods and continue even after selling of goods.
- Such activities include identification of customer needs, collection of information for developing package and giving it a brand name.
- Many follow up activities are required for maintaining good customer relations for procuring repeat sale.

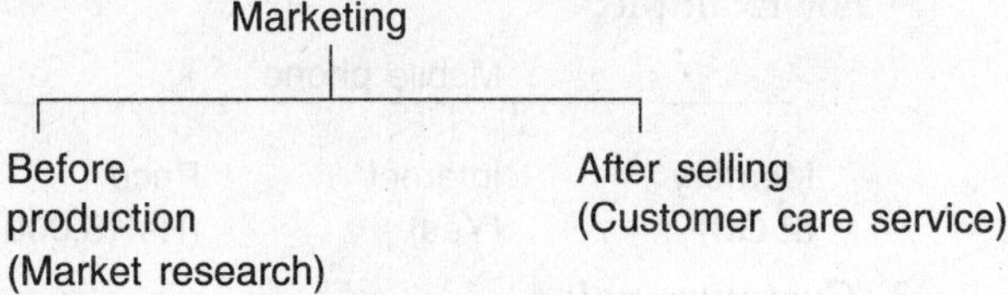

Q4. Explain the features of marketing

Ans. The features of marketing are:

1. ***Need and want***

- The focus of the marketing process is on satisfaction of the needs and wants of individuals and organizations
- A need is a state of felt deprivation or feeling of being deprived of something. Needs are basic to human beings and don't pertain to a particular product

For Example:

Hunger is a basic need.

- Wants are culturally defined objects that are potential satisfiers of needs. Human needs shaped by such factors as culture, personality and religion are called wants.

For Example:

Hunger can be satisfied through rice, chapattis, etc.

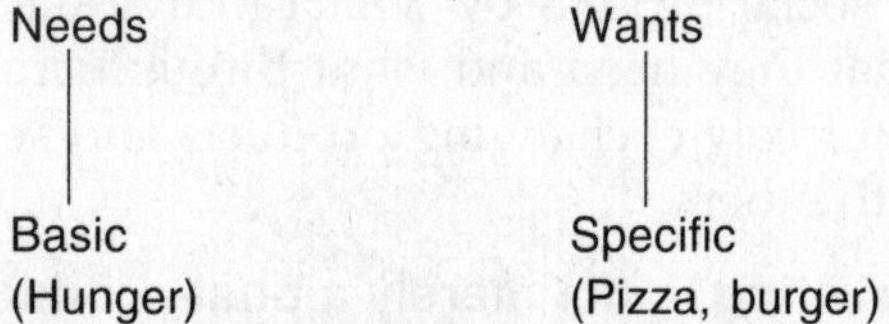

2. *Creating a market offering*
   - Market offering refers to a complete offer for a product or service having given features like:
     - Size
     - Quality
     - Taste

     At a certain price, place and promotional activities
   - A good 'market offer' is one which is developed after analyzing the preferences of the potential buyers

   For Example:

   Mobile phone

Memory	Internet	Price	Camera
(2 GB)	(Yes)	(Rs.15,000)	(2.0 MP)

3. *Customer value*
   - The process of marketing facilitates exchange of products and services between the buyers and sellers

- The buyers make buying decisions based on their perceptions of the value of the product or service in satisfying their needs in relation to its cost
- The job of a marketer is to add to the value of the product so that the customers prefer it in relation to the competing products and decide to purchase it.

4. *Exchange mechanism*
   - The process of marketing involves exchange of products and services for money or any other thing considered valuable.
   - Exchange refers to the process through which 2 or more parties come together to obtain the desired product or service from someone, offering the same by giving something in return
   - Exchange is referred to as the essence of marketing. For any exchange to take place, certain conditions must be satisfied.
     - Involvement of at least 2 parties viz. buyers and sellers
     - Each party should be capable of offering something of value to other

   For Example:

   Seller offers product, buyer offers money
     - Each party should have the ability to deliver the product or service
     - Each party should have the freedom to accept or reject other party's offer
     - The parties should be willing to enter into transaction with each other.

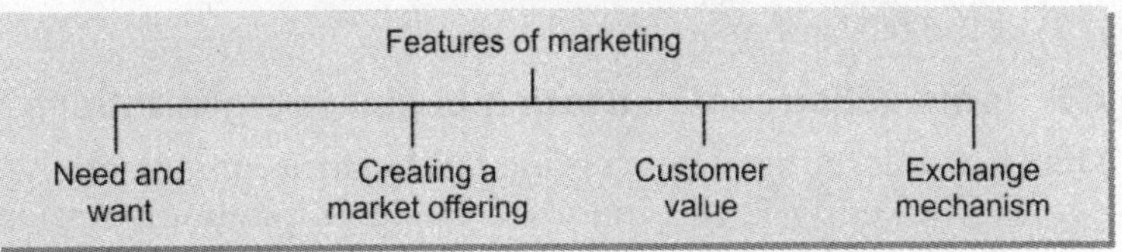

Q5. Differentiate between Need and Want.

Ans. The differences between need and want are:

Table 11.1

Basis	*Need*	*Want*
Meaning	It is a state of felt deprivation or feeling of being deprived of something	They are culturally defined objects that are potential satisfiers of needs
Nature	They are basic in nature	They are more specific in nature
Example	Hunger is a basic need	Food like rice, pizza can satisfy hunger

Q6. In the light of the statement "Exchange is the essence of marketing", state the conditions that are required to facilitate an exchange.

Ans. The following conditions are required to facilitate an exchange:

1. Involvement of at least 2 parties viz. the buyer and the seller
2. Each party should be capable of offering something of value to the other

For Example:

The seller offers a product and the buyer offers money for it.

3. Each party should have the ability to communicate and the deliver the product or service
4. Each party should have the freedom to accept or reject other party's offer
5. The parties should be willing to enter into transaction with each other. Thus, the acceptance or rejection of the offer takes place on voluntary basis rather than on the basis of any compulsion.

Q7. Is marketing confined to only business organizations?

Ans. No, marketing is not confined to business organizations.

- Marketing is not merely a business phenomenon or confined to business organizations

- Marketing activities are equally relevant to non-profit organizations such as hospitals, schools, sports clubs, religious and social organizations
- It helps these organizations in achieving their goals such as spreading the message of family planning, improving the literacy standards of people and providing medication to the sick.

Q8. What can be marketed?

or

Define a product with suitable examples.

Ans.

- A product is a 'source of satisfaction' or a 'bundle of utilities', that can be used to satisfy human needs and wants
- Anything that is of value to the buyer can be termed as a 'product'. It can be tangible which can be felt, seen and touched physically such as a pen, cycle, etc. or intangible such as services rendered by an accountant, doctor, lawyer, etc.
- A product can be in the form of:
  - Physical products (DVD Players, cell phones)
  - Services (Insurance, banking)
  - Persons (For election of candidates for posts)
  - Ideas (polio vaccination, helpage)
  - Place (Visit Agra-city of love, Udaipur – The city of lakes)
  - Experience (Lunch with a celebrity, experience of mountaineering)
  - Properties (Intangible rights of ownership in financial property)
  - Information (Research organization, technology information)
  - Organization (For boosting their public imafe org. like Dabur, Ranbaxy)
  - Events (Sports events, Diwali, etc)

Q9. Who is a marketer?

or

Does the marketer refer to the seller only?

Ans. No, the marketer does not refer to the seller only.

- Marketer refers to any person who takes more active part in the process of exchange
- Normally, it is the seller who is more active in the exchange process
- However, in certain situations the buyer may be taking more active role in the exchange process, say in situations of rare supply

For Example:

Buyer may be taking extra efforts in persuading the seller to sell the product to him/her in situations of defense deals or where a country having installed a nuclear plant needs the supply of nuclear fuel or 'heavy water'.

Q10. Explain the meaning of marketing management.

or

Define marketing management.

Ans.

- Marketing management refers to.
  - Planning
  - Organizing
  - Controlling.
  - Directing

    Of activities which facilitate exchange of goods and services between producers and consumers or users of products and services
- Philips Kotler has defined marketing management as the act and science of choosing target markets and getting, keeping and growing customers through creating, delivering and communicating superior customer values of management.

Q11. State the process of marketing management.

Ans.

- Philip Kotler has defined it as the act and science of choosing target markets and getting, keeping and growing customers through creating, delivering and communicating superior customer values of management.

- The process includes:
  i. *Choosing a target market*: Say a manufacturer may choose to make readymade garments for children up to the age of 5 years.

  ii. *Creating demand:* In respect of the target market chosen, the focus of the process of management is on
     - Getting
     - Keeping —> Customers
     - Growing

     Meaning that the marketer has to create a demand for his product so that the target customers purchase it, keep them satisfied with the firm's products and also attract more customers to the firm's product so that the firm can grow.

  iii. *Superior customer values:* The mechanism for achieving the objective is through
     - Creating
     - Developing
     - Communicating

     Superior values for customers. This means that customers are attracted to the products and services and communicate these values to the prospective buyers and persuade them to buy these products.

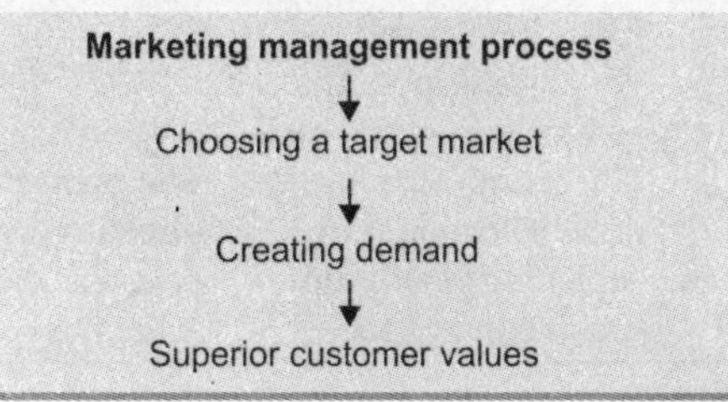

Q12. "Marketing management is not only concerned with creating demand but with managing the demand effectively". Explain.

Ans.

- Marketing management is generally related to creation of demand but in certain situations, the manager has to restrict the demand
- The job of marketing managers, in these situations would be to find ways to reduce the demand temporarily by:
  - Reducing the expenditure on promotion
  - Increasing the prices
- If the demand is 'irregular; such as in case of seasonal products (a/c, woolens) the marketer's job is to change the time pattern of demand through such methods as providing the buyers with short-term incentives. e.g. In early 90s, the excess demand for consumer products had to handled effectively by marketing managers.

Q13. Distinguish between marketing and selling.

or

Marketing and selling are synonymous. Comment

Ans. The difference between market and selling are:

Table 11.2

Basis	*Marketing*	*Selling*
Scope or wider term versus part of the process	It is a much wider term consisting of a number of activities viz. identification of customer's needs, developing the products to satisfy their needs, fixing prices and persuading potential buyers to buy the same	It is a narrower term and is a part of the process of marketing and is concerned with promoting, transfer of possession and ownership of goods from seller to buyer
Focus on satisfying customer needs vs. transfer of	Marketing activities put greater focus on achieving maximum satisfaction of the	The main focus is on affecting transfer of title, possession of goods from sellers to consumers/users

Contd.

Table 11.2 *(Contd.)*

Basis	*Marketing*	*Selling*
title	customer's needs and wants	
Objective of profit maximization through customer satisfaction vs. maximizing sales	It is aimed at customer satisfaction and thereby increasing profit in the long run.	It is directed at maximizing sales and profits of the firm, Thus emphasis is on profit maximization through maximization of sales
Duration or start and end of activities	Marketing activities start much before the product is produced and continue even after the sale of the product	They start after the product has been developed
Difference in emphasis	The emphasis is to develop the product and other strategies as per customer needs	The emphasis is on bending the customer according to the product
Difference in strategies	It uses integrated marketing efforts involving strategies in respect of: i. Product ii. Promotion iii. Physical distributioni v. Pricing	It involves promotion and persuasion

Q14. What is meant by *selling*?

Ans. Refer to the differences.

Q15. Which marketing philosophy existed during industrial revolution? Explain

Ans. Production concept existed during the industrial revolution.

- In those days, the demand for industrial goods was more than the supply.
- The focus of business activities was on production of goods as demand was greater than supply.
- It was believed that profits could be maximized by producing at large scale, thereby reducing the average cost of production.
- Consumers would prefer those products which were widely available at an affordable price.

- Availability and affordability of the product were considered to be key to the success of a firm.
- Emphasis was placed on improving the production and distribution efficiency of the firms.

Q16. Which marketing management philosophy focuses on quality rather than quantity? Identify and Explain.

or

Explain the product concept as a marketing philosophy.

Ans.

- With increase in the supply of the products, customers started looking for products which were superior in quality, performance and features.
- The emphasis of the firms shifted from quantity to the quality of products.
- Under the concept of product orientation product improvement became the key to profit maximization of a firm,

Q17. Making sale through any means became important in one of the marketing philosophies. Identify and Explain.

Ans. Selling concept laid emphasis on making sale through any means.

- It was assumed that the customers would not buy, or not buy enough, unless they are adequately convinced and motivated to do so.
- Therefore, firms must undertake aggressive selling and promotional efforts to make customers buy their products.
- The use of promotional techniques such as :
  - Advertising
  - Sales promotion
  - Personal selling
  - Publicity

  It was considered essential for selling of products.
- The focus of business firms shifted to pushing the sales of products through aggressive selling techniques with a view to persuade, lure or coax the buyers to buy the products.

Q18. What factor was ignored in the selling concept?

Ans. Customer satisfaction was ignored in the selling concept.

Q19. What factor was ignored in the product concept?

Ans. Selling and promotional techniques were ignored in the product concept.

Q20. What was ignored in the production concept?

Ans. Quality of products was ignored in the production concept.

Q21. Identify and explain the concept in which the basic role of a firm is to "identify a need and fill it".

or

State the pillars of marketing concept.

Ans. Marketing concept is the case in point.

- As per this concept, customer satisfaction becomes the focal point of all decision making.

For example:

What product will be produced by the firm, with what features and at what price it will be sold depends on the customer's wants.

- The basic role of a firm is to "identify a need and fill it".
- The pillars of this concept are:
  - Identification of market or customers who are chosen as the target of marketing effort.
  - Understanding needs of customer in the target market.
  - Development of products or services for satisfying needs of the target market.
  - Satisfying needs of target market better than the competitor.
  - Doing all this at a profit.

Q22. Identify the marketing philosophy which is considered to be the extension of marketing concept.

Ans. The societal marketing concept is the case in point.

- It was realized that the business orientation should not be short-sighted to serve only customer's needs but should also consider large issues of long-term social welfare.

- This concept is the extension of the marketing concept as supplemented by the concern for the long-term welfare of the society.
- This concept holds that the task of any organization is to identify the needs and wants of the target market and deliver the desired satisfaction in an effective and efficient manner so that the long-term well-being of the consumer and the society is taken care of.
- It pays attention to the social, ethical and ecological aspects of marketing like deforestation, inflation, environmental pollution, population explosion, etc.

Q23. What factor was ignored in the marketing concept?

Ans. Long term social welfare was ignored in the marketing concept.

Q24. Distinguish between the various marketing management philosophies.

Ans. The differences between the marketing management phihosophies are:

Table 11.3

Basis	*Production concept*	*Product concept*	*Selling concept*	*Marketing concept*	*Societal concept*
Starting point	It starts at the factory	It starts at the factory	It starts at the factory	It starts in the market	It starts in the market and the society.
Main focus	Focus is on quality of product	It focuses on quality, performance features of product	It focuses on the existing product	It focuses on the customer's needs	It focuses on customer's needs and society's well being.
Means	The means used is the availability	The means is product improvement and affor-dability of product	The means is selling and promoting	The means is integrated marketing	The means is integrated marketing
Ends	It aims at profit through volume of production	It aims at profit through product quality	It aims at profit through sales volume	It aims at profit through customer satisfaction	It aims at profit through customer satisfaction and social welfare.

Q25. With the help of suitable examples identify the factors which affect marketing decisions.

Ans.

- The factors affecting marketing decisions can be divided into:
  1. Controllable factors
  2. Non-controllable factors
- Controllable factors are those factors which can be influenced at the level of the firm.
- They include decisions related to:
  - Product
  - Place
  - Price
  - Promotion

Example:

To offer a product, i.e. soft drink, various decisions related to price, place, promotion, etc have to be taken.

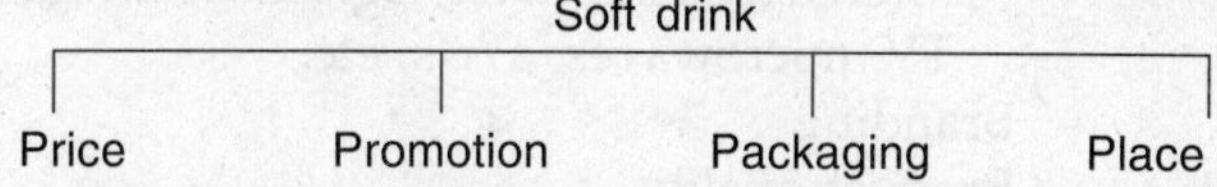

- Environmental variables are certain factors which affect the decision but are not controllable at the firm's level.
- They may arise due to these changes:
  - Political
  - Economic
  - Legal
  - Technological

  } Environmental variables

Example:

Political factors like govt. policy, production or economic factors such as rate of inflation or credit policy of the central bank.

Q26. What is meant by *marketing mix*?

or

Explain the various elements of marketing mix.

Ans.

- Marketing mix refers to combination of variables or marketing tools chosen by a firm to prepare its market offering. It is also known as the 4Ps of marketing namely:

1. Product
2. Price
3. Place
4. Promotion.

1. ***Product***
   - It refers to a bundle of utilities or source of satisfaction that can be used to satisfy human needs and wants.
   - Product can be in the form of:
     i. Physical product
     ii. Ideas
     iii. Services
     iv. Persons, etc.
   - The concept of product also includes:
     - Product mix
       - It refers to the total number of products being offered by a marketer, e.g. LG electronics offers TV, microwaves, a/c's, etc.
     - Branding
     - Product quality
     - Design
     - Packaging
     - Labeling, etc
2. ***Price***
   - It is the amount of money customers have to pay to obtain the product.
   - The pricing decisions include the following:
     - Price level
     - Pricing policy
     - Pricing strategies
     - Margins
     - Price change.
   - The marketers not only decide about the objectives of price setting but also analyze the factors affecting the price and fix a price for the firm's products.
3. ***Place/physical distribution***
   - They include activities that make firm's products available to the target customers.
   - The important decisions in this area include:

- *Channel of distribution:* Includes selecting middlemen like wholesalers, retailers in order to reach the final customer.
- *Physical distribution:* This is the physical movement of goods from the producers to the customers. The important areas include:
  - Transportation
  - Warehousing
  - Inventory
  - Order processing.

4. ***Promotion***
   - They include activities that communicate availability, features, merits etc of the products to the target customers and persuade them to buy it.
   - Most marketing organizations undertake different promotional activities and spend substantial amount of money on the promotion of their goods through these tools:
     - Advertising
     - Publicity
     - Personal selling
     - Sales promotion

   For Example:

   In respect of advertising, it is important to decide about the message and the media to be used (print media, newspaper)to promote the message.

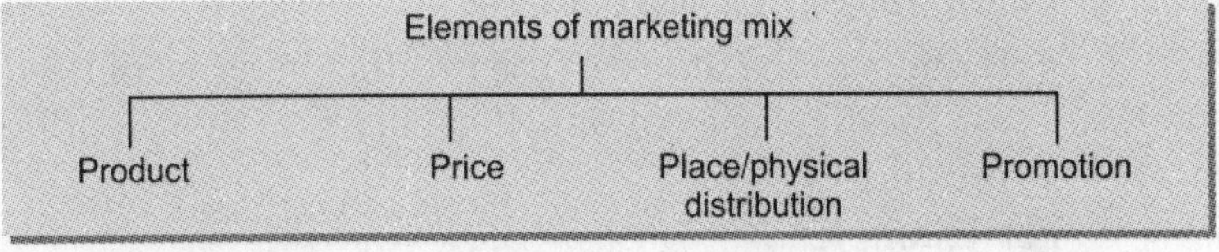

Q27. What determines the success of a market offer?

Ans. The 4 Ps of marketing:

1. Product
2. Price
3. Place
4. Promotion

Determine its success. These must be mixed to create superior value for customers and thus achieve their sale and profit objectives.

Q28. Explain the meaning of product

Ans. Refer to previous answer

Q29. Identify the element of marketing mix which has both tangible and intangible attributes.

Ans. Product is the mixture with both the above attributes.

Q30. State the 3 types of benefits the customers seek to satisfy from the purchase of product.

Ans. The 3 types of benefits the customers seek to satisfy from the purchase of products are:

1. ***Functional benefits:***
   - It refers to a basic utility or a functional benefit derived from the usage of product.

   For Example:

   The purchase of motorcycle provides functional utility of transportation.
2. ***Social benefits:***
   - It refers to the benefit in terms of acceptance from a group in the society, i.e. related to the social status.

   For Example:

   Driving a BMW attaches social status to the person.
3. ***Psychological benefits:***
   - It refers to the utility of the product in terms of need for prestige, esteem or self-satisfaction by using the product.

   For Example:

   A consumer derives psychological benefit by driving a Honda, Toyota, etc.

Q31. Classify products into 2 broad categories.

Ans. Products can be classified into:

1. Consumer products
2. Industrial products

Q32. With the help of suitable examples explain consumer products.

Ans.

- Consumer products are purchased by the ultimate consumers or users for satisfying their personal needs and desires.

For Example:

Soap, edible oil, textiles, fans, etc.

- They are further classified on the basis of
  a. *Shopping efforts involved:* On the basis of time and effort buyers are willing to spend on the purchase of a product, we can classify them into:
     - *Convenience products:* They are purchased frequently, immediately and with least time and effort.
     - *Shopping products:* Buyers devote considerable time in purchase of these products to compare quality, price, style, suitability, etc at several stores before undertaking final purchase.
     - *Specialty products:* They have certain special features because of which people make special efforts in their purchase.
  b. *Durability of products*: On the basis of durability, they can be classified into:
     - *Non-durable products:* Tangible products which are normally consumed in one or few uses.
     - *Durable products:* Tangible products which survive many uses.
     - *Services:* Intangible activities, benefits or satisfaction offered for sale.

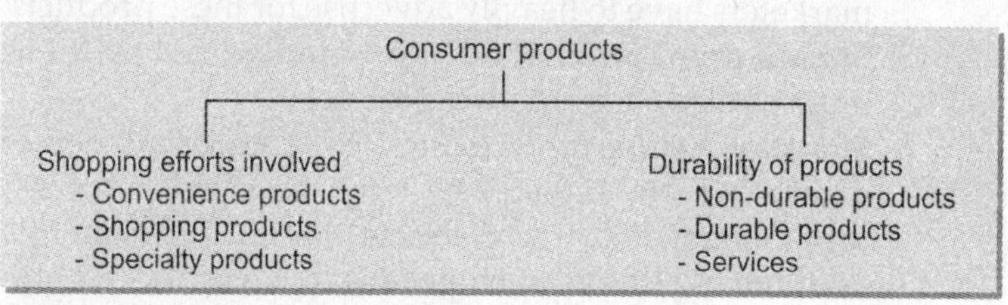

Q33. Identify and explain the features of those consumer products which are purchased frequently with the least time and effort.

Ans. Convenience products are purchased frequently.
For Example:
Cigarettes, ice-cream, medicine.

Fig. 11.1: Convenience products

1. ***Convenient location:*** These products are purchased at convenient locations with least time and efforts.
2. ***Regular and continuous demand:*** They have a regular and continuous demand, as these generally come under the category of essential products.
3. ***Low unit price:*** They have small unit of purchase and low prices.

For Example:
Eggs are sold at Rs. 28 per dozen and customers purchase them in small numbers

4. ***High competition:*** The competition in these products is high as the supply is greater than the demand. The marketers have to heavily advertise for these products.
5. ***Standardized price:*** They have standardized prices as most of these are branded products.
6. ***Short term sales incentives:*** Sales promotion schemes or short term incentives such as sales contests, promotional discount offers, etc play an important role in the marketing of such products.

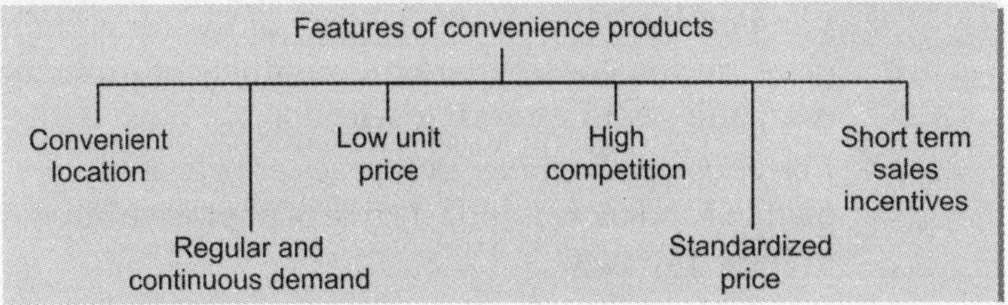

Q34. Identify and explain the characteristics of those consumer goods which require a considerable time in order to purchase the goods.

Ans. Shopping products require a considerable time in order to make their purchase.

Fig. 11.2: Shopping products

- They are those consumer goods, in the purchase of which buyers devote considerable time to compare the quality, price, style, etc. at several stores before the final purchase.

For Example:

Clothes, shoes, TV, washing machine, mobile phones, jewellery

Their characteristics are.

1. ***Durable nature***: They are generally of a durable nature, i.e. they normally survive many uses.
2. ***High unit price:*** The unit price as well as profit margin of shopping products is generally high.

3. ***Comparison of products:*** Because of their high unit price, customers compare the products of different companies before making selection.
4. ***Pre-planned shopping:*** Purchases are generally pre-planned and there is little degree of impulsive buying in these products.
5. ***Persuasive efforts:*** Retailers generally play an important role in the sale of shopping products as a lot of persuasive effort is needed to convince the buyers to purchase them.

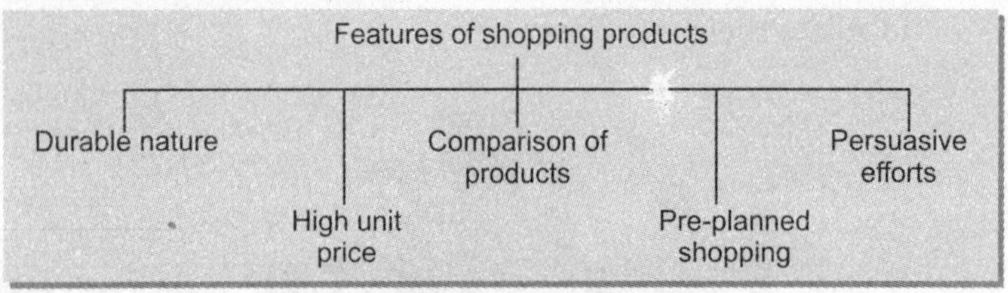

Q35. Identify the consumer goods which have a brand loyalty of the highest order. State its characteristics.

Ans. Specialty products are those consumer goods which have certain special features because of which people make special efforts in their purchase.

Fig. 11.3: Specialty products

- These products have reached a brand loyalty of the highest order with a significant number of buyers. The buyers are willing to spend a lot of time and efforts on their purchase.

For Example:

Rare collection of art work, antiques

- The demand for these goods is relatively inelastic, i.e. even if the price is increased the demand does not come down. Their characteristics are:
  1. ***Limited demand***: The demand is limited as relatively small number of people buy these products.
  2. ***High unit price:*** These products are generally costly and their unit price is very high.
  3. ***Aggressive promotion:*** An aggressive promotion is required for their sale, in order to inform people about their availability, features, etc.
  4. ***Sale at selected places:*** These products are available for sale at few places as number of customers is small and are willing to take extra efforts in the purchase of these products.
  5. ***After sales services***: After sales services are very important for many of the specialty products.

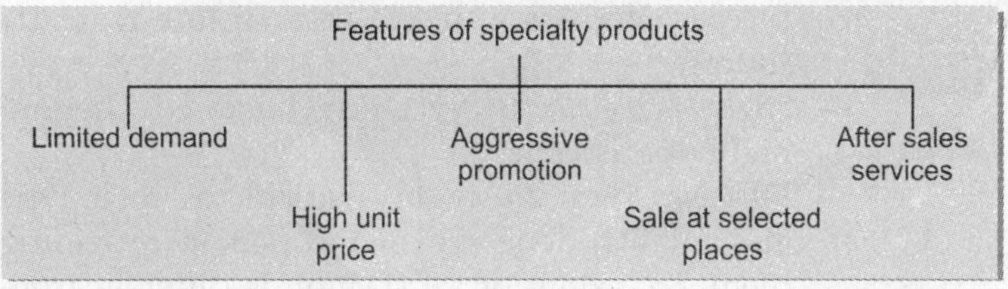

Q36. Explain consumer products on the basis of shopping efforts involved.

Ans. Explain all 3 with 3 characteristics each.

Q37. Explain the 3 types of consumer goods on the basis of durability.

Ans. On the basis of durability, consumer products are of 3 types

1. *Non-durable products*
   - They are tangible and are normally consumed in one or few uses.
   - They generally command a small margin, should be made available in many locations and need to be heavily advertised.

2. ***Durable products***
   - They are tangible consumer products which normally survive many uses.
   - These goods are generally used for a long period, command a higher per unit margin, require personal-selling efforts, guarantees and after sales services, on the part of the seller.

   For Example:

   Refrigerator, radio, bicycle.
3. ***Services***
   - By services we mean those activities, benefits or satisfaction which are offered for sale. They are intangible in form.

   For Example:

   Dry cleaning, nail cutting, water repairs, postal services. Their characteristics are:
   - *Intangible:* They are intangible, i.e. we can't see, touch, feel them.
   - *Inseparable:* A service is inseparable from its source.
   - *Highly perishable:* Services can't be stored. They are highly perishable.
   - *Variable:* They are highly variable as their type and quality depends on the person providing them, i.e. extent of satisfaction is different from the different services provided by different people.

Q38. What is meant by industrial products?

Ans.

- They are those products which are used as inputs in producing other products.
- They are meant for non-personal and business use.
- The market for industrial products consists of insurance companies, mining companies and public utilities.

For Example:

Raw material, engines, lubricants, machines, tools, etc.

Q39. Explain the characteristics of industrial and consumer products.

or

Distinguish between Industrial and Consumer Products.

Ans. The differences between industrial and consumer product are:

Table 11.4

Basis	*Industrial product*	*Consumer product*
Number of buyers	The number of buyers are limited.	As compared to industrial products, the number of buyers are more.
Channel levels	Because of limited buyers, the sale is made with the help of short channels of distribution, i.e. direct selling or one level selling.	Because of more buyers, the sale is made with the help of longer channels of distribution, i.e. multiple level selling.
Geographic concentration	Because of location of industries at certain regions, industrial markets are highly concentrated geographically, e.g. demand for power loom comes from Bombay, Sholapur where textile industry is concentrated.	Because of more buyers, the sale is made through longer channels of distribution, i.e. multiple level selling.
Derived demand	Their demand is derived from the demand of consumer products, e.g. Demand for leather is derived from demand for shoes.	Their demand is direct.
Role of technical considerations	They assume greater significance in the purchase of industrial products as they are complex products.	In consumer products, it is relatively less since the products are less complex.
Customer attitude and motive	An industrial buyer is expected to be more rational and will study the cost of different available brands, their technical specification, goodwill of supplies.	A consumer product buyer may be more impulsive and emotional who is susceptible to advertising and various sales promotion schemes

Note: Only for industrial products*

7. *Reciprocal buying**
   - It refers to a two-way transaction between two companies, i.e. from the buying perspective. Both companies buy from each other.

   For Example:

   Ashok Leyland may buy tyres from MRF and MRF may buy trucks from Ashok Leyland.
8. *Leasing out*
   - A growing trend in industrial product market is to lease out rather than to purchase the products on an outright basis. This is because of the heavy price of these products.

Q40. With the help of an example explain reciprocal buying.

Ans. Refer ans. 39

Q41. Categorize the industrial products.

Ans. The industrial goods can be classified into:

1. *Materials and parts*
   - These include goods that enter the manufacturer's products completely. They are of 2 types:
     - Raw materials
       - Farm products (cotton, sugar cane, oil seed)
       - Natural products (fish, lumber)
     - Manufactured materials and parts
       - Component parts (tire, electric bulb, battery)
       - Component materials (glass, iron, plastic)
2. *Capital items*
   - These are such goods that are used in the production of finished goods. They include:
     - *Installations:* Like elevators, computers, mainframe
     - *Equipments:* Like hand tools, personal computer, fax machines.
3. *Supplies and business services*
   - These are short lasting goods or services that help in developing or manufacturing the finished product. They include:
     - *Maintenance and repair items:* Like paint, nails
     - *Operating supplies:* Like lubricant, computer stationery, writing paper.

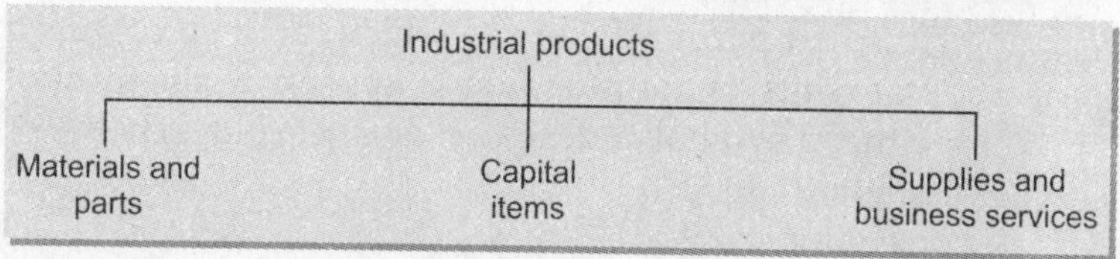

Q42. What is a generic name?

Ans.

- Generic name refers to the name of the whole class of the product.
- If products were sold by generic names it would become difficult for the marketer to distinguish their products from that of their competitors.

For Example:

A book, a wristwatch, soap, detergent, etc.

Q43. Explain the following terms:

Ans.

1. ***Brand***
   - A brand is a name, term, sign, symbol, design or some combination of them, used to identify the product – goods or services of one seller or group of sellers and to demarcate them from those of other competitors

   For Example:

   Some common brands are Bata, Lifebuoy, Ponds, etc.
   - It is a competitive term which has 2 components:
     - Brand name
     - Brand mark

   For Example:

   Asian paints has the symbol of Gattu on its pack.
2. ***Branding***
   - It is the process of giving a name or a sign or a symbol, etc to a product.
3. ***Brand name***
   - It is the part of a brand which can be spoken. In other words, it is the verbal component of a brand

   For Example:

   Asian paints, Safola, Maggie.
4. ***Brand mark***

- It is that part of the brand which can be recognized but which is not utterable. It appears in the form of either a symbol, a design, a distinct color scheme or a letter.

For Example:
Gattu of Asian Paints, Devil of Onida

5. *Trade mark*
   - It is a brand or a part of a brand that is given legal protection.
   - The protection is given against its use by other firms. Thus, the firm which has got its brand registered gets the exclusive rights for its use. No other firm can use such name or mark in the country.

Q44. Branding offers several advantages to the marketers. Discuss.

Ans. The various advantages are:

1. *Product differentiation*
   - Branding helps a firm in distinguishing its products from that of its competitors.
   - This enables the firm to secure and control the market for its product.
2. *Differential pricing*
   - Branding enables a firm to charge different prices for its products than that charged by its competitors.
   - This is possible because if customers like a brand and become habitual of it, they don't mind paying a little extra for it.
3. *Advertising and display programs*
   - A brand aids a firm in its advertising and display programmes.
   - Without a brand name, the advertiser can only create awareness for the generic product and can never be sure of the sale for his product.
4. *Ease in Introduction of new product*
   - If a new product is introduced under a known brand, it enjoys reflected glory of the brand and is likely to start off excellently.
   - Many companies with established brand names decide to introduce new products in the same name.

For Example:

Food specialties Ltd had a successful brand Maggie (noodles). It extended this name to many of its new products such as tomato ketchup, soup, etc.

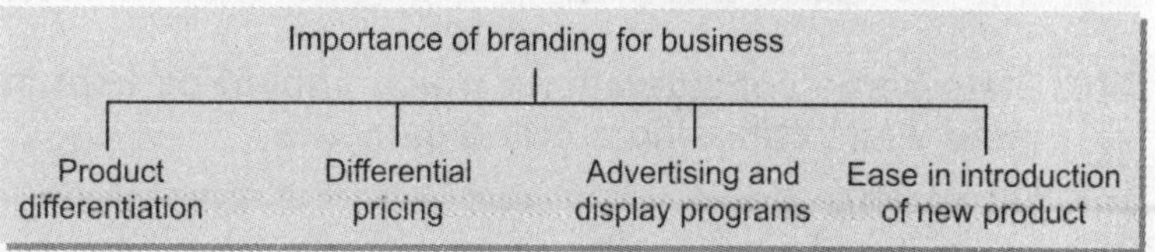

Q45. Identify a process which involves giving a name, sign or symbol which is used to identify the products. Discuss the advantages of this process to the customers.

Ans. Branding is the process which is being talked about. The advantages are:

1. ***Helps in product identification***
   - It helps the customers in identifying the products. Branding greatly facilitates the repeat purchase of the product.

   For Example:

   If a person is satisfied with a particular brand of soap, he need not make a close inspection every time he has to buy that product.
2. ***Status symbol***
   - Some brands become status symbols because of their quality.
   - The consumers of those brands of products feel proud of using them and adds to the level of satisfaction of the customers.
3. ***Ensures quality***
   - It ensures a particular level of quality of the product. Whenever there is any deviation in the quality, the customers can have recourse to the manufacturer or marketer.
   - This builds up confidence of customers and helps in increasing their levels of satisfaction.

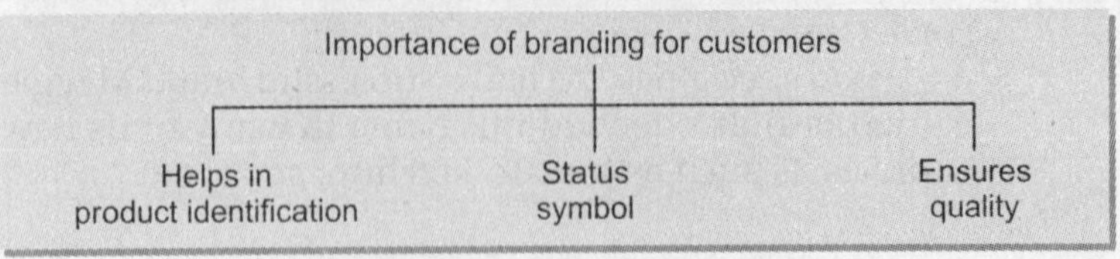

Q46. State some considerations which should be kept in mind while choosing a brand name.

Ans. The various considerations are:

1. *Short and easy*
   - The brand name should be short, easy to spell, recognize and remember.

   For Example:
   Ponds, Lux.
2. *Suggestive*
   - A brand name should suggest the product's benefits and qualities. It should be appropriate to the product's function.

   For Example:
   Rasna, Promise, Boost.
3. *Distinctive*
   - A brand name should be distinctive, i.e. different from that of the competitors.

   For Example:
   Liril, Spirit, Zodiac, Safari.
4. *Versatile*
   - The brand name should be sufficiently versatile to accommodate new products, which are added to the product line.

   For Example:
   Maggie, Colgate.
5. *Adaptable*
   - The brand name should be adaptable to packing or labeling requirements, to different advertising media and to different languages.
   - Chosen name should have staying power, i.e. it should not get out of date.
6. ***Registered:*** It should be capable of being registered and protected legally.

Q47. What is meant by packaging?

Ans. Packaging refers to the act of designing and producing the container and wrapper of the product.

Q48. State the 3 levels of packaging.

Ans. The 3 levels of packaging are:

1. *Primary package*
   - It refers to the product's immediate container.
   - In some cases, the primary package is kept till the consumer is ready to use the product (e.g. plastic packet for socks); whereas in other cases, it is kept throughout the entire life of the product (e.g. a toothpaste tube, a match box).

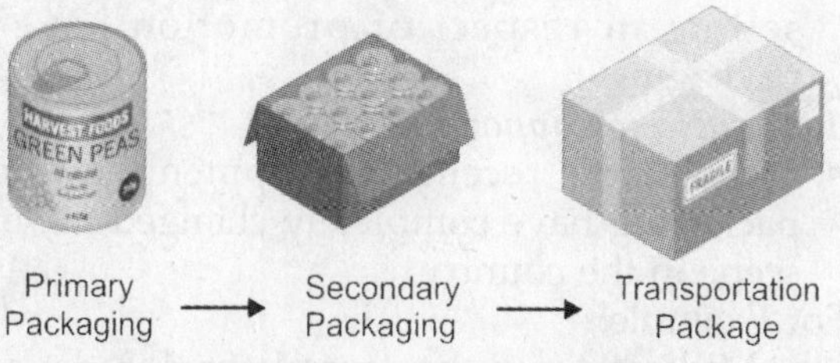

Fig. 11.4: Levels of packaging

2. *Secondary package*
   - It refers to additional layers of protection that are kept till the product is ready for use.

   For Example:

   A tube of shaving cream usually comes in a cardboard box.
   - When consumers start using the product they will dispose off the box but retain the primary package.
3. *Transportation packaging*
   - It refers to the further packaging components necessary for storage, identification or transportation.

   For Example:

   A toothpaste manufacturer may send the goods to retailers in corrugated boxes containing 10, 20, 100 units.

Q49. What is the importance of packaging?

or

Why has packaging acquired great significance in the marketing of goods and services?

Ans. Packaging has acquired greater significance because:

1. ***Rising standards of health and sanitation***
   - Because of the increasing living standards in the country, more and more people have started purchasing packed goods as the chances of adulteration in such goods are minimized.
2. ***Self service outlets***
   - They have become extremely popular, particularly in major cities and towns.
   - Some of the traditional roles assigned to personal selling in respect of promotion have gone to packaging.
3. ***Innovational opportunity***
   - Some of the recent developments in the area of packaging have completely changed the marketing scene in the country.

   For Example:

   Milk can now be stored for 4–5 days without refrigeration in the recently developed packaging material.
   - As a result the scope for marketing of such products has increased.
4. ***Product differentiation***
   - It is a very important means of creating product differentiation. The colour, size, etc. of package makes ample difference in the perception of customers about the quality of product.

   For Example:

   By looking at the package of a paint/chips/shampoo/hair oil, we can guess about its quality.

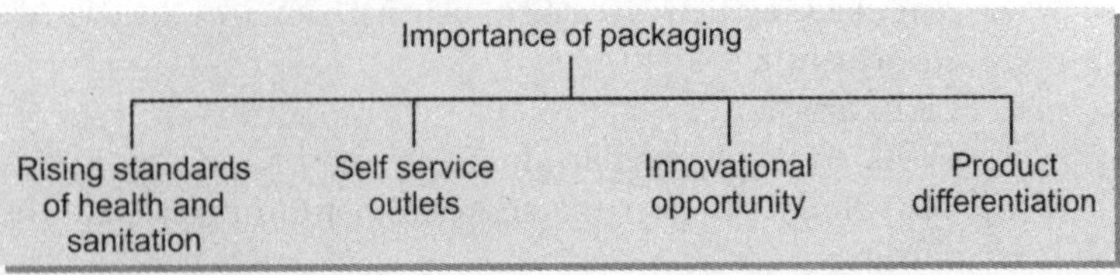

Q50. Packaging acts as a silent salesman. In the light of this statement explain the functions of packaging.

Ans. The functions of packaging are:

1. ***Product identification***
   - It helps in identification of the products.

   For Example:

   Colgate in red colour, or Ponds cream jar can be easily identified by its package.
2. ***Facilitating use of the product***
   - The size and shape of the package should be such that it should be convenient to open, handle and use for the consumers.

   For Example:

   Cosmetics, medicines, toothpastes
3. ***Product protection***
   - It protects the product from spoilage, breakage, leakage, pilferage, damage, climatic effect, etc. This kind of protection is required during storing, distribution and transportation of the product.
4. ***Product promotion***
   - It is used for promotion purposes. A startling colour scheme, photograph or type face may be used to attract attention of the people at the point of purchase.
   - Sometimes, it may work even better than advertising. In self-service stores, this role of packaging becomes all the more important.

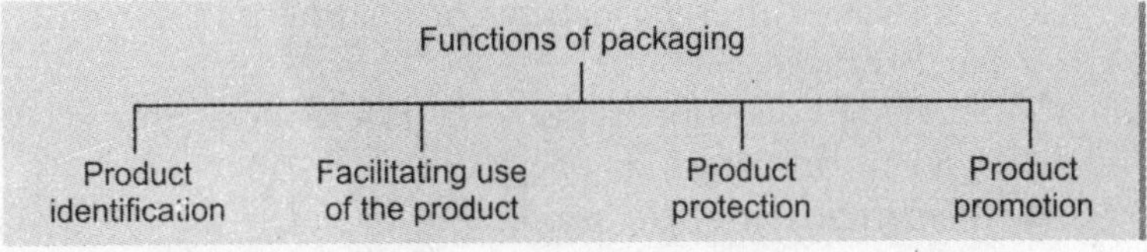

Q51. What is meant by labeling?

Ans.

- Labeling is a process of designing the label to be put on the package.
- It may vary from a simple tag attached to the product (such as in the case of local unbranded products like

sugar, wheat) indicating some information about the quality or price, to complex graphics that are part of the package.

For Example:

The graphic of boat and patwar on the package of an after shave lotion.

- They are useful in providing detailed information about the product, its contents, method of use, etc.

Q52. Labeling is an important process and plays a significant role in marketing of goods. Discuss.

Ans. It is important as it performs the following functions:

1. *Describe the product and specifies its contents*
   - Package of fast food products like ready to eat dosa, idli or noodles, describe the procedure of cooking these products, the package of a tooth paste brand lists the 'ten teeth and gum problems', which the product claims to fight with 'complete germ check formula'.
   - One of the most important functions of labels is to describe the product, its usage, cautions in use, etc and specify its contents.
2. *Grading of products*
   - Grading refers to the process of classifying the products into different groups on the basis of its important characteristics like quality, size, etc.
   - Labels help to grade products into different categories. Sometimes marketers assign different grades to indicate different features or quality of the product.

   For Example:

   Hair conditioners come in different categories say for normal hair, dry hair, etc.
3. *Identification of the product or brand*
   - An important function of labels is to help in identifying the product or brand.
   - Other common identification information provided by the labels includes name and address of the manufacturer, net weight when packed, manufacturing date, MRP and batch no.
4. *Helps in promotion of products*

- A carefully designed label can attract attention and give reason to purchase. We see many product labels providing promotional messages.

For Example:

Amla hair oil's pack states 'baalon mein dum, life mein fun.

- Labels play an important role in sales promotional schemes launched by companies.

For Example:

Label on a pack of potato chips states '33% extra free'

5. *Providing information required by law*

- Labeling provides information required by law.

For Example:

Statutory warning on the pack of pan masala or cigarettes –'smoking is injurious to health.

- Such information is required on processed food, drugs and tobacco products. In case of hazardous/poisonous material, appropriate safety warning need to be put on the label.

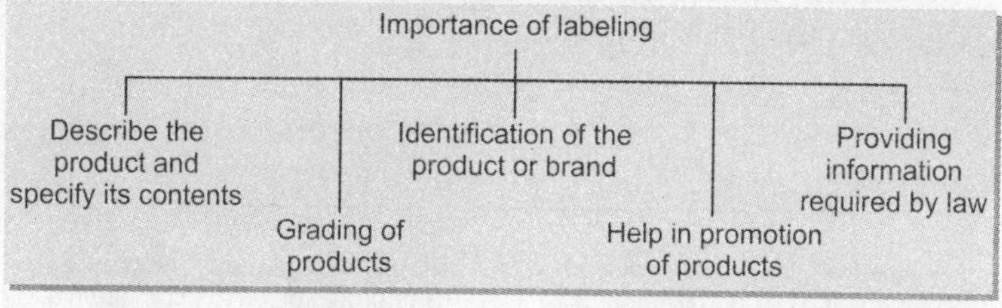

Q53. Identify and explain the element of marketing mix which is directly related to revenue and profits of a firm.

Ans. Price is directly related to revenue and profits.

- It may be defined as the amount of money paid by a buyer (or received by a seller) in consideration of the purchase of product/service. It occupies an important place in marketing of goods and services.

1. ***Helps in launching the product:*** No product can be launched in the market without a price tag or some guidelines for pricing.

2. *Regulator of demand of product:* It is often used as a regulator of the demand of a product. Generally, if the price of a product is increased, its demand comes down and vice-versa.

Q54. Pricing plays an important role in the marketing of goods and service. Explain

Ans. Pricing is an important element of marketing as:

1. *Helps in launching the product:* No product can be launched without a price tag or some guidelines for pricing.
2. *Regulator of demand of product:* It is often used as a regulator of the demand of a product. Generally, if the price of a product is increased, its demand comes down and vice-versa.
3. *Affects revenue and profits of the firm:* It is the single most important factor affecting the revenue and profits of a firm. Most firms give high importance to the fixation of price for their products and services
4. *Acts as a competitive weapon:* It is an effective competitive weapon. In the conditions of perfect competition, most of the firms compete with each other on the basis of pricing.

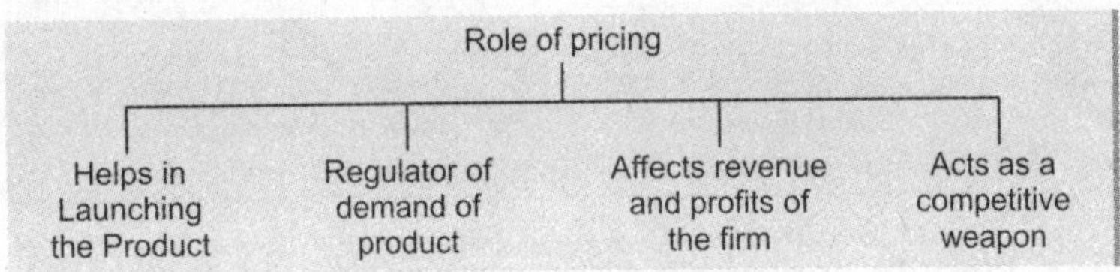

Q55. Give an example of a product when the price is paid for services.

Ans. Fare for the transport service, premium for insurance policy and fee to a doctor.

Q56. Discuss the factors affecting the fixation of the price of a product. (6 Marks)

Ans. The various factors are:

1. ***Product cost***
   - This includes the cost of producing, distributing and selling the product.
   - The cost sets the base level or the floor price at which the product may be sold
   - The firms aim at earning a margin of profit over and above the costs.
   - There are broadly 3 types of costs:
     - *Fixed cost:* Those costs which don't vary with the level of activity of a firm, i.e. with volume of production/sale.

     For Example:

     Rent of building, salary of sales manager.
     - *Variable cost:* Those costs which vary in direct proportion with the level of activity of a firm.

     For Example:

     Costs of raw materials, labour, power.
     - *Semi variable cost:* Those costs which vary with the level of activity but not in a direct proportion with it.

     For Example:

     Compensation of a sales person may include a fixed salary of Rs.10,000/- plus a commission of 5% on sales.
2. ***Utility and demand***
   - The product costs set the lower limits of the price and the utility provided by the product and the intensity of demand sets the upper limit of price which a buyer would be prepared to pay.
   - The price must reflect the interest of both the parties to the transaction, the buyer (in terms of utility) and the seller (in terms of cost of product). The price of the product is affected by the elasticity of demand of the product.
     - The demand is said to be elastic if a small change in price results in a large change in the quantity demanded.
     - In case of inelastic demand, the total revenue increases when the price is increased and goes down when the price is decreased. In case of

inelastic demand of a product, the firm is in a better position to fix higher prices.

3. *Extent of competition in the market*
   - The price will tend to reach the upper limit in case there is lesser degree of competition while under conditions of free competition, the price will tend to be set at the lowest level.

     Lowest price ⟶ High competition

     Highest Price ⟶ Low Competition
   - Competitor's prices and their expected reactions must be kept in mind before fixing the price of a product.
   - Not only the price but the quality and features of the competitive products must be examined carefully, before fixing the price.
4. *Government and legal regulations*
   - Govt. can intervene and regulate the price of commodities. It can declare a product as an essential product and regulate its price.

   For Example:

   In case the cost of a drug to a manufacturer is Rs.20 and in lieu of no competition he fixes a price of Rs.200 for it. In such cases, govt. can intervene and regulate its price.
   - The Govt. doesn't allow the firms to charge such a high price and intervenes to regulate the price of commodities.
5. *Pricing objectives*
   - Profit maximization is one of the main pricing objective:

   Profit maximization (Short term) ⟶ Price will be high

   Profit maximization (Long term) ⟶ Per unit price is lower to attain lager market share.
   - The other pricing objectives are:
     a. *Obtaining market share leadership:* If a firm aims to attain larger market share, it will keep the price of its products at lower levels so that greater number of people are attracted to purchase it.

b. *Attaining product quality leadership:* Normally higher prices are charged to cover high quality and high cost of research and development

c. *Survival in a competitive market:* If a firm is facing difficulties in surviving in the market due to intense competition then it may resort to discounting its products or running a promotion campaign to liquidate its stock.

6. **Marketing methods used**
   - Price fixation process is affected by other elements of marketing such as:
     - Distribution system
     - Type of packaging
     - Quality of salesmen employed
     - Quality and amount of advertising
     - Sales promotion efforts
     - Credit facility
     - Product differentiation
     - Customer services.

For Example:

If a company provides free home delivery, it has some flexibility in fixing prices.

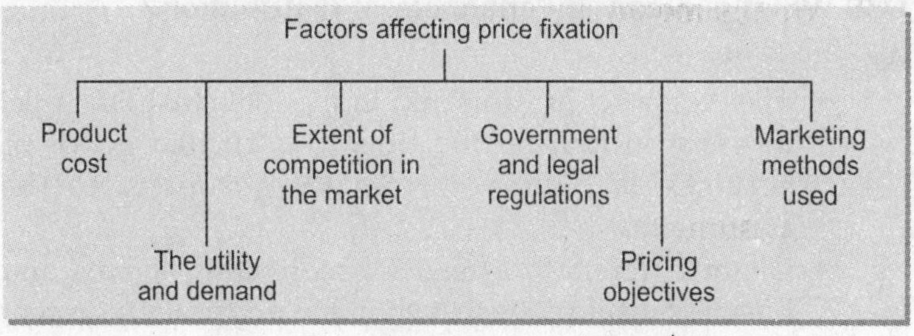

Q57. State the various pricing objectives of a firm

or

Apart from profit maximization, identify the other pricing objectives of a firm

Ans. Refer to the previous answer

Q58. Identify and explain the element of marketing mix which is concerned with physical distribution of goods and services.

Ans. Place/physical distribution/distribution/distribution mix is concerned with the physical distribution of goods and services.

- It is concerned with making goods and services available at the right place, so that people can purchase them.
- There are two important decisions relating to this aspect.
  - Regarding the physical movement of goods from producers to customers/users known as physical distribution.
  - Regarding the channels or using intermediates in the distribution process known as channels of distribution.

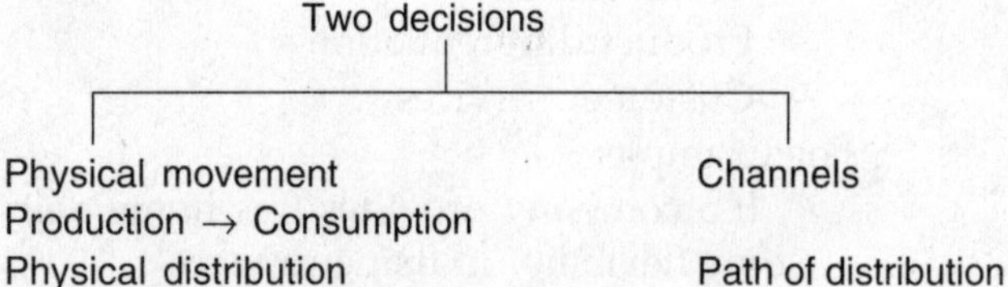

Q59. What is meant by channels of distribution?

Ans.

- They are a set of firms and individuals that take title, or assist in transferring title, to particular goods or services as it moves from the producer to the consumers.
- Channel refers to a team of merchants, agents and business institutions that combine physical movement and title movement of products to reach specific destinations.
- Goods and services are mostly distributed through a network of marketing channels.

For Example:

We buy merchandise of our need such as salt, bulb, tea, sugar, etc from retail sellers.

Q60. "The channels bring economy of efforts". Explain

Ans.

- Channel is a term which refers to a team of merchants, agents and business institutions that combine physical movement and title movement of products to reach specific destinations.

For Example:

- Let us say we have 4 things viz. sugar, bulb, coffee and toothpaste. Most probably we would walk into a general merchant's shop and buy all articles from one place.
- Imagine what would happen if there were no middlemen or general merchants available. We would have to buy directly from the manufacturers of these products. We would have to make 4 contacts each with the producer of the 4 different products.
- Now let us assume that there are 4 customers needing same 4 articles. In all 16 contacts would have to be made and if middlemen are used, only 8 contacts would be needed.

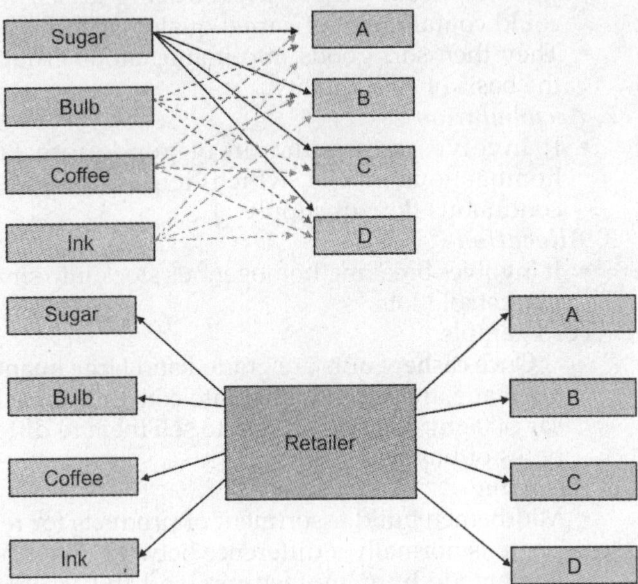

Fig. 11.5: Channels bring economy in efforts

- The other benefits of middlemen include:
  - Cover large geographical area.
  - Bring efficiency in distributing including transportation, storage, negotiation.
  - Bring convenience to consume as they make various items available at one particular place.
  - Serve as authentic source of market information as they are in direct contact with the customer.

Q61. What are the other benefits of channels?

Ans. Refer to the previous answer

Q62. Discuss the functions performed by the distribution channels.

Ans. The various functions are:

1. ***Sorting***
   - Middlemen procure supplies from a variety of sources which is often not of the same quality, nature and size.

   For Example:

   A wholesaler of cashew nuts may procure a large quantity from different producing areas, which could contain nuts of varied quality and size.
   - They then sort goods into homogenous groups on the basis of size, quality.
2. ***Accumulation***
   - It involves accumulation of goods into larger homogenous stocks, which help in maintaining continuous flow of supply.
3. ***Allocation***
   - It involves breaking homogenous stock into smaller, marketable lots.

   For Example:

   Once cashew nuts are graded and large quantities are made, they are divided into convenient packs of say 500 gm, 250 gm, 100 gm to sell them to different types of buyers.
4. ***Assorting***
   - Middlemen build assortment of products for resale. There is normally a difference between the product lines made by manufacturers and the assortment desired by the users.

For Example:

A cricket player may need a bat, ball, wickets, gloves, T-shirt, shoes and no one manufacturer produces these in the desired combination.

- Middlemen procure variety of goods from different sources and deliver them in combinations desired by the consumer.

5. ***Negotiation***
   - Channels operate with manufacturers on one hand and customers on the other.
   - Arriving at deals that satisfy both the parties is an important function of middlemen.
   - They negotiate the price, quality, guarantee and other related matters with customers so that transfer of ownership is properly affected.
6. ***Product promotion***
   - Most advertising and other sales promotion activities are organized by manufacturers
   - Middlemen participate in certain activities such as demonstrations, special displays, controls etc to increase sale of products
7. ***Risk taking***
   - In the process of distribution of goods the merchant middlemen take title of goods and thereby assume risks on account of price and demand fluctuations, spoilage, destruction , loss, etc.

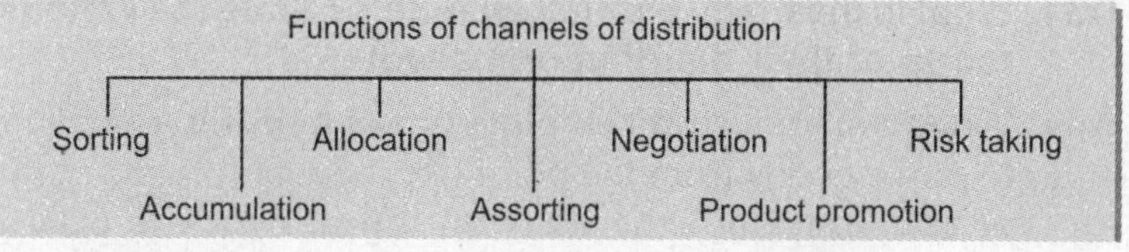

Q63. What is meant by direct channels? State the various methods of direct selling.

Ans.

- The simplest and the shortest mode of distribution is direct channel distribution, where in goods are made directly available by the manufacturers to customers without involving any intermediaries.

- This is also called zero level channel. A straight and direct relationship is established between the manufacturer and the customer.

Direct channel (zero level)

Manufacturer ⟶ Customer

The various types of direct selling are

1. ***Mail order selling:*** It refers to selling, shopping by post where the manufacturers sell directly to the customers through postal services.
2. ***Internet selling:*** It is a popular method wherein the customer can place an order to the manufacturer directly through internet. Also, the manufacturer makes himself available to customers directly on the internet.
3. ***Telemarketing:*** It involves selling-through TV Products are offered and complete information is available on TV and orders can be placed through telephones.

For Example:

Tele sky shop.

4. ***Personal/direct selling through own sales force:*** The manufacturers may resort to direct selling by appointing their own sales people.
5. ***Setting up your own retail outlets***

Q64. What is meant by indirect channels? State the various forms of their distribution network

Ans. When a manufacturer employs one or more intermediary to move goods from the point of production to the point of consumption, the distribution network is called indirect.

The various types are:

1. ***Manufacturer-retailer-consumer (one level channel)***
   - An intermediary, i.e. retailer is used between the manufacturers and customers.

For Example:

Maruti Udyog sells its cars and vans through company approved retailers

- This type of network enables the manufacturers to cover wide area of market while retaining control over channels.

Manufacturer ⟶ Retailer ⟶ Consumer

2. ***Manufacturer-wholesaler-retailer-consumer (two level channel)***
   - This is the most commonly adopted distribution network for most consumer goods like soaps, shampoos, oils, clothes, rice, sugar, pulses.
   - Here the wholesaler and retailer function as connecting links between the producer and consumer. Thus, it enables to cover a larger market area.

Manufacturer ⟶ Wholesaler ⟶ Retailer ⟶ Consumer

3. ***Manufacturer – agent – wholesaler – retailer – consumer* (three level channel)**
   - Manufacturers use their own selling agents/brokers who connect them with wholesalers and then the retailers.
   - It is done particularly when the manufacturer carries a limited product line and has to cover a wide market.

   For Example:

   De Beers is a diamond manufacturing company which has agents in India to further sell to wholesalers and retailers.

Manufacturer ⟶ Agent ⟶ Wholesaler ⟶ Retailer ⟶ Consumer

Q65. Which channel of distribution is generally used for consumer goods?

Ans. Manufacturer – Wholesaler – Retailer – Customer (two level channel) is used for consumer goods.

Q66. Explain the various factors which determine the choice of channels of distribution.

Ans. The various factors are:

1. *Product related factors*
   - Industrial goods Vs. consumer goods
     – Industrial products are usually technical, made to order, expensive and are purchased by few

buyers. They require short channels, i.e. direct distribution involving few middlemen.

- Consumer products are usually standardized, less expensive, less bulky, non-technical and frequently bought products and therefore can be distributed by long network of channels with many middlemen.

- Unit value of product
  - If the unit value of a product is low, then long channels are preferred.

  For Example:

  Convenience products.

  - If the unit value is high, then shorter channels are preferred.

  For Example:

  Specialty Products.

- Perishable goods Vs. non-perishable goods
  - Perishable products get easily spoiled and are best sold through short channels.

  For Example:

  Fruits, vegetables, dairy products.

  - Non-perishable products are not liable to get easily spoiled and require long channels to reach wide spread consumers,

  For example:

  Soap, shampoo, oils, creams.

- Degree of complexity of product
  - In case of complex goods requiring technical details, shorter channels are preferred.

  For Example:

  Industrial, engineering goods.

  - Non-complex goods can be sold through long channels with many middlemen.

  For Example:

  Consumer goods.

2. *Company characteristics*
   - Financial strength of company
     - Direct selling involves lot of funds to be invested in fixed assets for starting own retail outlets or engaging large sale force.

- Indirect selling through intermediaries doesn't involve deployment of huge funds in these aspects.
- Degree of control desired
  - If the management wants to have greater control on the channel members, short channels are used.
  - If the management doesn't want excess control over the middlemen, it can go in for longer channels.

3. *Competitive factors*
   - The firm may like to select channels similar to that of their competitors.

   For Example:

   If the competitors have selected a particular channel for sale of toiletry products then the firm may wish to do the same.
   - The firm may want to avoid the channels used by the competitors.

   For Example:

   If other cosmetic producers have chosen big retail stores for the sale of their products, a particular firm may adopt door to door selling.
   - Thus, it will depend upon the policy of the firm – whether it wants to follow the competitors or be different from them.
4. *Market factors*
   - Size of market
     - In case the number of buyers is small, short channels are used.

     For Example:

     Industrial goods.
     - In case the no. of buyers is large, longer channels are used.

     For Example:

     Consumer goods.
   - Geographical concentration
     - If the buyers are concentrated in a small place, short channels may be used.
     - If the buyers are widely dispersed over a wide geographical area, long channels are used.

- Quantity purchased
  - If the size of the order is small, long channels are used.

  For Example:

  Consumer goods.
  - If the size of the order is large, short channels are used.

5. *Environmental factors*
   - Other important factors affecting the choice of channels of distribution include environmental factors like:
     - Economic condition
     - Legal constants
   - In a depressed economy, marketers use shorter channels to distribute their goods in an economic way.

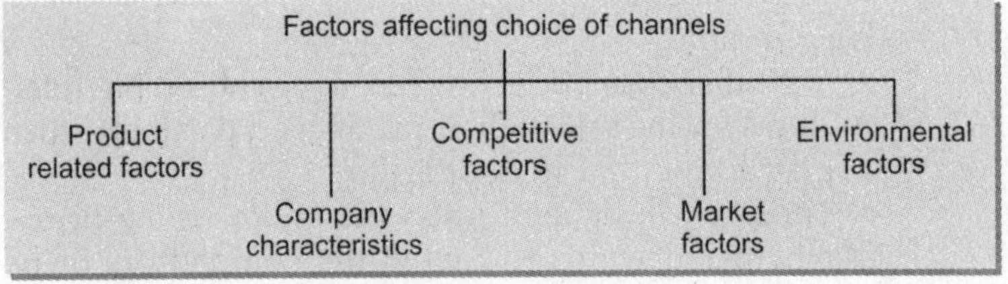

Q67. What is meant by physical distribution?

Ans. Physical distribution is an important element of marketing mix. It is concerned with making goods and services available at the right time and right place. It involves 2 important decisions:

1. *Channels of distribution*: Refers to a team of agents/ merchants that combine physical movement and title movement of products to reach a specific destination.
2. *Physical movement:* Physical movement and handling of goods from place of production to the place of distribution. Also called physical distribution. It involves 4 important components.
   - Order processing
   - Transportation

- Warehousing
- Inventory control

Physical distribution: Two decisions

Physical movement — Production → Consumption — Physical distribution

Channels — Path of distribution

Q68. Explain the 4 important factors of physical distribution.

Ans. The factors are:

1. *Order processing*
   - Order placement is the first step in a buyer-seller relationship
   - While products usually move from manufacturers to customers through members of the channel, orders flow in the reverse direction from customers to manufacturers.
   - A proper physical distribution system ought to provide for an accurate and speedy processing of orders, in the absence of which goods are likely to reach the customers late or in wrong quantity or in undesired specifications. This would result in customer dissatisfaction which can lead to the loss of business and goodwill.
2. *Transportation*
   - Is carrying of goods and raw materials from the point of production to the point of sale.
   - Till the goods are physically made available, the sale cannot be completed and thus transportation is a key component of physical distribution of goods.
3. *Warehousing*
   - Is the act of storing and assorting products in order to create time utility in them.
   - There is a need for warehousing as there is a significant time gap between the production of a product and its consumption.
   - The efficiency of a firm will depend on where these warehouses are located and where are the products to be delivered

- The firm has to strike a balance between the cost of warehousing and the level of customer service.
- For products such as agricultural produce that require long term storage the warehouses are located near production sites thereby reducing the charges of transportation of goods whereas the products which are bulky, need to be shipped (machinery, automobiles) as well as perishable products (bakery, meat) are kept at different locations near the market.

4. ***Inventory control***
   - Deciding about the level of inventory is a very important decision in inventory management
   - Higher the level of inventory, faster is the service to customers
   - The cost of carrying the inventory will also be high since capital is tied up in stocks of inventory
   - A balance is to be maintained in respect of cost and customer satisfaction.
   - With advancements in computers and IT the need for keeping higher inventory is reducing and the new concept of Just in Time inventory decision is becoming popular in companies. In this, a correct estimate of the demand helps to hold inventory and cost level down to minimum. The major factors determining inventory are:
     - *Cost of inventory:* It includes holding cost of inventorry such as cost of warehousing, locked in capital and the manufacturing cost.
     - *Accuracy of sales forecast:* The need for keeping very high level of inventory can be minimized if more accurate estimates are available
     - *Customer service:* Higher the level of service greater will be the need to keep more inventories.
     - *Responsiveness of the distribution system:*
       - It is the ability of the system to transmit inventory needs back to factory and get products in the market.
       - If the time required to respond to additional demand is high, there is a need to maintain higher inventory.

- But if it can be met in less time then inventory required is low.

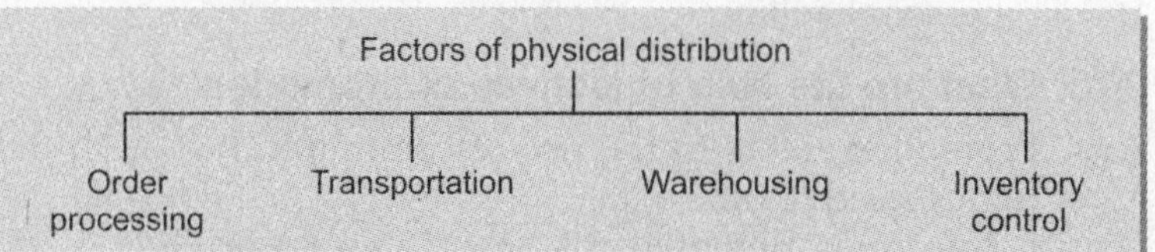

Q69. What is the relationship between warehousing and customer service?

Ans. Larger the amount of warehouses a firm has, lesser would be the time taken in serving customers at different locations but greater would be the cost of warehousing and vice versa.

Q70. What is the relationship between level of inventory and customer service?

Ans. Refer to Ans. 68

Q71. State the factors which determine the inventory levels of a firm.

Ans. Refer to Ans. 68

Q72. What is meant by promotion/promotion mix?

Ans.

- Promotion is the use of communication with the twin objective of :
  - Informing potential customers about a product.
  - Persuading them to buy it.
- Promotion mix refers to a combination of promotional tools used by organizations to achieve its communication objectives.
- These promotional tools include:
  - Sales promotion
  - Publicity
  - Advertising
  - Personal selling
- These tools are also called the elements of promotion mix and can be used in different combinations to achieve the goals of promotion.

For Example:

Consumer goods firms may use more of advertising through mass media while capital goods firms may use personal selling.

Q73. What are the twin objectives of promotion?

Ans. Promotion refers to the use of communication with the twin objective of:

1. Informing potential customers about a product.
2. Persuading them to buy it.

Q74. State the elements of promotion mix.

Ans. Promotion mix refers to a combination of promotional tools used by organizations to achieve its communication objectives.

- The promotional tools include:
  - Advertising
  - Publicity
  - Personal selling
  - Sales promotion
- These are called the elements of promotion mix and can be used in different combinations to achieve the goals of promotion.

For Example:

Consumer goods firms may use more of advertising through mass media while capital goods firms may use personal selling.

Q75. State the factors which will determine the use of various promotional tools by a firm.

Ans. The various factors are:

1. Nature of product
2. Nature of market
3. Objectives of promotion
4. Promotions budget

Q76. What is meant by advertising? State the features of advertising.

Ans.

- Advertising is an impersonal form of communication which is paid for by the marketers (sponsors) to market some goods or services among the intended target segments

- The most common tools of advertising are:
  - Newspapers
  - Magazines
  - TV
  - Radio

  The important features are:

  1. ***Paid form***: It is a paid form of communication, i.e. the sponsor has to bear the cost of communication with the prospects.
  2. **Impersonality*:*** There is no direct face to face interaction between the potential customer/target segment and the advertiser. It is therefore an impersonal method of promotion. Advertising creates a monologue and not a dialogue.
  3. ***Identified sponsor:*** It is undertaken by an individual/company, who makes the advertising efforts and also bears the cost.

Q77. Advertising creates a monologue and not a dialogue. Explain.

Ans. There is no direct face to face cóntact between the prospect and the advertiser. It is therefore an impersonal method of promotion. Thus its is said that advertising creates a monologue and not a dialogue.

Q78. State the various benefits of advertising as a medium of communication.

Ans. The various benefits are:

1. *Enhancing customer satisfaction level and confidence*
   - It generates confidence and trust amongst prospective buyers as they feel more comfortable and assured about the product quality and hence feel more satisfied.
2. *Expressiveness*
   - Advertising has developed into one of the most forceful mediums of communication on account of the new techniques that have taken shape in art, computer designs, effects and graphics

- With the special effects that can be created, even simple products and messages can look attractive.

3. *Mass reach*
   - It is a medium through which a large number of people can be reached over a large geographical area.

   For Example:

   An advertisement message placed in a national daily reaches lakhs of its subscribers

4. *Economy*
   - It is very economical if a large number of people are to be reached.
   - Because of its wide reach, the overall cost of advertising gets spread over numerous communication links established. As a result per unit cost of reach becomes low.

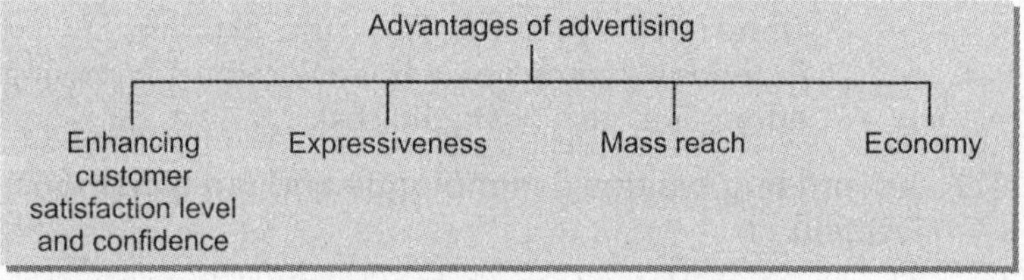

Q79. What are the limitations of advertising?

Ans. The various limitations are:

1. ***Less forceful***: It is an impersonal form of communication and is thus less forceful than personal selling as there is no compulsion on the prospects to pay attention to the message.
2. ***Inflexibility:*** It is less flexible as the message is standardized and is not customized to suit the requirements of different customer groups.
3. ***Lack of feedback:*** The evaluation of its effectiveness is very difficult as there is no immediate and accurate feedback mechanism of the message delivered.
4. ***Low effectiveness:*** As the volume of advertising is increasing it is becoming difficult to make the advertising messages heard by the target prospects as there is excessive cluttering thereby affecting its effectiveness.

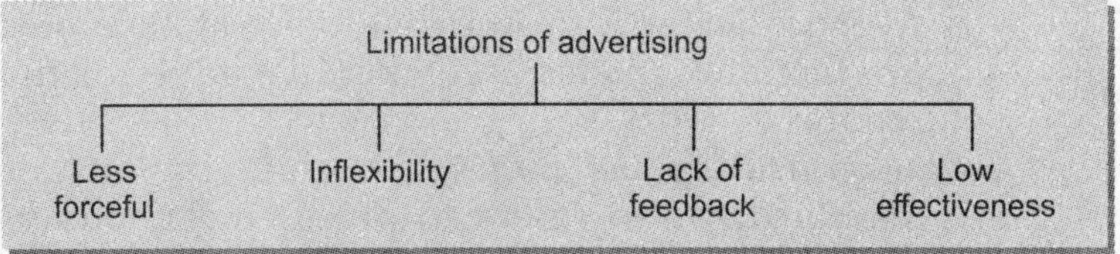

Q80. Explain the various functions of marketing.

Ans. The various functions are:

1. *Market planning*
   - A marketer has to develop appropriate marketing plans so that the marketing objectives of the organization can be achieved.

   For Example:

   The marketer aims at enhancing his market share from say 10% to 50%.
   - He will have to develop a complete marketing plan covering various important aspects including:
     - Plan for increasing level of production.
     - Promotion of product.
     - Specify action programs to achieve these objectives.
2. *Gathering and analyzing market information*
   - Required to identify the needs of the target customers and take various decisions for the successful marketing of products and services.
   - Crucial for conducting an analysis of the available opportunities and threats as well as strengths and weaknesses of the organization and helps in deciding what opportunities can best be pursued by the firm.

   For Example:

   Rapid growth is predicted in Indian economy in the use of internet, market for mobiles, etc.
   - The new segments in which the organization should enter or the existing segments in which it should expand requires a careful scanning of the strengths and weaknesses of the firm which is done with the help of careful market analysis.
3. *Product designing and development*
   - The design of the product is the key to making product attractive to the target customers.

- A good design can improve performance of a product and creates a competitive edge for the product

4. *Standardization and grading*
   - Standardization refers to producing goods of predetermined specifications, which helps in achieving uniformity and consistency in the output.
   - It gives confidence to buyers that goods conform to the well defined standards of quality, price and packaging
   - It reduces the need for inspection, testing and evaluation of the products.
   - Grading is the process of classification of products into different groups, on the basis of some important characteristics such as quality, size, etc.
   - It is particularly necessary for products which are not produced according to predetermined specifications such as in the case of agricultural products like wheat, rice, oranges, etc.
   - It ensures that goods belong to a particular quality and helps in realizing higher prices for high quality output.
5. ***Packaging and labeling:*** Refer to earlier questions
6. ***Branding:*** Refer
7. ***Customer support services***
   - These include support services like :
     – Sales service
     – Maintenance and repair services
     – Handling customer complaints, adjustments
     – Providing credit services
     – Technical services
   - These are targeted at providing maximum satisfaction to the customers, which is the key to marketing success in modern days.
   - Customer support services prove very effective in bringing repeat sales from the customers and developing brand loyalty for a product.
8. ***Pricing of product:*** Refer
9. ***Physical distribution***: Refer
10. ***Promotion:*** Refer

11. ***Transportation:*** Refer
12. ***Warehousing:*** Refer

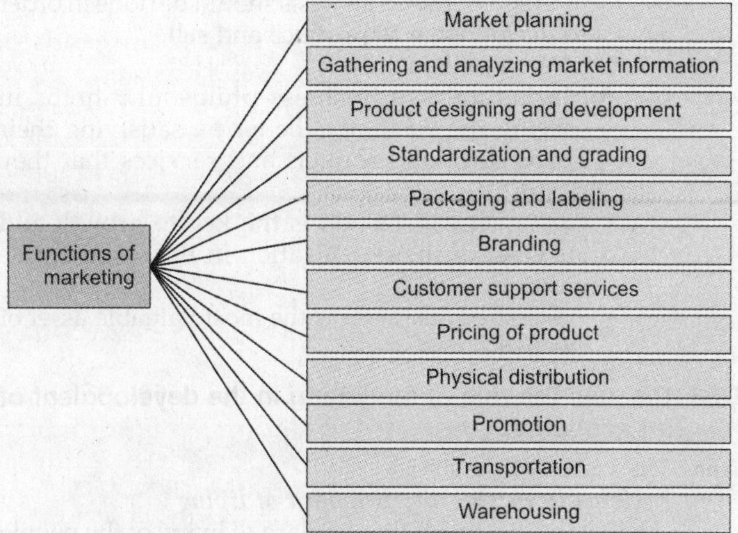

Q81. What type of products generally require grading?

Ans. Goods which are usually produced according to a predetermined specification or defined standard require grading.

For Example:

Agricultural products – wheat, rice, oranges.

Q82. Explain the role of marketing in a firm.

Ans.

- Marketing helps consumers in raising their standard of living by making available the products and services that satisfy their needs and wants.
- Marketing also plays a significant role in the economic development of a nation.

Role of marketing in a firm is as follows:

1. ***Adopting market orientation***
   - By adopting market orientation, an organization whether profit making or non-profit making, can achieve its goal in the most effective manner.

- It helps the organization to focus its efforts on the needs and wants of the customers.

For Example:

Customer need analysis should be done in order to decide what to produce and sell.

2. **Customer satisfaction**
   - Marketing as a business philosophy helps in serving the customers better by satisfying their needs through products and services that they desire
   - Customer satisfaction is the key to growth and survival of the organization in this competitive environment.
   - A satisfied customer is the most valuable asset of the firm.

Q83. Discuss the role of marketing in the development of an economy.

Ans. The various roles are:

1. ***Helps in raising the standard of living***
   - It helps in raising the standard of living of the people by providing quality products and services.
   - Development of a nation can be judged by the level of standard of living of its people.
2. ***Development of an economy***
   - Marketing plays a significant role in developing any economy.
   - It acts as a catalyst in the economic development of a country
3. ***Helps in increasing the per-capita income***
   - Helps in ensuring that the products and services offered to the customers are as per their needs.
   - Per-capita income of an average citizen of a country is an important indicator of its level of development.
   - It helps to increase the standards of living and PCY of an individual.
4. ***Helps to reduce the imbalance between the levels of production and consumption***
   - Marketing inspires people to undertake new activities and set up production units to meet the growing demand of the consumers.

- This thus, helps in overcoming problems related to high prices due to imbalances in the level of production and consumption.
- Thus, marketing acts as an important link between production and consumption centers, accelerates economic activity leading to higher incomes, more consumption and increased savings and investment.

Production unit ⟶ Marketing ⟶ Consumption centre

5. ***Helps in ensuring smooth flow of goods from producers to consumers:*** Marketing helps in ensuring smooth flow of goods through efficient and effective movement of goods through transportation, warehousing, inventory control and timely execution of orders.

Q84. Various objections are raised against advertising. Are these fully justified? Discuss.

Ans. No the objections raised to advertising are not fully justified, as explained below:

1. *Objection raised - Undermines social values*
    - It undermines social values and promotes materialism.
    - It breeds discontent among people as they come to know about the new products and feel dissatisfied with their present state of affairs.

    Counter arguments
    - It helps buyers by informing them about the new products, which may be an improvement over the existing products.
    - The final choice to buy/not to buy anyway rests with the buyers.
    - They will buy if the advertised product satisfies some of their needs.
2. *Objection raised - Adds to cost*
    - The opponents of advertising may propose that it eventually adds to the cost of the product, which is eventually passed on to the buyers in the form of high prices.
    - The money spent adds to the cost, which is an important factor in fixation of price of a product.

Counter arguments

- Advertising helps to increase the demand for the product as a large number of potential buyers come to know about the availability of the product.
- The increased demand leads to higher production which brings with it economies of scale as a result of which per unit cost of production comes down as the total cost is divided by larger number of units.

3. ***Objection raised - Encourages sale of inferior products***
   - It doesn't distinguish between superior and inferior products and persuades people to purchase even the inferior product.

   Counter arguments
   - Superiority and inferiority are however relative concepts and depend on quality.
   - The desired level of quality will depend on the economic status and preferences of the target customers.
   - If a firm makes a false claim it can be prosecuted for it.
4. ***Objection raised - Confuses the buyers***
   - So many products are being advertised which make similar claims that the buyers gets confused as to which one should be relied upon.

   Counter arguments
   - We are all rational human beings who make our decisions for purchase of products on factors such as price, style, size, etc.
   - Thus the buyers can clear their confusion by analyzing the information provided on the advertisements and other sources before making the purchase.
5. **Objection raised - Some advertisements are in bad taste**
   - A criticism against advertisements is that some of them are in bad taste. They distort relationships like those between employees and employer.

   Counter argument
   - Taste is a matter of perception and can vary from one person to the other. As social values evolve, tastes also changes from one generation to the other

Conclusion

- There may be some chances of misuse of advertising which can be properly safeguarded by the law or be avoided by the advertisers through self regulation.
- In this changed economic environment of globalization, advertisement is considered an important tool of marketing.
- It is not a social waste, rather it adds value to the social cause by giving a boost to production and generating employment.

Q85. What is meant by personal selling? State its features.

Ans.

- Personal selling includes the oral presentation of messages in the form of conversations with one or more prospective customers for the purpose of making a sale.
- It is a personal form of communication. Companies appoint salesperson to contact prospective buyers and create awareness about the product and develop product preferences with the aim of making sale.

Its features are:

1. ***Facilitates the development of relationship***: It allows a salesperson to develop personal relationships with prospective customers, which may become important in making sale.
2. ***Personal form:*** In personal selling a direct face to face dialogue takes place that involves an interactive relationship between the seller and the buyer.

Q86. State 3 merits of personal selling.

Ans. The various merits are:

1. ***Direct feedback:*** As there is direct face to face communication between the salesperson and the prospective customer, it is possible to take a direct feed back from the customer and to adapt the presentation according to the needs of the prospects.
2. ***Flexibility:*** It has a lot of flexibility. The sales presentation can be adjusted to fit the specific needs of the individual customers.
3. ***Minimum wastage:*** The wastage of efforts in personal selling can be minimized as company can decide the target customers before making any contact with them.

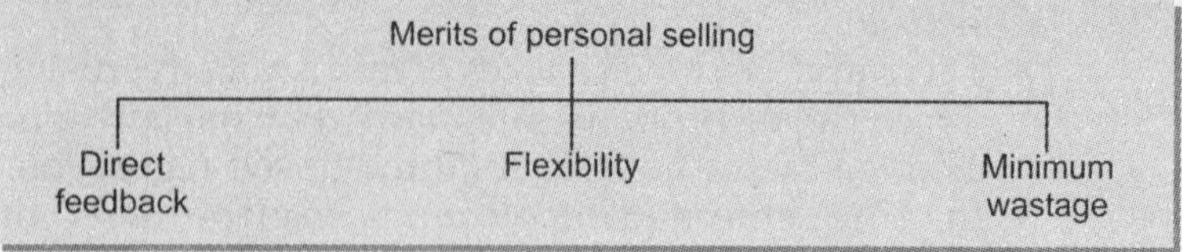

Q87. Personal selling plays a very important role in the marketing of goods and services. Discuss.

Ans. Explain all three components in detail - Business + Customers + Society

Q88. Personal selling is a powerful tool for creating demand and making the sale of products effective for a business organization. Discuss.

Ans. It is effective because of:

1. ***Effective promotional tool:*** It is a very effective promotional tool, as it helps in informing the prospects about the merits of a product and thereby increasing sale.
2. ***Role in introduction stage:*** It plays a very important role in the introduction stage of a new product as it helps in persuading customers about the merits of the product through face to face interactions.
3. ***Minimizes wastage of efforts:*** Compared with other tools of promotion the possibility of wastage of efforts in it is minimum. It helps the business in bringing economy in its efforts.
4. ***Flexible tool:*** It is more flexible than other tools of promotion such as advertising and sales promotion. It helps business persons in adapting their good/service offering to varying purchase situations.
5. ***Consumer attention, lasting relationships and personal rapport***
   - There is an opportunity to detect the loss of consumer attention and interest in a personal selling situation. This helps the business in successfully completing the sales by taking remedial action or customizing the offering

- It helps to build a lasting relationship by helping the company's salesperson establish a personal rapport with the buyers.

6. *Link business with customers*
   - Sales people play 3 roles:
     - Persuasive role
     - Service role
     - Informative role and thereby link a business to its customers

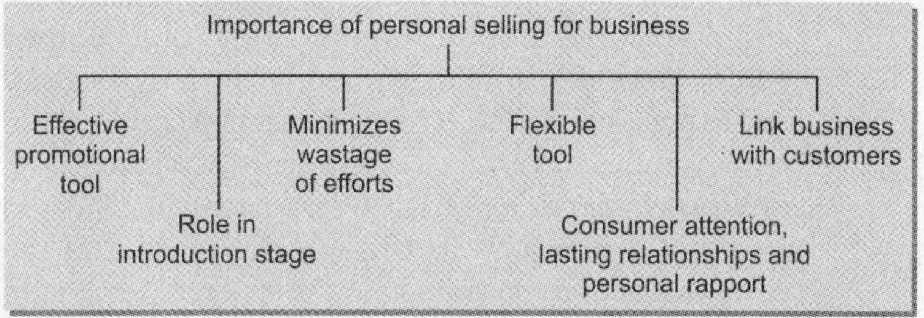

Q89. Personal selling is one of the most effective promotional tools for customers and especially for the illiterate and rural customers. Do you agree? Give reasons.

Ans. Yes, I agree with the statement. It is so because of:

1. ***Provides latest market information:*** Customers get latest market information regarding price changes, product availability and shortages and new product introduction which help them in taking purchase decisions in a better way.
2. ***Helps in identifying needs:*** It helps the customers in identifying their needs and wants and in knowing how these can be best satisfied.
3. ***Induces new product purchases:*** It induces customers to purchase new products that satisfy their needs in a better way and thereby helps in improving their standards of living.
4. ***Expert advice:*** Customers get expert advice and guidance in purchasing various goods and services, which help them in making better purchase.

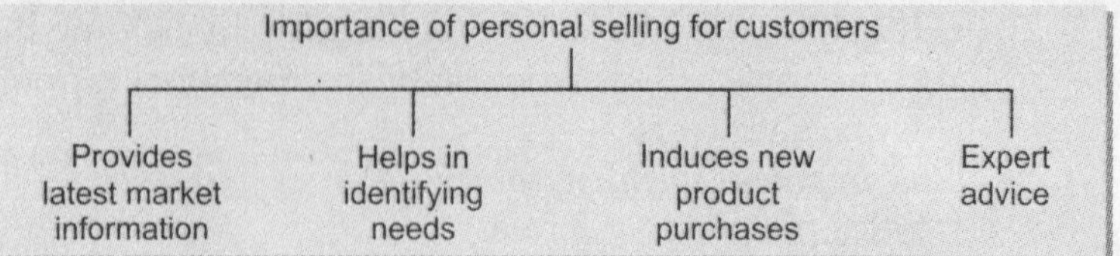

Q90. Personal Selling plays a productive role in the economic progress of a society. Discuss.

Ans. It plays a productive role through:

1. ***Employment opportunities:*** It offers greater income and employment opportunities to the unemployed youth. Since demand and economic activity increase due to personal selling, it helps in creating employment opportunities in various departments of a firm
2. ***Converts latent demand:*** It converts latent demand into effective demand. It is through this cycle that the economic activity in the society is fostered, leading to more jobs, more incomes and more products and services.
3. ***Product standardization:*** It increases product standardization and uniformity in consumption pattern in a diverse society.
4. ***Career opportunities:*** It provides attractive career options with greater opportunities for advancement and job satisfaction as well as security, respect, variety, interest and independence.
5. ***Mobility of sales people:*** There is a greater degree of mobility in sales people, which promotes travel, tourism in the country.

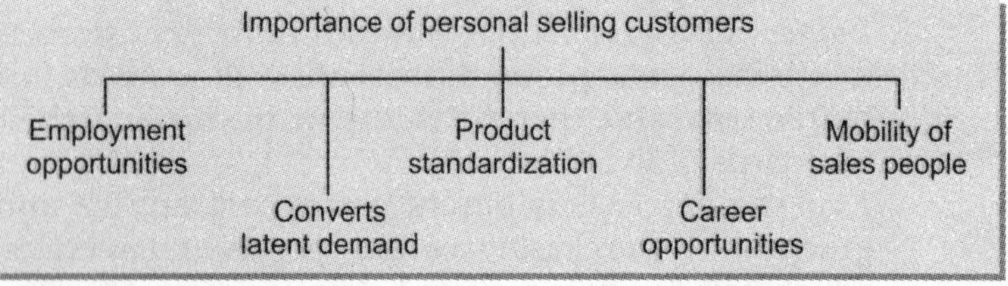

Q91. What is meant by sales promotion?

Ans.

- It refers to short term incentives, which are designed to encourage the buyers to make immediate purchase of a product or service.
- Sales promotion activities include
  - Free gift offers
  - Free sample distribution
  - Offering cash discounts
  - Sales contests
- It is usually undertaken to supplement other promotional efforts such as advertising and personal selling.

Q92. Which promotional tool is referred to as a short term incentive to increase the sales of a firm?

Ans. Sales promotion

Q93. Are sales promotional tools designed to promote sales to customers only?

Ans. No they are used to promote sales to

- Customers (e.g. free samples, discounts, contests)
- Tradesmen or middlemen (e.g. cooperative advertising, dealer discounts, dealer incentives and contests.)
- Salesperson (e.g. bonus, salesmen contest, special offers)

Q94. State the advantages and limitations of sales promotion.

Ans. The various merits are:

1. ***Useful in new product launch:*** Sales promotion tools can be very effective at the time of introduction of a new product in the market. It induces people to break away from their regular buying behavior and try the new product.
2. ***Attention value:*** These activities attract attention of the people because of the use of incentives
3. ***Synergy in total promotional efforts:*** Sales promotion activities are designed to supplement personal selling and advertising efforts used by a firm and add to the overall effectiveness of the promotional efforts of a firm.

4. ***Helps to counter competition in the market:*** These techniques are used by a firm to counter competition in the market by offering different and innovative schemes.

For Example:

Colgate offers a free tooth brush with tooth paste.

5. ***Tool to reduce old stock:*** It plays an important role in clearing the old dead stock which may not have buyers in the market by offering extensive discounts.

The demerits are:

1. ***Can adversely affect product image:*** Use of these tools may affect the image of a product. The buyers may start feeling that the product is not of good quality or is not appropriately priced.
2. ***Reflects crisis:*** If a firm frequently relies on sales promotion, it may give buyers the impression that the product is not doing well in the market

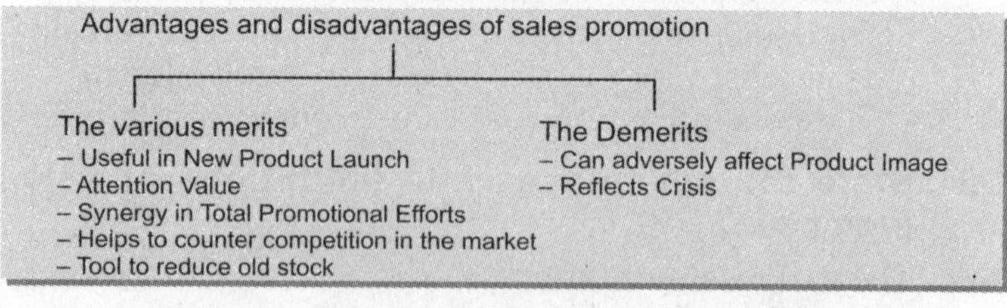

Q95. Explain the various sales promotion tools available.

Ans. The various tools are:

1. ***Discount:*** Offering products at less than list price (as a decreased percentage of original price).

For Example:

A cellphone company's offer of a discount upto 50% or a shoe marketer's offer of 50+40% discount.

2. ***Rebate:*** Offering products at special prices to clear off stock (as a decrease in price).

For Example:

A car manufacturer's offer to sell a particular brand at a discount of Rs. 10,000 for a limited period.

3. ***Product combinations:*** Offering another product as a gift along with the purchase of a product.

For Example:

An offer of a pack of ½ kg of rice with purchase of a bag of wheat, or get a free 512 MB memory card free with a digicam or Buy a TV of 25+ and get a vacuum cleaner free or 100 gm bottle of sauce free with 1 kg detergent.

4. ***Refunds***: Refunding a part of price paid by customer on some proof of purchase, say return of empty wrappers. This is commonly used by food product companies to boost their sales.
5. ***Quantity gifts:*** Offering extra quantity of the product commonly used by marketer of toiletry products.

For Example:

A shaving cream's offer of 40% extra or a Hotel's offer of take a 2 nights 3 days package at the hotel and get an extra night stay at just Rs. 500 or Buy 2 get 1 free.

6. ***Instant draw and assigned gift***

For Example:

'Scratch a card' or 'burst a cracker' and instantly win a refrigerator, car, t-shirt, computer with the purchase of a TV.

7. ***Lucky draw***

For Example:

Offer of a soap company to win a gold coin on lucky draw, coupon for free petrol on purchase of certain quantity of petrol from given petrol pump or lucky draw coupon on purchase of easy undergarment and win a car offer.

8. ***Usable benefit***

For Example:

Purchase goods worth Rs. 3000 and get a holiday package worth Rs. 3000 free or get a discount voucher for accessories on apparel purchase of Rs. 1000 and above.

9. ***Full finance @ 0%:*** Many marketers of consumer durables such as electronic goods, automobiles, etc offer easy financing schemes to boost sales

For Example:

24 easy installments, eight up front and sixteen to be paid as post dated cheques. However, one should be careful about the file charges, which sometimes are nothing but the interest recovered in advance.

10. ***Sampling***: Offer of a free sample or product

For Example:

Detergent powder or tooth paste to potential customers at the time of launch of a new brand.

11. ***Contests***: Competitive events which engage buyers through the application of skills or luck.

For Example:

Solving a quiz, answering some questions.

Q96. A company manufacturing mobile phones offers a free internet facility along with it. Identify it and also explain any 2 other sales promotion activities.

Ans. Usable benefit is being referred to here.

Q97. What is meant by publicity? What are its features?

Ans.

- It is a non-paid form of communication.
- It generally takes place when favorable news is presented in the mass media about a product or service.

For Example:

If a manufacturer achieves a breakthrough by developing a mobile phone battery, which runs on solar energy instead of electricity, and this news is covered by TV or radio in the form of news item, it will be publicity

The features are:

1. ***Unpaid form:*** It is an unpaid form of communication. It does not involve any direct expenditure by the marketing firm.
2. ***No identified sponsor:*** There is no identified sponsor for the communication as the message goes as a news item.

Q98. What is the similarity between publicity and advertising?

Ans. Publicity and adverstising, both, are non-personal forms of communication.

Q99. State the merits of publicity.

Ans. The merits of publicity are:

1. ***Higher reach:*** As the message is sent in the form of a news rather than direct sales communication it can reach even to those persons who otherwise may not pay attention to paid communication.
2. ***Higher degree of credibility:*** As the information is disseminated by an independent source, the message has more credibility than if the information comes as a sponsored message in advertising.

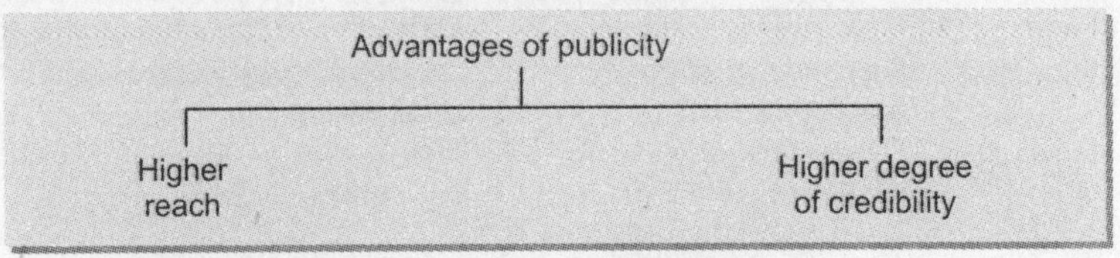

Q100. State the limitations of publicity.

Ans. The demerits are:

1. ***No control of the firm:*** As a medium of promotion, it is not within the control of a marketing firm.
2. ***Can't be used actively for promotion:*** The media would cover only those pieces of information, which are news worthy and which symbolize some achievement in the field. Thus, the firm can't use publicity to actively promote its products.

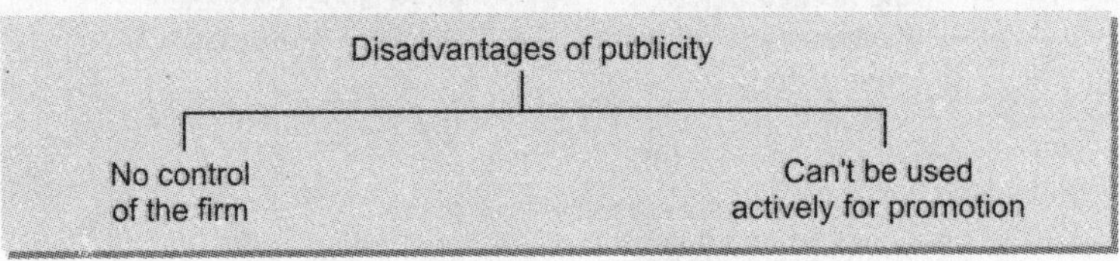

Q101. Differentiate between advertising and personal selling,

Ans. The differences between advertising and personal selling are:

Table 11.5

Basis	*Advertising*	*Personal selling*
Form	It is an impersonal form of communication.	It is a personal form of communication.
Nature of message	It involves transmission of standardized messages, i.e. same message is sent to all customers in a market segment.	The sales talk is adjusted keeping in view of customer's background and need.
Flexibility	It is inflexible as the message can't be adjusted to needs of buyers.	It is highly flexible as the message can be adjusted.
Reach	It reaches the masses, i.e. a large number of people can be approached.	Only a limited number can be contacted because of time and cost considerations.
Mode	It makes use of mass media such as TV, radio, newspaper and magazines.	It makes use of sales staff, which has limited reach.
Cost per person	The cost per person is very low.	The cost per person is high.
Time period to cover market	It can cover the market in a short time.	These efforts take a lot of time to cover market.
Nature of buyers	It is more useful in marketing to the ultimate consumers who are large in number	It is more helpful in selling products to the industrial buyers and to intermediacies such as dealers, retailers who are relatively few in number
Feedback	It lacks direct feedback. Marketing research efforts are needed to judge customer's reactions to advertising.	It provides direct, immediate feedback. Sales persons come to know about customers' reactions immediately.
Role	It is more useful in creating and building interest of the consumers in the firm's product.	It plays an important role at the awareness stage of decision making.

Q103. What is the difference between advertising and publicity.

Ans. The differences between advertising and publicity are:

Table 11.6

Basis	*Advertising*	*Publicity*
Purpose	As a promotional tool, it includes a persuasive message designed to convince the customer to favor a product or a service.	As a promotional tool, it involves an informative message designed only to inform the public at large.
Payment	It is a paid form to communication, i.e. the advertiser has to bear the cost of communication.	It is an unpaid form of communication where the firms do not have to pay
Control	The sponsor exercises control over the contents and timing of the message.	Content and timing of the message are not within the control of firm.
Sponsor	Advertising has an identified sponsor, i.e. advertising is undertaken by an identified individual or a company.	There is no identified sponsor for the communication as the message goes as a news item.

Q104. 'Product is a mixture of tangible and intangible attributes'. Discuss.

Ans. Explain the meaning of product. Explain the 3 benefits of product. One's decision to buy a product is not only affected by its physical qualities, but also by certain non tangible and psychological factors.

For Example:

Brand name, reputation, guaranty, packaging, etc.

12

Consumer Protection

Q1. Who is the king in a free market economy?

Ans. Consumer

Q2. What is meant by '*caveat emptor*' and '*caveat venditor*'?

Ans. Caveat emptor means 'let the buyer beware' and was subsequently changed to caveat venditor which meant 'let the seller beware'.

Q3. Why is there a need to provide adequate protection to consumers?

Ans.

- Manufacturers and service providers may be tempted to engage in unscrupulous, exploitative and unfair trade practices in order to counter competition or to increase sales, such as:
  - Hoarding
  - Black-marketing
  - Defective and unsafe products
  - Adulteration
  - False and misleading advertisement
- Thus consumers might be exposed to risks due to unsafe products, might suffer from bad weather due to adulterated food products, might be cheated due to misleading advertisements or might have to pay higher prices. Thus there is a need to provide protection.

Q4. Consumer protection has a wide agenda. Explain

Ans.

- Consumer protection includes educating consumers about their rights but also helps in getting their grievances redressed
- It has a special significance for business too.It not only requires a judicial machinery for protecting the interests of consumers but also requires the consumers to get together and form themselves into consumer associations for protection and promotion of their interests.

Q5. Discuss the importance of consumer protection from consumer's point of view.

Ans.

1. *Consumer ignorance*
   - In the light of widespread ignorance of consumers about their rights and reliefs available to them, it becomes necessary to educate them about the same so as to achieve consumer awareness
2. *Unorganized consumers*
   - Consumers need to be organized in the form of consumer organizations
   - In India, we do not have consumer organizations which are working in this direction, and adequate protection is required to be given to consumers till these organizations become powerful enough to protect and promote the interests of consumers.
3. *Widespread exploitation of consumers*
   - Consumers might be exploited by unscrupulous, exploitative and unfair trade practices like
     - Defective and unsafe products
     - Adulteration
     - Black-marketing
     - Hoarding
     - False and misleading advertisements

     Consumers need protection against such malpractices of sellers

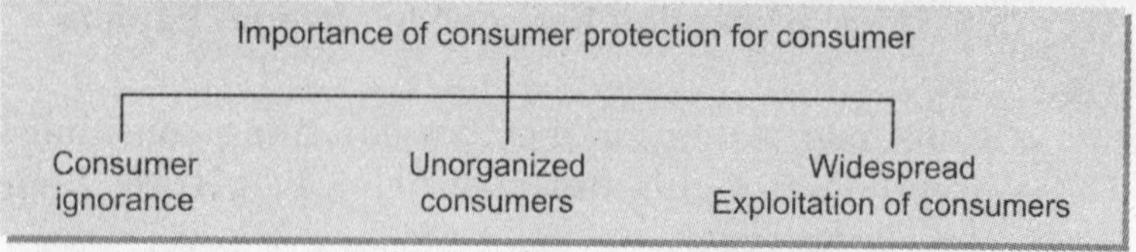

Q6. A businessman should lay emphasis on protecting the consumers. In the light of the statement discuss the importance of consumer protection from the point of view of business.

Ans.

1. *Long term interest of business*
   - Enlightened businesses realize that it is in their long term interest to satisfy their customers
   - Satisfied customers not only lead to repeat sales orders but also provide good feedback and cross referral to prospective customers and thus, help in increasing the customer base of business
   - Thus, business firms should aim at long term profit maximization through customer satisfaction
2. *Business uses society's resources*
   - Business organizations use resources which belong to the society. They, thus, have a responsibility to supply such products and render such services which are in public interest and would not impair public confidence in them.
3. *Moral justification*
   - It is the moral duty of any business to take care of consumer's interest and avoid any form of their exploitations
   - A business must avoid unscrupulous, exploitative and unfair trade practices like:
     - Defective and unsafe products
     - Adulteration
     - Black-marketing
     - False and misleading advertisements
     - Hoarding
4. *Social responsibility*
   - A business has social responsibilities towards various interest groups. Business organizations make

money by selling goods and providing services to consumers

- Consumers form an important group among the many stakeholders of business and like other stakeholders, their interest has to be well taken care of.

5. *Government intervention*
   - A business engaging in any form of exploitative trade practices would invite government actions
   - This can impair and tarnish the image of the company. Thus, it is advisable that business organizations voluntarily resort to such practices where the customers' needs and interests are well taken care of.

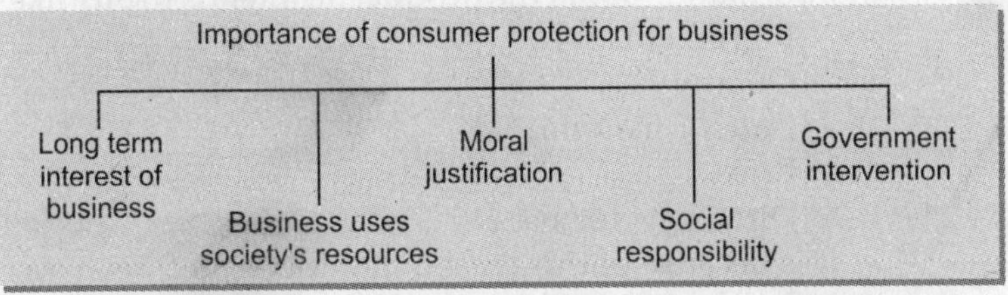

Q7. What does the consumer protection act seek?

Ans. The Consumer Protection Act 1986 seeks to protect and promote the consumers' interest through speedy and inexpensive redressal of their grievances

Q8. How can we say that scope of the Consumer Protection Act is very wide?

Ans. The scope of the act is very wide. It is applicable to all types of undertakings:

i. Big or small
ii. Supplying goods or providing services.
iii. Private or public or co-operative sector
iv. Manufacturer or trader

Q9. Discuss the various consumer rights mentioned in the Consumer Protection Act 1986.

Ans.

1. *Right to safety*

- The consumer has a right to be protected against goods and services which are hazardous to life and health.

For Example:

Electrical appliances which are manufactured with substandard products or don't conform to the safety norms might cause serious injury to the user

- Consumers are educated that they should use electrical appliances which are ISI marked as this would be an assurance of such products meeting quality specifications

2. *Right to be informed*
   - The consumer has a right to have complete information about the product he intends to buy like:
     - Ingredients
     - Quantity
     - Date of manufacture
     - Price
     - Directions for use
   - It is because of this reason that the legal framework in India requires the manufacturers to provide such information on package and label of product.
3. *Right to choose*
   - The consumer has the freedom to choose from a society of products at competitive prices
   - This implies that the marketers should offer a wide variety of products in terms of quality, brand, prices, etc. and allow the consumer to make a choice from amongst these.

For example:

A consumer who wishes to buy ice-cream has the choice of Amul, Mother Diary, Kwality Walls, Vadilal, etc.

4. *Right to be heard*
   - The consumer has a right to file a complaint and to be heard in case of dissatisfaction with goods/service
   - Many consumer organizations are also working towards this and helping consumers in the redressal of their grievances.

- It is because of this reason that many enlightened businesses have set up their own consumer service and grievance cells

5. *Right to seek redressal*
   - The consumer has a right to get relief in case the product/service falls short of expectations
   - The CPA provides a number of reliefs to the consumers including:
     - Replacement of product
     - Compensation paid for any loss or injury suffered by the consumer
     - Removal of defects in product
6. *Right to consumer education*
   - The consumer has a right to acquire knowledge and be a well informed consumer throughout life
   - He should be aware about his rights and the reliefs available to him in case of a product/service falling short of his expectation
   - Many consumer organizations and some enlightened businesses are taking an active part in educating consumers in this respect

Q10. Removal of defect in a product is a right available to customer. Identify this right

Ans. Right to seek redressal

Table 12.1: 3-tier judicial machinery for redressal of consumer complaints

Basis	*District forum*	*State commission*	*National commission*
Consists of	President and 2 other members one of whom should be a woman	President and not less than 2 other members one of whom should be a woman	President and at least 4 other members one of whom should be a woman
Appointed by	The concerned state government	The concerned state government	The central government
Total claim	A complaint can be made to the appropriate district forum when value of goods and services in question along with compensation claim can't exceed Rs. 20 lakhs	A complaint can be made to the appropriate state commission when value of goods and services in question along with compensation claim exceeds Rs. 20 lakhs but not Rs. 1 Cr.	A complaint can be made to the national commission when value of goods and services in question along with compensation claim exceeds Rs. 1 Cr.

Contd.

Table 12.1: 3-tier judicial machinery for redressal of consumer complaints (*Contd.*)

Basis	*District forum*	*State commission*	*National commission*
Process	i. On receiving a complaint, the district forum shall refer the complaint to the party against whom it is filed	i. Same	i. Same
	ii. If required goods/sample thereof, shall be sent for testing to specified laboratories	ii. Same	ii. Same
	iii. The district forum shall pass an order after considering the test report from the laboratory and hearing to the party against whom the complaint is filed	iii. Same	iii. Same
	iv. In case the aggrieved party isn't satisfied with the order of the district forum, it can appeal before state commission within 30 days of passing of the above the order	iv. In case the aggrieved party is not satisfied with the order of the state commission, it can appeal before the national commission within 30 days of the passing of the order	iv. In case the aggrieved party isn't satisfied with the order of the national commission, it can appeal before the Supreme Court
Hierarchy of authority/ Maximum authority where a complaint can be filed	District forum ↓ State Commission ↓ National Commission (Can't approach Supreme Court)	State Commission ↓ National Commission (Can not approach Supreme Court)	National Commission ↓ Supreme Court

Q11. State the various responsibilities to be kept in mind by a consumer.

Ans.

1. *Be aware of availability of goods*

- Be aware about various goods and services in the market so that an intelligent and wise choice can be made.

2. ***To learn about risks associated with product***
   - Learn about the risks associated with products and services, follow manufacturer's instructions and use the products safely
3. ***Buy only standardised products***
   - Buy only standardized goods as they provide quality assurance
   - Thus look for ISI mark on electrical goods, FPO mark on food products, Hallmark on jewellery, Agmark for agricultural products
4. ***To read labels carefully***
   - Read labels carefully so as to have complete information about prices, net weight, manufacturing and expiry dates
5. ***To be honest in your dealings***
   - Be honest in your dealing. Choose only legal goods and services and discourage unscrupulous practices like black-marketing, hoarding, etc.
6. ***To be assertive***
   - Assert yourself to ensure that you get a fair deal
7. ***Insist on a cash memo***
   - Always ask for a cash memo on purchase of goods or services. This would serve as a proof of the purchase made
8. ***To file a complaint in an appropriate consumer forum***
   - File a complaint in an appropriate consumer forum in case of a shortcoming in the quality of goods purchased or services availed. Do not fail to take action even when the amount involved is small.
9. ***To protect the environment***
   - Respect the environment. Avoid waste, littering and contributing to pollution
10. ***To form consumer societies***
    - Form consumer societies which would play an active part in educating consumers and safeguarding their interests

Q12. Discuss the various ways and means of consumer protection/How can the objective of consumer protection be achieved?

Ans. The objective of consumer protection can be achieved through:

1. *Self regulation by business*
   - Enlightened business firms realize that it is in their long term interest to serve the customers well
   - Socially responsible firms follow ethical standards and practices in dealing with their customers
   - Many firms have set up their customer service and grievance cells to redress the grievances of their customers
2. *Consumer awareness*
   - A consumer who is well informed about his rights and reliefs available to him would be in a position to raise his voice against any unfair trade practices or unscrupulous exploitation
   - An understanding of his responsibilities would enable him to safeguard his interest
3. *Business association*
   - The associations of trade, commerce and business like Federation of Indian Chambers of Commerce and Industry (FICCI) and Confederation of Indian Industry (CII) have laid down their code of conduct which lays down the guidelines for members in their dealing with customers
4. *Consumer organizations*
   - They play an important role in educating consumers about their rights and providing protection to them
   - They can force business firms to avoid malpractices and exploitation of consumers.

   For example:

   Consumer Coordination Council, Delhi; Common Cause, Delhi
5. *Government*
   - It can protect the interests of the consumers by enacting various legislations
   - The legal framework in India encompasses various legislations like Consumer Protection Act, 1986, which provide protection to consumers

- The Consumer Protection Act provides for a 3-tier machinery at the
  - District
  - State
  - National

  Levels for redressal of consumer grievances

Q13. How is self regulation by business firms a means of consumer protection?

Q14. Name 2 business associations which lay down the code of conduct for business firms in dealings with customers

Ans. Refer to Ans.12

Q15. Define a consumer under Consumer Protection Act, 1986

Ans

- A 'consumer' is generally understood as 'a person who uses/consumes goods or avails any service.'
- Under CPA it is defined as
  1. Any person who buys any goods for a consideration, which has been paid or promised, or partly paid and partly promised, or under any scheme of deferred payment. It includes any user of such goods, when such use is made with the approval of the buyer, but does not include a person who obtains for re-sale or any commercial purpose
  2. Any person who hires or avails of any service, for a consideration which has been paid or promised, or partly paid and partly promised or under any scheme of deferred payment. It includes any beneficiary of services when such services are availed of with the approval of the person concerned, but does not include a person who avails of such services for any commercial purpose.

Q16. Who can file a complaint?

Ans. A complaint before the appropriate consumer forum can be made by:

1. Any consumer
2. Any registered consumer association

3. One or more consumers, on behalf of numerous consumers having common interest
4. The central govt. or any state govt.
5. A legal heir or representative of a deceased consumer

Q17. In case of a deceased consumer, who can file a complaint?

Ans. Legal heir/representative

Q18. State the various reliefs available to a consumer if his complaint is genuine

Ans

1. *Remove the defect*
   - To remove the defect in goods or deficiency in service
2. *Replace the defective product*
   - To replace the defective product with a new one free from any defect
3. *Pay reasonable compensation*
   - To pay a reasonable amount of compensation for any loss or injury suffered by the consumer due to the negligence of the opposite party
4. *Refund the price*
   - To refund the price paid for the product or the charges paid for the service
5. *Pay punitive damages*
   - To pay punitive damages in appropriate circumstances
6. *Not to offer goods*
   - Not to offer hazardous goods for sale
7. *Discontinue unfair/restrictive trade practices*
   - To discontinue unfair/restrictive trade practices and not to repeat it in the future
8. *Withdraw the hazardous goods*
   - Withdraw the hazardous goods from sale
9. *To cease manufacture of hazardous goods*
   - To cease manufacture of hazardous goods and to desist from offering hazardous services
10. *Credit specific amount to consumer welfare fund*
    - To pay any amount(not less than 5% of the value of the defective goods or deficient services provided) to be credited to consumer welfare fund or any other

organization/person, to be utilized in the prescribed manner

11. *Issue corrective advertisement*
    - To issue corrective advertisement to neutralize the effect of a misleading advertising
12. *To pay adequate costs to appropriate party*

Q19. Identify NPOs which aim at promoting the welfare of the consumers

Ans. NGOs. For example: Common Cause, Delhi

Q20. Identify NPOs which have a constitution of their own and are free from govt. intervention

Ans. NGOs

Q21. State the functions performed by consumer organizations/NGOs

Ans.

1. *Educating general public*
   - Educating general public about consumer rights by organizing training programmes, seminars and workshops
2. *Comparative testing of consumer products*
   - Carrying out comparative testing of consumer products in accredited labs to test relative qualities of competing brands and publishing the test results for the benefit of consumers
3. *Publishing periodicals to impart knowledge*
   - Publishing periodicals and other publications to impart knowledge about consumer problems, legal reporting, reliefs available, etc.
4. *Encouraging consumers*
   - Encouraging consumers to strongly protest and take action against unscrupulous, exploitative and unfair trade practices of sellers
5. *Filing complaints*
   - Filing complaints in appropriate consumer courts on behalf of the consumers
6. *Providing legal assistance*
   - Providing legal assistance to consumers by way of providing aid. Legal advice in seeking legal remedy

7. *Taking initiative*
   - Taking initiative in filing cases in consumer courts in the interest of the general public, not for any individual.

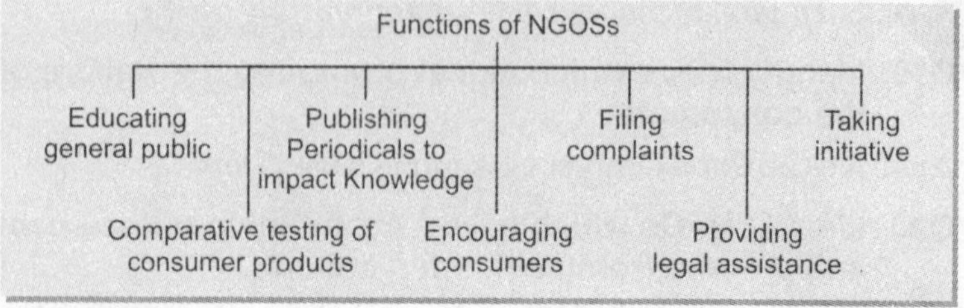

Q22. State the cases which are appealable in the supreme court

Ans.

- An order passed by the national commission in a matter of its original jurisdiction is appealable before Supreme Court
- Only those appeals where the value of goods and services in question, along with the compensation claimed exceeded Rs. 1 Cr. and where the aggrieved party was not satisfied with order of national commission, can be taken to the Supreme Court
- In a case decided by district forum, the appeal can be filed before state commission and thereafter the order can be challenged before national commission and no further

Q23. Name some of the important consumer organizations and NGOs engaged in protecting and promoting consumers' interests

Ans.

1. Consumer Co-ordination Council, Delhi
2. Common Cause, Delhi
3. Voluntary Organization in Interest of Consumer Education (VOICE), Delhi
4. Consumer Protection Council (CPC), Ahmedabad
5. Consumer Education and Research Centre (CERC), Ahmedabad

6. Karnataka Consumer Service Society, Bangalore
7. Consumer Unity and Trust Society (CUTS), Jaipur
8. Consumer's Association, Kolkata
9. Consumer Guidance Society of India (CGSI), Mumbai
10. Mumbai Grahak Panchayat, Mumbai

Q24. What are the 2 aspects of *consumer protection*?

Ans.

1. Educating consumers about rights and responsibilities
2. Redressal of grievances

Q25. Which is the standardized mark for the following:

Ans.

1. Jewellery – Hallmark
2. Processed Food products – FPO
3. Woollen – Woolmark
4. Agriculture – Agmark
5. Eco – friendly products – Eco mark scheme

Q26. Explain the various provisions under the legal protection to consumers

Ans.

1. *The Consumer Protection Act, 1986*
    - The act seeks to promote and protect the interests of consumers. It provides safeguards to consumers against defective goods, deficient services, unfair trade practices, etc.
    - It provides for the formation of consumer protection councils in every district, state and at the apex level
    - It provides for the setting up of a 3-tier machinery consisting of:
        - District forums
        - State commissions
        - National commission
2. *The Contract Act, 1982*
    - It lays down the conditions in which the promises made by parties to a contract will be binding on each other
    - It also specifies the remedies available to parties in case of breach of contract

3. *The Essential Commodities Act, 1955*
    - It aims at controlling production, supply and distribution of essential commodities, checking inflationary trend in their prices and ensures equal distribution of essential goods
    - The act also provides for action against anti-social activities of profiteers, hoarders and black marketeers
4. *The Sale of Goods Act, 1930*
    - It provides some safeguards and reliefs to the buyers of the goods in case the goods purchased don't comply with expressed or implied conditions/ warranties
5. *The Agriculture Produce (Grading and Marking) Act, 1937*
    - It prescribes grade standards for agricultural commodities and livestock products
    - It stipulates the conditions which govern the use of standards and lays down the procedure for grading, marking and packing of agricultural produce
    - The quality mark provided under the act is known as AGMARK, acronym for 'agricultural marketing.'
6. *The Prevention of Food Adulteration Act, 1954*
    - The act aims to check adulteration of food articles and ensure their purity so as to maintain public health
7. *The Trade Marks Act, 1999*
    - This act has repealed and replaced the Trade and Merchandise Marks Act, 1958
    - It prevents the use of fraudulent marks on products and thus, provides protection to consumers against such products
8. *The Competition Act, 2002*
    - It has repealed and replaced the Monopolies and Restrictive Trade Practices Act, 1969(MRTP).
    - It provides protection to the consumers in case of practices adopted by business firms which hamper competition in the market
9. *The Standards of Weights and Measures Act, 1976*
    - The provisions of this act are applicable in case of those goods which are sold or distributed by weight, measure or number,
    - It provides protection to consumers against the malpractice of under-weight or under-measure

10. *The Bureau of Indian Standards Act, 1986*
    - The BIS has been set up under the act
    - It has 2 major activities:
      - Formulation of quality standards for goods
      - Certification of goods through BIS certification scheme
    - Manufacturers are permitted to use ISI mark on their products only after ensuring that goods conform to the prescribed quality standards
    - The bureau has set up a grievance cell where consumers can make a complaint about the quality of the products carrying the ISI mark.

Q27. Mr. Anurag bought an electric iron from a reputed showroom of a manufacturing company but it caused electric shock to his wife while she was using it. He claimed a compensation of Rs. 15 lacs. Where can he file his complaint. Give reasons and 2 features.

Ans. District forum

Q28. (a). Piyush claimed a compensation of Rs. 60 lacs for the damaged caused to him while using a company's product. What forum will he approach

(b). If he does not get a favorable verdict from this body, what other options are available to him ?

Ans. (a). State commission (b). Appeal before national commission within 30 days of passing order

Q29. Dushyant was a vegetarian. He went to a snack bar for having French fries and later found that it had non veg. Neither the advertisement nor the packaging displayed that the product has non vegetarian content. Will he be able to claim compensation? Which right of consumer is being violated?

Ans. Right to information

Q30. Akhil, a consumer purchased medicine without noticing the date of expiry. He also did not obtain the cash memo. Do you think he'll be able to protect himself by the loss. Give reasons.

Ans. No.

1. He did not behave in a responsible manner
2. He did not obtain the cash memo which is a proof of purchase and it is a must for filing any complaint
3. He did not go through the packing instructions and did not notice the expiry date. He is not a cautious consumer.

Q31. Dushyant purchased a book from a book seller. Took the cash memo of Rs. 220 which he paid for the book. Later, he found that the actual price of the book is Rs. 180 but bookseller had put a sticker of Rs. 220 on original price. Can he recover the extra money he has paid? What other options are available to him?

Ans. He is a cautious consumer. He had taken the cash memo for the book. Thus he can recover the extra money. Other options available to him under CPA are:

1. He can return the book and ask for a refund of Rs. 220
2. He can sue the bookseller for using unfair and restrictive trade practices.

Q32. Which consumer right suggests the business firm to set up their own grievance cell?

Ans. Right to be heard

Q33. What is *BIS*?

Ans. BIS is a seal certifying that the goods conform to the prescribed quality standards.

Q35. Who can file a complaint on behalf of a deceased consumer?

Ans. Legal heir/representative

Q36. Name the apex institution under CPA

Ans. National commission

Reader's Notes

Reader's Notes